André Breton

and the

Basic Concepts of Surrealism

STUDIES IN THE HUMANITIES
PHILOSOPHY

André Breton
and the
Basic Concepts of
Surrealism

BY

Michel Carrouges

TRANSLATED BY

Maura Prendergast, S.N.D.

The University of Alabama Press
University, Alabama

CONTENTS

TRANSLATOR'S PREFACE

Man, says Heidegger, is a fundamentally poetic being. It is this poetry at the heart of man—man who has "lost heart"—that the surrealists set out to restore, to raise to the surface of the conscious mind, to free from the rubble (by artistic detonation, if necessary) of time, habit, sclerotic ways of thinking and seeing and speaking. Michel Carrouges presents surrealism as a dialectical humanism in which man becomes "le foyer vivant où s'unissent les mondes antagonistes mais indissociables de l'objectif et du subjectif." No one incarnates the spirit of surrealism more than André Breton; his presence animated the movement from its beginnings until Breton's death in 1966. It is as one of the surrealist group and as a friend of Breton that Carrouges writes of surrealism. The text translated here, published originally in 1950, was well received by Breton as well as by those interested in the movement. Yet, strangely enough, it seems the remote cause of Carrouges' expulsion from the surrealist movement.

As a Catholic in the anticlerical and, if not completely atheistic, at least agnostic movement, Carrouges retains a certain distance from it and, given this perspective, a clarity of vision that is reflected in his study. As he points out in the postscript, Carrouges refrains from taking any position in the present work on the relationship of surrealist poetry with religion and atheism. This deliberate avoidance of bias by one who belongs to the movement is what gives Carrouges' book a unique value above and beyond that which derives from its intelligent examination of surrealism's major themes. If the latter value was of special appeal to Breton, the former was a reason for Carrouges to be regarded as a good spokesman for surrealism to those outside the movement. On one such occasion, in February, 1951, he was asked to speak about the movement to the *Cercle des Intellectuels catholiques de France* at the Salle Saint-Séverin in Paris. There were protests by some of the surrealists, an attempt was made to disrupt the lecture and, eventually, Carrouges was excluded from the group, not without reluctance on Breton's part.

That Carrouges, like many others, fell victim to the sometimes strange inner politics of the surrealist group in no way detracts from the value of his study, just as they do not diminish the value of the surrealist experiment.

INTRODUCTION

What we ordinarily call life is only the mediocre side of reality. Man despairs because he fails to recognize the other side of existence, infinitely more vast, more beautiful. He is either unaware of it, or else he believes it inaccessible.

The dominant trait of modern civilization is that never before has man so rigorously cloistered himself within banality. He has come to look on ordinary appearances as the exclusive limits of reality: like the fox of the fable, he takes pride in a would-be positivism which, though he considers it a setting free, is in fact a self-mutilation. Although he cannot help feeling from time to time, in the depths of his being, the impulses of that cosmic mystery from which, all unknown to himself, he proceeds, he stifles these appeals like so many absurdities.

In this respect, the appearance of surrealism in the land of Descartes and of Voltaire, in the heart of a world enslaved by abstract philosophies and the classical arts, by a bourgeois mentality and a laborite economy, is an extraordinary phenomenon. Surrealism is, indeed, a radical revolt against that civilization. It demands not only an intellectual and artistic revolution but a social revolution as well and, above all, a total liberation of humanity.

It is self-evident that, at every point, surrealism goes beyond the conceptual framework of its adversaries, and even beyond these provisional means it uses to reach each stage of its development. The final goal of surrealism can be no less than the full satisfaction of its passionate thirst for total liberty. For the man who looks at it from the outside, surrealism is an absurd monstrosity. But for anyone who has penetrated within, it is the most extraordinary of human revelations. The one thinks he has a monopoly on common sense, while the other knows the intoxication of entering into the unknown worlds of surreality—not into the unreal, but into the heart of the real.

Surrealism is, first of all, an immense force for divisiveness. The way in is not by means of probes and tests, but by a brusque mutation of the spirit which overthrows in an instant every means of thought and feeling. This does not mean that surrealism is, as its detractors would have it, an absurd wager, but only that it will not enter the Procrustean bed of their conceptions; nor should it be supposed that this indispensable mental mutation is not within the reach of everyone. Every man can, if he wants, discover within himself an interior domain where it becomes possible to set foot within the boundaries of surrealist worlds. If they are separated from these worlds, it is because they are first of all separated from themselves, cut off from their own secret domain. Understanding surrealism is nothing more than understanding one's self. That is possible, however, only on the condition of breaching deeply that wall which a classic, rationalist education has built in us, and which divides us stupidly from ourselves.

Surrealism is a human experience, and every human experience has meaning; it is that meaning which we are going to try to set forth here.

The works of André Breton cited or referred to by Carrouges are listed in Section I of the Bibliography. In the text, they are usually identified, immediately following their citation or reference, by a short form of the title and the page numbers involved. These short forms are given in the Bibliography (Section I).

ONE

The Birth of Surrealism

Surrealism is not a philosophy, in the scholarly sense of the word; it takes no stock in demonstrating theses by setting up a framework of abstract reasoning. It is plunged deep into life itself and not into the twilight zone of abstractions.

And yet it is a philosophy, in the full sense of that word, because it expresses a new conception of the world and seeks to possess the secret of the universe. It is not mere empiricism. It is action and at the same time reflection on the means and end of that action. Like religion, Marxism, and modern physics, it is both *praxis* and *weltanschauung*. These two aspects are inseparable. It is impossible to understand the concrete advances of surrealism while ignoring the tenets of surrealist cosmology and, by the same token, impossible to understand that cosmology if one is unaware of the concrete explorations on which it is built.

To penetrate this world, it is necessary to recall at least briefly the beginnings of the surrealist movement. Surrealism is above all a movement of revolt. It is not the result of intellectual caprice, but rather of a tragic conflict between the powers of the spirit and the conditions of life. It is born of an enormous despair prompted by the condition to which man is reduced on earth, and of a boundless hope in human metamorphosis.

1

That essential refusal which is the first step toward surrealist self-awareness is expressed many times by Breton, as when he cries: "Absolutely incapable of playing my role in the destiny which has been allotted me . . . I refuse to adapt my existence to the stupid conditions of existence in general." (*Pas,* 7)

All of surrealism is contained in embryo in this statement of the misery of the human condition, for the wealthiest or "happiest" of humans has nevertheless this desire to raise himself above his condition, if only by his stubborn refusal to participate in it. Moreover, if man is capable of becoming aware of the baseness and mediocrity of his life, it is because he feels within himself infinite strengths, unchangeably written on the heart of the human spirit, even though he is all too often forgetful of them. Surrealism's violence comes from the unbearable tension between the two poles of immediate life and that other existence that lies within our power. "Human life would not be such a disappointment for some if we did not feel constantly able to accomplish acts beyond our strength." (*Pas,* 7)

Above and beyond the usual and familiar forces which we use daily, there are indeed undreamed of powers within us, their presence revealed to us from time to time by mysterious signs, but which we do not yet know how to use. Before discovering the way by which one can come into their possession, the surrealists had first to experience bitterly their powerlessness before the laws of terrestrial existence.

This is the foundation of their experiment. Every truly strong doctrine is based upon a vital experiment, above all on an experiment which has known and won out over despair. No one can make about life a concrete judgment in which the whole being participates unless he has first felt himself tossed out of the mainstream of life. No one can arrive at a new conception of the world who has not first experienced in himself the emptiness of his previous conceptions. No one can reach the foundations of life who has not felt the old forms break apart and who has not then fallen down into those strange mines of the mind where he feels the heat of the fire within.

Natural satisfaction precludes self-awareness. Only pain awakens the consciousness; only despair throws it down to the bottom of that interior abyss through which it must inexorably journey before leaping back to the upper reaches of illumination.

Breton and his friends are the direct successors of that great line of hermetic, promethean poets born with Nerval and Baudelaire and continued in Mallarmé, Rimbaud, Lautréamont, Jarry, Apollinaire, Roussel. With Picasso, Duchamp, Picabia, and their followers, the same superhuman spirit enters and overwhelms painting.

Yet another description of that great and dramatic odyssey of the poetic conscience would serve no purpose here, but it is important to underscore the dual aspect of their genius. These great devastators call fire from heaven—or perhaps from hell—to strike down the beaux-arts centers where reign the recital-makers with earrings in their ears. They unleash the spirit of negation like a corrosive acid that will dissolve social and cultural prejudices, and even the most natural feelings. They try to dynamite structures of thought and, if possible, even of behavior, so as to enter into a new and flaming cloud of unknowing. Yet at the same time, they are the demiurges of new worlds in perpetual expansion. They preach revolt against the human condition and proclaim hope for the transfiguration of life through poetical magic.

Surrealism cannot be considered apart from its historical situation vis-à-vis the world tragedy of 1914. Like the dadaists, the first of the surrealists belong to the generation which came of age during that other war. For these young men who took a stand against positivism as well as against religion, the war was considered not a terrible plague, but a natural thing, not a trial of the spirit; it was an unprecedented catastrophe menacing with death the birth of new worlds.

From it came a deep wave of nihilism, a desperate effort of the spirit to affirm unconditionally its immediate supremacy over the machine of death. But war leaves to the combatant little leisure for the laying down of such challenges; Vaché's *Lettres de guerre* is one of the rare witnesses that we possess. And yet, it is in the Helvetic polygon, in the still eye of the storm, that the dadaist idea breaks out, about 1916, in a resounding explosion of the spirit. A kind of poetic *Zimmerwald*[1] was impelled into being by Val Serner, Hans Arp, and Tristan Tzara.

From the beginning of the postwar period, it was clear that the drama, far from dying out, was going to take on new life. Those artists and avant-garde writers who had lived through it, directly or on the sidelines, would no longer be satisfied, once peace had returned, to adhere to the values of a civilization which the war had compromised or—for them—definitely ruined. The spectacle of this so-called new world being reborn from the deluge seemed to them so derisory that the question of death which the war had posed was still being asked in all its violence. Having just come through this time of fire, they found it impossible to go back to applying themselves to the painting of china and heiresses, to the rhyming of sonnets. No longer could there be question of ornamenting walls and memories. When esthetics can no longer face death and nothingness victoriously, it has no more value. Arts and literature risked falling under the same condemnation; they would survive only in the measure in which they were capable of transcending themselves, of going beyond sentimental and decorative use to become convincing signs, perhaps even efficacious signs, of a superior human destiny.

Immediately after the war then, the dadaist movement quickly made itself felt in Germany by Val Serner and the German group, among them Max Ernst, and also in France through Duchamp, Picabia, Breton, Tzara, Eluard, Soupault, Aragon, Ribémont-Dessaignes, and many others. There appeared chaotically explosive little periodicals like *Littérature, Cannibale, 391,* and others, as well as scandal-making manifestoes. In 1919, Dada reached its apogee, but, torn by bitter intestine battles, it burned out and disappeared around 1921.

Struggles between powerful rival personalities and arguments over tumultuous ideas destroyed it. How could this be other than inevitable in a movement which questioned everything, absolutely everything?

It was, par excellence, a chemically unstable body since it was by definition the negation of any position. The ceaseless affirmation of mental anarchy, the practice of no other discipline but that of integral chaos was an intenable situation which could end only in suicide, as with Vaché and Rigaut, or in the sterile repetition of senseless anathemas. Or else there had to be someone beyond that region of quagmires and volcanoes in full eruption, someone who would know how to discover a way of entry into a totally new world, into a veritable promised land of magic and of marvels.

There was, of course, some of this hope in the dadaist spirit; Ribémont-Dessaignes gives us a glimpse of it, although much later, when he defines Dada as a desire to "replace submission to reality by the creation of a superior reality" (*Histoire de Dada*). This hope, however, remained dim, even at the height of dadaism, especially since the dadaists frequently wore themselves out trying to saw down the very branch they might have hung onto to cross over the abyss. With its stand against everything, even against itself, Dada by its very nature excluded all sustained action, all possibility of development; consequently, it turned round and round in the wilderness, never advancing toward the domain of marvels.

And yet, sterility did not result from this dadaist phase. Such might have been the case had the movement remained within itself; but as it was the essential moment preceding the birth of surrealism, it showed itself to be a magnificent source of fecundity.

The phases of negation are not empty and useless periods. One cannot pass directly from one affirmation to a contrary one. Logic makes an instantaneous changeover, but man cannot. He has to live through an intermediate period of doubts and negations. The deeper the ideas and the antagonistic experiences, the more grievous will be the crisis in the interval. It is nihilism's violent readying of being which subsequently permitted surrealism to reveal its depths and to liberate itself from the bonds of habit. Even today, one cannot understand surrealism without having undergone some analagous experience. It is not a question of abstract dialectic, but of the concrete dialectic of human life.

From the historical point of view, surrealism designates that movement which began about 1920 and which grouped a pléiade of poets and painters under the direction of André Breton. Animated by the spirit of revolt of the dadaist movement, to which most of them had belonged originally, the surrealists reacted violently against its nihilism, its absurdity and blindness. They were in fact looking for what we must call, even from their point of view, a way of salvation. They thought they had found it in those vital moments in which a man is raised above himself and ordinary life; that is, in instants of ecstasy and of illumination.

This is why Breton threw himself heart and soul into the pursuit of the flash of poetic inspiràtion, for its light along still shone undiminished over the devastated landscape of dadaism. Rather than invent novels or philosophies or construct esthetic poems, he began to spy on his dreams, to lie in wait for those enigmatic words that are born spontaneously in the spirit, without any conscious direction, and to search out the signs of coincidences and premonitions.

Whatever the relationship of these phenomena to the art of letters and of painting, it was not at all artistic utilization that mattered most, but rather the placing of art at the service of these phenomena from which the surrealists expected the revelation of the mystery of the destiny of man and of the world.

Beginning in 1919, Breton had been struck by those words which one sometimes hears arising within one's self, quite involuntarily, especially when standing at the edge of sleep. His great discovery was, while wide awake, to listen in on his dreams so as to seize by broad day these nocturnal phrases.

Thus he arrived at a kind of interior dictation, first documented and presented in the collection entitled *Champs magnétiques*, written in collaboration with Philippe Soupault and brought out in 1921. That such an experiment in automatic writing was pursued, not by one man alone shut away in his subjectivity, but made in common by two persons, is quite remarkable and demonstrates that the question of automatic writing is much more complex than one would suppose.

Breton's essential work, on the experimental level, is first and foremost the discovery of the natural link existing between the automatism of dreams and the manifestations of poetry. The first is, in effect, the source of the others; the birth of surrealism dates from this discovery.

In this way, surrealism escapes from those two antagonistic forms of the arbitrary, classicism and dadaism, puts the machinery of subjective automatism at the disposition of the consciousness and proposes to make a systematic exploration of the depths of subjectivity.

And yet surrealism does not allow itself to become confined within this abstract category of subjectivity, precisely because it is only that: an abstract category, and because, within the interior perspective, one discovers not only a strictly interior spectacle, but also countless obscure manifestations of other modes of the presence of objectivity. At that moment obscure, they need only that the floodlights of surrealism be brought to bear on them and focused, to appear with blinding clarity.

The other and essential side of Breton's work is the discovery of the natural link existing between personal subjective automatism and universal automatism. Or, if one prefers, between personal unconscious, collective unconscious, and even cosmic unconscious. In Breton's language, this discovery is called objective chance, a formula that includes both premonitions and striking coincidences.

Far from being heterogeneous, these two basic elements of surrealism are inseparable. In every demonstration of automatic writing, the manifestations of objective chance can be held in abeyance, whether these be the foreshadowing of an individual future or telepathic communications. It makes little difference if their presence is not immediately identified. Besides, man being not an aberrant epiphenomenon added to the universe, but of a piece with nature, every human word engages all of nature, and every impression, even the most fleeting and most subjective, is a manifestation of the cosmos. Automatic writing is not then simply an exploratory psychological procedure; it is a means for the revelation of the world by man, that cosmic word. In exploring, along with another surrealist, the magnetic fields of the mind, Breton was counting on the pre-established harmony of the human unconscious and on the manifestation of a power of cosmic revelation. It was not a question of building a work of art, but rather of proffering, like the sibyls, a prophetic word; hence, the incantatory tone of Breton's writings and the sacral atmosphere of his thought.

In this way, surrealism breaks away from the purely negative attitude of Dada, without however, retracing its steps. With new strength, it reaffirms the superior power of poetry, capable of drawing to itself both the flow of interior necessity in the human unconscious and that of exterior necessity in nature, in order to reveal, through the thick shell of appearances, the apparition of a new world, a veritable hemisphere of marvels. Thus the stages of automatic writing, of objective chance, and of all the surrealist experiments become the phases of the conquest of a kind of *corps glorieux* for the use of man, to use Jacques Rivière's fitting expression. They tend simultaneously toward the manifestation of a new golden age, not pastoral, but superhuman and prodigious.

This is the period that saw the appearance of so many extraordinary works in which splendor was mingled with revolt, negation with hope: Breton's first *Manifeste*, in 1924, remarkable for the primacy it gives to dreams and for its desire to bring together in triumphant union revery and wakefulness; Benjamin Péret's often admirable poems, *Dormir, dormir dans les pierres;* Paul Eluard's *Capitale de la douleur; Corps et biens* by Desnos, as well as Louis Aragon's *Paysan de Paris* and Vitrac's *Connaissance de la mort.* The same climate made itself felt among the great painters: Chirico, Ernst, Masson, Picasso, Dali, Tanguy.

It seemed, when Breton published those two admirable works, *Nadja* (1928) and the *Second Manifeste* (1930), that surrealism was becoming more and more vigorous, that it would actually cross the boundaries of literature in order to take part in the exploration of the domain of the dream, the unconscious, and surrealist magic;

that it would completely reorganize the data of psychic science and penetrate to the very heart of fantastic realities.

Instead, this is the very time when it became completely embroiled in the crisis of materialistic Marxism. This, added to the lassitude of those who were looking for nothing but a literary adventure in surrealism, caused a gradually worsening break-up of the surrealist group. Yet this was a salutary experience to the extent that it kept surrealism from falling into subjective idealism, forcing it to a sharper awareness of the toughness of the obstacles that ordinary circumstances oppose to the flight of the fantastic.

This crisis did not in any case hold back the ever-widening circulation by the movement of the ideas and experiences brought about by surrealism. In spite of the ill-will of its sworn denigrators, surrealism has become the great nerve center of our era. The more we hear of the death of surrealism, the more it continues living and developing. The later writings of Breton continue to give the lie to its decline. It has traveled a long way from *Les Vases communicants to Flagrant délit,* and the road for the future remains open.

What are the basic questions brought up by the surrealist experience? This is what we shall try to analyze.

TWO

Esoterism and Surrealism

Surrealism appears first of all as that pure movement of revolt which was and remains in the avant-garde of the modern spirit. As such, nothing is more repugnant to it than being attached to a tradition. Animated by a particularly violent anti-religious spirit, it adhered to the atheistic materialism of Marx. This adhesion was only tempo-rary, but it expresses a deep and continuing tendency to reject all forms of spiritualism and to submit the surrealist mythology itself to a materialistic critique. It places itself in diametric opposition to all tradition, especially to all religious tradition. To omit this chief aspect of surrealism would be to disfigure it. It would be an even more serious omission, however, to pass over in silence the influence of esoterism on Breton's thought.

One has only to leaf through Breton's books to be struck by the numerous times the most famous names of alchemy and herme-ticism star these pages: Hermes, the Cabal, considered "one of the major problems dividing the ages," Flamel, Abraham Juif, Cornelius Agrippa, Paracelsus, Raymond Lully, Joachim de Flore, Eliphas Lévi, not to mention Sade and Lautréamont, those demigods of surrealism (cf. *Peinture*, p. 157). This fact alone is already strongly symptomatic; it is not a question here of picking up a few traces of esoterism in the sources of surrealism, in the vain hope of appearing erudite. It is much more important than that: for, as one penetrates more and more profoundly into surrealism, one realizes that hermeticism is the cornerstone that inspires its basic concepts.

There is no doubt but that esoterism and materialism are violently opposed one to the other. The uninitiated will judge them as incompatible as fire and water, and yet that does not prevent their being simultaneously the two poles of Breton's thought. For all that his path from one to the other seems capricious, disconcerting, bizarrely wandering, this is, nevertheless, the essential dialectical exercise of surrealism. One can even say that this name finds its highest justification in thus designating the attempt to carry forward progressively the synthesis of two most antagonistic points of view. It is from this very tension that surrealism receives its strength and determining factor.

The Supreme Point

The notion of the supreme point is the cornerstone of the surrealist cosmology, the living focal-point of real and surreal; it comes from esoterism. We have this formally from Breton himself. This is not just a notion inherited from the occultists; it expresses a desire so deep that one might say that it is doubtless from there that surrealism has taken its substance. (*Situation*, p. 26) The *Second Manifeste*, the great philosophic charter of surrealism, begins with these triumphal lines:

> Everything leads us to believe that there is a certain point in the spirit from which life and death, real and imaginary, past and future, communicable and incommunicable are no longer perceived as contradictories. It would be vain to look for any other motivation in surrealist activity than the hope of determining this point. (*Manifestes*, p. 92)

There is something Hegelian in the idea of thus bypassing all antimonies. However, the idea of the supreme point is not found in Hegel. Coming from another source, it adds something new; besides, this is not just philosophy. This supreme point must not be taken for a more theoretical viewpoint from which contraries can become reconcilable; it is a real point, truly surreal and central, situated both in the subjective reality of the consciousness and in the exterior universe. In a word, it is the living focal-point of the totality of the world in which it is no longer possible to perceive the diverse forms of being as essentially heterogeneous realities. It is not a theoretical point, but rather a superhuman domain which will not forever remain inaccessible to exploration by man.

The apex of the point, moreover, is exact only in relationship to the perspectives of ordinary existence. From beneath, there where the observer must of necessity remain, this region that is sovereign mediator of antimonies is so far removed that it seems no larger than a speck. It is just like a star, seemingly so tiny above earth's immensity, and yet which is a world infinitely more vast than this planet.

Even if we call this point supreme, in the sense that it dominates all the others, this does not mean that it is opposed to those others that we might call inferior, but that it includes them all in its dialectic totality. It is not the negation of what is below at the expense of what is above, as in idealism, nor the negation of what is above for the sake of what is below, as in materialism; it is the negation of their existential dislocation, the affirmation of their reciprocal positivity, the possession of their totality.

For the same reason, the surreal, of which this point is the focus, is no transcendental empyrean situated above earthly reality, but shot through by the beams of a fantastic light. Surreal is not to be confused with unreal; it is the living synthesis of the real and the unreal, of the immediate and the virtual, of the banal and the fantastic. Such a contention appears logomachy only to the extent that these words maintain their falsely compartimentalized sense, while surrealism implies becoming aware of their manifold overlapping.

Even in the period when Marxism exercised its strongest hold on Breton, the idea of surrealism's bringing about an *effective* conciliation of the most disparate realities did not disappear. Thus in 1932, in *Vases communicants*, Breton wrote:

> It is my desire that it (surrealism) be best recognized for having attempted to set up a line of communication between the over-disassociated worlds of sleep and wakefulness, of interior and exterior reality, of reason and folly, of the calm of knowledge and of love, of life for the sake of life and of Revolution. (p. 101)

One will notice in this text a brief eclipse of the symbol of the supreme point, indicative of a serious weakening of the surrealist cosmology, threatened with submersion by materialism. It is striking to notice in this regard that this new enumeration no longer mentions the antimonies of past and future, of life and death. To pose the problem is, in effect, to compromise materialistic principles. On the other hand, surrealist prometheism undergoes a veritable *capitis deminutio:* it no longer envisages anything but a kind of rearranging within the human condition; gone are the plans to dynamite its basic foundations. (The same winding-down appears in *Position politique,* published in 1935, p. 63.)

But Breton's thought triumphs over this crisis of self-criticism, since two years later, in *Limites non frontières du surréalisme* (N.R.F., February 1, 1937), he again writes:

> It is by calling upon automatism and automatism alone, under all its forms that one can hope to resolve, other than on an economic basis, *all* those antimonies which, because they existed prior to the form of social regime under which we live, may well outlast it. These antimonies, cruelly felt, must be gotten rid of, implying as they do a servitude deeper, more definitive than any temporal servitude; this suffering, no more than any other, must not find man resigned. These antimonies are those of waking and sleep (of reality and dream), of reason and folly, of the objective and the subjective, of perception and representation, of past and future, of the collective sense and love, and even of life and death.

These lines show decisively surrealism's stand in regard to Marxism, not in any way denying it, but engulfing it in a vaster, more comprehensive synthesis. This time, the limitless nature · of surrealism's metaphysical ambitions is reaffirmed without any possible equivocation. No less clear is this commentary in *L'Humour noir:*

> The whole Nietzchian enterprise tends to bolster up the "surmoi" as a growth and enlargement of the ego (pessimism presented as a source of good will, death as a form of liberty, sexual love as the ideal realization of the union of opposites: "to annihilate one's self in order to become once more.") This is no more than giving back to man all the power that he has been capable of attributing to God's name. (p. 97)

It goes without saying that, while writing these lines about Nietzsche, Breton could not see surrealism as aiming lower. They show the human will to arrive at an absolute sovereignty over the cosmos and fate. It is not surprising, then, that in publishing *Situation de surréalism* in 1945, Breton reaffirms more strongly than ever the same terms he had used in *Le Second Manifeste* to insist on the existence of the supreme point and on the willingness of surrealism to lead humanity to it.

This essential idea of surrealism comes from the hermetic tradition; it can be found in the Cabal and plays an essential role in *Le Zohar*,[1] in whose metaphysics it is creation's point of origin, the point of action in which God created the world and in which everything is contained *ab ovo*. It is, in a certain sense, the throne of the Creator. It is God in action tending toward the exterior.

> A tradition teaches us that when the Holy One, may he be blessed, created the world, he wrote in the unintelligible world the letters which represent the mysteries of the faith; he wrote there the letters Yod, He, Vav, He, which sum up every world, above and below. Yod represents *the central point, the cause of all things*, which remains hidden from all the worlds, which is unknown and will remain forever unknown; it is the supreme mystery of the Infinite. There emanates from this mysterious point a thin net of light which receives the vibrations of the One who does not vibrate, from the mysterious point, and reflects the light of the One who sheds no light, the mysterious point. The vibrations felt by the thin net form luminous waves around it; and this light brought about by the waves constitutes

the "charm of the charm", that is, the thin net of light constitutes the charm of the mysterious point and the light of the waves constitutes the charm of the thin net of light. . . . Thus it is that the thin net gives birth to a world of light brought on by the waves, which world illumines all other worlds.[2]

In a footnote, the translator adds this commentary:

The central mysterious point is Kether; the thin net of light coming out from it is Hochma. Kether is the brain of all creative emanations and the crown of the sephirotic tree which is in some sort the genealogical tree of creative manifestations in the world as seen by the Cabal.

We do in fact know that the doctrine of the Sephiroths has an immense value for the cabalists and forms the backbone of their conception of the world.

The notion of a supreme point reappears several times in the *Zohar*, notably in this passage that stresses how it is the heart of all worlds, the quintessence of the real from which radiate all the spheres of reality.

Beginning with the mysterious supreme point and reaching to the most infinitesimal degree of creation, everything serves as vesture for a superior thing and so on . . . The supreme point threw out an immense light of such subtlety that it penetrated everywhere. In this way, a palace was formed around this point and clothed it. The light of the supreme point being of an almost inconceivable subtlety, that of the palace, which is inferior, forms a dark circle around it. . . . But the light of the first palace, even though inferior to that of the supreme point, possessing even so an immense splendor, ends by forming around this palace another which serves it as a kind of vesture, and so on: Thus, beginning with the supreme point, each graduation of creation fits like a skin around another.[3]

It must be noted that the vehement criticism made of de Pauly's translation has nothing to do with the matter at hand. We are not at this moment looking to tabulate historically the exact ideas of the cabalists of the Middle Ages, but rather to indicate what influences have indeed come down to us from their era. A possible error in the former case would be no less historical matter in the latter.

This same notion of supreme point is found at the heart of the esoteric geometry of John Dee, the English cabalist. John Dee speaks of it under the name of hieroglyphic monad and writes notably that "It is by virtue of the point and of the monad that things began in principle to be." [4] Grillot de Givry, in his commentary, notes that this point has the same meaning in the Cabal as the letter Yod, "the generative and phallic symbol." This theme is used by another cabalist, Khunrath, as well as by Paracelsus.

It is striking to notice in the works of Cardinal de Cuse the presence of an analogous cosmology founded equally on the concept of the point as the integral generator of the universe, containing it wholly and potentially or even from a superior and supra-worldly point of view, actually. He writes:

> The indivisibility of the point is but the image of the indivisibility of the one itself . . . Let the point communicate itself in the measure of its communicability, and that is its volume. . . In the indivisibility of the point are contained all indivisibilities, for one finds in them only the development of the punctual indivisibility. Everything to be found in the volume is but one point, that is to say, the image of itself.[5]

Since the point has no volume, to add it to itself is to add one nothingness to another, so that the immense multitude of points of which the universe seems to us to be made is only an illusion due to the fact that we are immersed in them; seen, however, from the outside, the whole world would be reduced to a single point which would be both the origin and the university of the cosmos.

> Nor is the spheric rotundity of the world divisible, because it consists of an indivisible and unmultipliable point . . . The extremity of the world, then, is not composed of points, but this extremity is a roundness which consists of one point . . . If it were possible for an observer to place himself outside the universe, the latter would be invisible to him, just as an indivisible point would be.[6]

The supreme point is not unreal, but on the contrary contains the totality of the real, a concept which is valuable not only for Cardinal de Cuse, but also for the Cabal and for surrealism. It is true that, seen from the interior of the sphere of the cosmos, it seems to evade the grasp, to be purely ideal, since man is literally submerged by the flooding multiplicity of appearances and dominated by the contradiction of antimonies.

It can be said that it is central, inasmuch as it is the focus of all reality, but it is not simply the geometric midpoint situated in the center of space: it takes in the totality of the cosmos, which is why it cannot be grasped from the interior of space. It could become so only for the man who would stand at the tangential point of the universal sphere and the exterior darkness, because this point of origin could be grasped only at the same time in which one would grasp the world as being some other than this very point.

In the same way, it cannot be reduced to the point located in the center of time (supposing, in any case, that such a notion had meaning) and which would then designate a mid-moment, because such a moment, the passive result of calculation, would have in itself no reason for being more privileged than any other moment in time; it would contain no extra measure of reality. Just as it encompasses all space, so does the supreme point encompass all of time. From the basis of an instant situated in time, we cannot grasp it either, since to grasp it means precisely to surmount the antimonies of the present, the past, the future, and eternity. Just as there is a super-point encompassing all of space, so there is a super-instant encompassing all of time. It could be grasped only by a deified man whose awareness would encompass the totality of space and of time.

The direct influence of the Cabal is also found in this commentary by Auriger on the *Noces chymiques de Christian Rosenkreuz:*

> The center of the circle is the point of perfect equilibrium where He (God) exists potentially. He manifested himself six times at equal intervals, from the center to the circumference, and these were the six days of creation. Seeing that the work was complete, He retired

within himself, and on the seventh day, the day of rest, the creative Power rejoined the center of the circle upon which He had acted.[7]

This idea of a supreme point is, moreover, at the heart of all occultist doctrines. René Guénon points this out in his study of the symbolism of the cross in esoterism:

> The center of the cross is then the point at which all oppositions are conciliated and resolved; within this point is established the synthesis of all contrary terms which, in reality, are contrary only from the exterior and particular viewpoint of a distinctive kind of knowledge. This central point corresponds to what Moslem esoterism designates as the "divine station," which is "that which reunites contrasts and antimonies"; it is what the tradition of the Far East calls the "Invariable Middle," the place of perfect equilibrium, represented as the center of the "cosmic wheel", and which is also at the same time the point at which "the activity of heaven" is directly reflected. This center directs all things by its "unacting activity" which, even though not manifest, or rather, because it is not manifest, is in reality the fullness of activity, for it is that of the Principles from which are derived all particular activities." [8]

Guénon adds quite justly that this point cannot be situated because it is absolutely independent of space, which is but the result of its expansion,[9] recalling the antimony we pointed out in connection with the Cardinal de Cuse and which a theory alone cannot surpass.

The same notion shows up again in the bardic Triads which speak of a certain "point of liberty", "in which is the equilibrium of all opposition".[10] Finally, it is Eliphas Lévi who evokes for us the same conceptions in a promethean statement which responds quite closely to Breton's:

> The Great Work is the conquest of the central point in which resides the equilibrant force. Everywhere, the reactions of the equilibrated force conserve universal life by the perpetual movement of birth and of death. . . . Those who have reached this central point are the real experts, the miracle-workers of knowledge and of reason. They are the masters of all the riches of the world and of the worlds,

the confidants and the friends of the princes of heaven; nature obeys them because their wish is the wish of the law that governs nature.[11]

That the idea of the supreme point is of esoteric and religious origin must now be evident. So how is it that surrealism could have been tempted to take it over for itself? It is because the idea is, if one may use the word, laicizable. It has been said that Descartes' world was self-constructed, the role of God therein being limited to the initial flick of the finger, so that with a slight "progression" it could be possible completely to abstract from this divine initiative and to close the world in on itself. God is present there only transparently to the eye of the believer, since he remains transcendent to his action. This is true even for the hermeticists who admit the divine immanence, for if they remove the barrier of the divine transcendence, they substitute for it the esoteric notion by which God still remains hidden, even though for other reasons and in another way. Even an atheist can grasp the idea of the supreme point; to adopt it, he has only to suppress that divine presence hidden in the background. In other words, for him the divine is only an abstraction representing the chief life-forces spread throughout the universe, and somehow concentrated in this point which is their source. Thus, the supreme point can remain for the surrealists the place, at once real and ideal, where all antimonies are resolved, the meeting-place of all the divine energies that Nietzsche dreamed of recuperating.

In spite of its extreme boldness, such an idea is not particularly idealist, since it in no way denies matter, but considers it as a constituent of reality. In this sense, surrealism can validly claim to bring about a synthesis between materialism and certain forms of pantheism and idealism. Only the affirmation of the primacy of matter was illogical and contrary to the very idea of surrealism; besides, this marked only a stage of the time when surrealism was at its most Marxian. Every time that surrealism fully affirms the notion of the supreme point, it rejects at least implicitly the primacy of matter and rises above the dialectic conception of Marxism which, choked by the affirmation of the primacy of matter, remains relative. It rises above the idealistic conception of dialectic also, which was the case of the Hegelian conception (at least, according to the Marxist interpretation) and it opens the perspectives of absolute dialectic.

This doctrine of the supreme point and this ambition to conquer it give surrealism a position quite apart from the atheist philosophies, because they place it in radical opposition to nihilism. They also set up an essential difference between surrealism's cosmology and that of Nietzscheism which remains cyclic, eternally subjecting man to the torture of the cosmic wheel.

Winning Back Lost Powers

Surrealism is not a passive philosophy, but a metaphysical going forward. It does not see the supreme point as some dead star whose position it would suffice to establish, but as a land of wonders to be conquered or, more precisely, reconquered. This is the desire expressed in the second main proposition of the *Second Manifeste:*

> Let us recall that the idea of surrealism is directed simply to the total regaining of our psychic power by that means which is none other than the dizzying descent into ourselves, the systematic illumination of the hidden places and the progressive darkening of others, a perpetual walking about in the heart of the forbidden zone; recall, also, that there is no possibility of this activity's ending as long as man manages to distinguish an animal from a flame or from a stone. (*Manifestes,* p. 111)

This idea of recuperation also is specifically hermetic. It opposes surrealism to all prometheisms based on a darwinian conception and which represent the evolution of the world and of humanity as a progressive ascent beginning from the lowest point; from the inanimate to the animal, from the animal to "primitive" man, from "primitive" to civilized. The curve described by surrealism is quite different, and is based in a belief in a lost paradise where man lived in a sort of wonderland, in perfect harmony with the forces of nature and the divine energy. Man was then infinitely closer to the supreme point than he is today, even taking into account his prodigious historical progress. Everything was possible and permitted, or almost so. However, it is by this mysterious *almost* that ruin was introduced, that is, the fall which accounts for man's miserable condition on earth. The essential role of religion and of hermeticism is to repair the consequences of this fall and to reintroduce man into a definitive wonderland. The particular task which hermeticism assigns itself is to allow certain initiates to anticipate the moment of this regaining of the lost powers.

This brief schema is generally valid for Judeo-Christian and Moslem hermeticism; one finds analogous conceptions in all primitive mythologies as well as in China and India. It is then remarkable to find this idea of the regaining of the lost powers reappearing at the center of the surrealist perspective, in spite of atheistic correctives and the fact that the idea poses insoluble problems. When Breton, starting on the first page of *Nadja*, asks himself how to give a really authentic response to the question, "Who am I?", and finds that he cannot do so other than by appealing to the idea of the phantom, one must see something more than the mark of the influence of the gothic novels. Through them, and by their mediation—I was going to say their medium—the word "haunted" strikes deeply responsive chords in him: "While I am alive, he makes me play the role of a phantom; evidently he is alluding to the fact that I had to cease to be, in order to become *who* I am" (*Nadja*, p. 7). For him, then, the way he pictures the phantom "is valuable above all . . . as the finished image of a torment which can be eternal" (*Nadja*, p. 8): an avowal that he is tempted here by the feeling that humanity is destined to a cyclic, and therefore irremedial, unhappiness. "It is possible," he adds, "that my life is but an image of this kind and that I am condemned to retrace my steps in the belief that I am exploring, condemned to trying to discover that which I ought very well to know, to learning some small part of what I have forgotten." (*Nadja*, p. 8)

Atheism, however, impels him to challenge in part the implications of such a conception. "This view of myself seems to me false only to the extent that it takes me for granted, that it arbitrarily situates at a previous level a completed figure of my thought which has nothing to do with time, that it implies in this time an idea of irreparable loss, of repentance, or of a fall which, to my mind, is indisputably without any moral basis." (*Nadja*, p. 9)

Even though this conclusion, flowing from atheism, seems to me inadmissible, Breton's thought is profound. It shows how, outside all religious dogma, surrealism aims to discover in the depths of the human person a mysterious domain where it will be in continuous communication with the supreme point. The obstacle separating us from it is within ourselves rather than outside us, and consists of that enigmatic threshold separating the ordinary self from the deeper self, where the singular immerses itself totally in the universal, where lucidity is completely one with the sense of cosmic mystery.

That is why the instant of ecstasy and illumination holds such a tremendous fascination for the surrealists, because it seems to realize that marvelous hope of a human plunge into timelessness. It is the instant of Proust, of Nietzsche, in which man believes that he can effectively surmount within himself the antimonies of time. Does he really do so? That is another question. In fact, it seems nothing more than a powerless effort allowing us to glimpse the act of casting off the bonds of time, but never going beyond the threshold of subjectivity, because it is as weak as the hand of a shadow, incapable of seizing for itself any objective reality.

One can see how surrealism throws doubt on the apparently most unshakeable ideas, even that of man's nature. Arnaud Dandieu [12] said, speaking of Proust, that modern man had discovered in Descartes' "*Je pense*" an abyss of heterogeneities: but in the case of surrealism, just as with Proust, it is not just a question of an immense psychological complexity, it is a calling into question of the very idea of psychology. The intermittences of the heart are but little compared to the intermittences of time. In the depths of the human spirit, there is found an immense fault running between its more or less comfortable adaptation to the earthly necessities and its abyssal life. However bundled up by the body's participation in the usual forms of society and nature, the human spirit is already, by its very presence, a witness, a fragment detached from the living source of surreality.

This is not true only of certain exceptional states. If man only knew how to open his eyes and observe, he could discover that already here below he is immersed in a kind of beyond. This is indeed what Breton suggests in this meditation on the word phantom: "By it I understand that what I take to be the objective manifestations of my existence, more or less deliberate manifestations, is only the passage within the boundaries of this life of an activity whose real extent is quite unknown to me." (*Nadja*, p. 7)

The human mind is no dead-end, nor a mere extension of the body enclosed within the brain; it is an immense chasm whose point of intersection with material life is located within the brain but which, from there, radiates in all directions, binding man to all regions, even the most secret, of the visible and invisible universe. It is in the mind, in that abyss, that is found the road leading to the conquest of superhuman worlds.

There is a mysterious region in man, hidden in his very depths, which goes beyond the human condition and is in communication with the supreme point. Here Archimedes' lever can be forged, capable of lifting the weight from the world and of restoring to man the full powers of his liberty. This is the domain that Breton is talking about in the second passage of the *Second Manifeste* where we have heard him call for the "dizzying descent into ourselves . . . a perpetual walking about in the heart of the forbidden zone." More enigmatic is the ending, where he writes that the activity of surrealism is faced with no serious chance of ending "as long as man manages to distinguish an animal from a flame or from a stone." This idea, however, ought not to disturb us even though it seems in overwhelming accord with the idea of the "darkening" of the places not presently hidden. Breton is not proposing as his goal an inorganic confusion of the awareness, like that of the infant still incapable of differentiating among the three realms of matter. This darkening is only a methodological necessity; it results from that tyrannical law of compensations which decrees that our awareness will make no progress in the immense domain open to its exploration if it does not abandon its usual stopping-places at least while en route. It will never go very far without first deciding to emigrate for a long time outside the boundaries of its birthplace. It is easy to imagine the contrary, since the eye of the spirit sees something of what is happening even very far off; but it is the same as for the eye of the body, our body does not live there where our look carries, because it cannot simultaneously occupy two different positions nor go very far abroad if we bring it back every evening under the same roof. And so it is for the human mind.

One must go beyond so-called normal sensations and "positive" knowledge, for they imprison us; how can we claim to be liberated so long as we remain within their keep? If we sometimes have the impression of escaping from this conditioning of the mind, it can be true only to the extent that we draw nearer, however little, to the supreme point—not by plunging into irreality, but by the discovery of a deeper perspective on human and cosmic reality.

This text shows also how a whole area of surrealist activity, which when seen from the outside appears purely negative and chaotic, can hide a positive meaning infinitely more important than its apparent role. By boycotting all the ideas received by ordinary means, by summoning forth an inconceivable and apparently unlocalized world, surrealism burns its bridges, constraining itself to continue forward into the midst of an unparalleled storm on the far side of which it hopes to enter into the forbidden domains. The darkening is only a phase on the way leading to the total recuperation of our psychic force.

In his works, Breton comes back a number of times to this idea that the conquest is rather a reconquering; and discovery, rediscovery. It plays an important role in his conception of love. Thus he says to the woman he loves: "Seeing you for the first time, I recognized you without the slightest hesitation." (*Arcane*, p. 35) Such a statement makes no sense in a materialistic philosophy, for it presupposes a whole background of ideas more or less analogous to the Platonic doctrine of the pre-existence of souls and of metaphysical memory.

It is the same as when Breton asserts that true love "restores to all things the lost colors of the time of the ancient suns." (*Amour*, p. 12) If one thinks of all the prestige that Breton gives to childhood or to primitive life, the objection could be made that it is hardly necessary to go so far back in order to situate the paradises he is alluding to. Yet that would be insufficient, for who could prove that such states approach the supreme point or the wonderland in any really appreciable way, or that they eliminate that radical alienation which man experiences in relationship to his true self and to the true life which must both be situated nowhere else but in the supreme point? There is an evident difference between today's city-dweller, mechanized and exhausted, and the child or the primitive. By the ordinary standards of our present-day life, it is an immense difference, and yet it remains infinitesimal compared to the immeasurable distance that separates us from the supreme point. Doesn't the primitive know servitudes other than ours? and the happiest euphoria of children, their wonderland—is not powerlessness its price? Only traces of the original state remain in them.

Breton, moreover, recognizes this in another passage where he points out how the separation of the subjective and the objective result from an initial and real prehistoric rupture: "Perception and representation are to be taken only as products of the dissociation of a unique original faculty, to which the eidetic image bears witness, and of which one finds some trace in the primitive and the child." (*Point*, p. 250) He adds immediately: "All those who care about defining the real human condition aspire more or less clearly to rediscover this state of grace."

He takes up the same idea again in making the brief summary contained in *Situation de surréalisme*, written during the war:

> For surrealism—and I think that one day this will be its glory—everything has been put to good use to overcome those oppositions wrongly presented as insurmountable and gouged deeply into the course of time; these are the true refiners of suffering: the opposition between insanity and so-called "reason" which refuses to take irrationality into consideration, the opposition between mental representation and

physical perception, both of them products of the dissociation of a unique original faculty whose trace remains in the primitive and the child, and which removes the curse from an insurmountable barrier between the interior and the exterior worlds; rediscovered, it would be man's salvation. (p. 27)

The extremely close resemblance of these two texts, written almost ten years apart, is amazing; it shows how unswerving Breton was in his basic intentions.

And yet, even the state of ecstasy and illumination which the poet sometimes attains is only a foreshadowing of liberation, and not that liberation itself. It is a sensible image of the wonderland, a sort of felt anticipation, but it is not yet the wonderland in fact. However, its heightened awareness brings with it a sort of regaining of the privileges of the primitive and the child. The whole value of these forms of existence lies in their having preserved traces of the original and future glory of man; but these are only traces.

The present life, no longer a paradise, is gray and miserable, offering a characteristic ruinous aspect: we live in the wreckage of paradise. And yet it is therein that we find the hope of attaining the supreme point; for if we had always been confined within the limits of a degenerate space and time, where would we have found the strength to go beyond them and to establish ourselves at a point and at an instant that stand outside this world? If, on the contrary, we had once in some way been there, then even if we are now fallen away, we shall perhaps be able to make up for the consequences of that catastrophe and to reintegrate ourselves into that former state—definitively, this time, for we shall have overcome the ordeal and the dizziness of the fall. If it is true that the fall took place, then it is also true that that former wonderland existed, as well as the passage from a superior place and time to an inferior. There would remain but to reverse the movement of destiny.

It is true that in the preliminary meditation of *Nadja*, Breton refuses the idea of the fall. Yet he is as it were, ceaselessly thrown upon the banks of this myth by the current of his thought. As soon as man becomes aware of the unhappiness of his earthly situation and proposes to himself the recuperation of a world of marvels, it becomes by definition evident that, at the beginning of history, there must have occurred that cosmic catastrophe called the "fall". Basically, it would probably be more exact to say that Breton does after a fashion recognize the fact of a primordial fall, but that he rebels violently against the idea that it could be the result of man's *fault*. It would be rather the result of a weakness of man faced with the blind hostility of fate. Surrealism aims to be the total renewal of the will to victory over destiny.

Calling On the Powers of Darkness

Although Breton states that he cannot accept the idea of a fall understood as just punishment, he has not the same trouble, it would seem, assenting to the notion of a primitive curse. But while believers try to win over to their side the celestial powers so that they will once more show themselves propitious, Breton means to have recourse to the powers of darkness, as though the alliance of all evil forces, both human and superhuman, could give a victorious power to the cosmic revolt.

This is one of the particular aspects of Breton's position: contrary to most atheists, contrary in any case to all materialists, he admits a superior source of reality and man's falling away from an original glory; at the same time, however, he is in opposition to believers because he does not count on celestial powers, but rather on a kind of cooperation from evil powers to attempt the great work of the regaining of the lost powers.

Even though for an atheist like Breton, God can be no more than an abstract symbol of fate, he nevertheless reveals himself as an agressive and vengeful Being in the myth of the curse. This myth seems very much alive to Breton's eyes when he writes—inspired perhaps by Vigny *(Eloa)*, by Victor Hugo *(La Fin de Satan)*, and by certain occultists—that human love is capable of regenerating the world and that by it "the great curse is raised." *(Arcane,* p. 80) It is true that, in this passage stating the theme of malediction, it would seem that it is love to which recourse is made; however, the sentiment of love is itself peculiarly envisaged by Breton. Indeed, he writes in *L'Amour fou:*

> Love, the only love that is, carnal love, I adore and have never ceased to adore your mortal shadow, your venomous shadow. The day will come when man will recognize you for his only master and will honor you even in those mysterious perversions with which you surround yourself. (p. 109)

A few pages further on he adds:

> The sex of the man and that of the woman are drawn to each other only on the condition that there be present between them a web of ceaselessly renewed uncertainties, a flight of humming-birds whose feathers have perhaps been smoothed in hell itself. (p. 118)

It would be indeed fallacious to see in the end of this passage nothing more than an episodic and superficial figure of speech; on the contrary, it springs up at the end with a strange sort of boldness, and, set off by its supernatural background, reveals the venomous basis of this love in a sort of infernal secret. Nor would it be out of place here to recall the well-known adage: *in cauda venenum:* no animal is entirely venomous, but it is enough to call one so for the poison of his sting to be mortal. Equally well-known is the symbol that assures us that a serpent is hidden under the flowers of love.

In addition, the whole of surrealism is itself envisaged, at least at certain moments, not only as an agent of rebellion, but even as an accursed thing which turns on the curse, no doubt to defy it; this is how Breton sees surrealism when, hoping to forbid it to the uninitiated, he writes: "Down with those who would scatter the evil bread to the birds." (*Manifestes,* p. 109)

We will see many other traces of this attitude in Breton's writings. I will at present, however, stress the fact that the idea of malediction is linked to the notion of the existence of evil powers in the darkness. Naturally, in virtue of Breton's materialistic tendencies and his atheism, the idea of evil spirits is almost as repugnant to him as that of a divinity, and logically so. This becomes evident in the reading of certain passages such as that in which he states that the existence of "spirits" smacks of a "nauseous terminology", that the idea of "guardian spirits" is a "sorry joke" from "lamentable spiritual literature." (*Point*, p. 237) Elsewhere, he ridicules the "poor mortals who used to take upon themselves the doubtful honor of admonishing the devil, which finally led him to decide, we are told, to show himself". (*Manifestes*, p. 203)

On the same page, however, he congratulates himself that a contact has always been maintained between evil poetry and the evil sciences. These are not mere idle words, for he had occasion to praise Desnos during the "period of sleep" for being lifted up by the "powers of the dark" (*Manifestes*, p. 151); Dali, for being the "envoy" of "mysterious powers" (*Point*, p. 88); and Max Ernst, for being "the most magnificent haunted brain in existence". (*Point*, p. 84)

We see then that there is a new light to be shed on that initial passage of *Nadja* in which Breton looks on himself as a phantom astray in the world for the purpose of haunting his own sensitive outer self. We have pointed out there an allusion to mankind's primordial fall and a hidden reference to the supreme point; attention must be drawn to the opposite view as well, contained in an allusion to the powers of darkness and to the bonds which unite them to man.

In Breton's language, the term "haunted" is all the more striking in that it distinguishes a place specially privileged in the mythical topology of surrealism: the theme of the haunted castle recurs continually as an essential leitmotiv of Breton's symbolism. It is the place par excellence for calling upon the powers of the supernatural. This attraction is noticeable from the very beginning of Breton's work. In *Les Pas perdus*, for example, he writes: "In the presence of a supernatural phenomenon, we express either delight or fear, nothing else. The most skeptical among us live in a haunted house". (p. 96). Further on, speaking of Chirico and the shocking nature of his painting, Breton goes one step more—a step accompanied by a curious reservation: "Nevertheless Chirico doesn't suppose that a ghost could get in other than through the door". (*Pas*, p. 112)

Even in these early notations there is manifest surrealism's characteristic wavering between modern skepticism, on the one hand, and belief in supernatural phenomena, on the other. These two tendencies never stop interfering with each other, but their strength is variable and depends on the degree of influence brought on by a wrong social state; but the meaning of the word phantom has varied in surrealism, tending sometimes to become narrowed down, absorbed into the concept of a psychic phantom, reduced, in a certain sense, almost to psychoanalysis, while, at other times, Breton has been able to avail himself of this means for the disintegration of pure materialism which the conjunction of the idea of dialectic with that of materialism has opened at the very heart of Marxism. He has, then, always been able to preserve in the idea phantom a certain measure of the marvelous which can be totally reduced neither to Marxism nor to psychoanalysis.

The origin of the theme of the haunted castles which people Breton's imagination seems to antedate that strange series of stories, the gothic novels and, before them, the chivalrous novel. In the midst of the Marxist period, he admits to the taste he has for gothic novels and to the long searches he undertakes in Paris to collect them: those of Lewis, of Maturin, even those of Clara Reeve, *Le Vieux Baron anglais* (*Vases*, p. 104), *Les Amants somnambules* (*Vases*, p. 122). "There is nothing more exciting," he writes, "than this wildly romantic, ultra-sophisticated literature. All those chateaux of Otranto, Udolpho, the Pyrenees, Lovel, Athlin, Dunbayne, rent with great cracks, honeycombed by tunnels, persist in leading their fictitious life, in presenting their strange phosphorescence, in the darkest corner of my mind" (*Vases*, p. 117). Later, praising once more this type of novel, he says of Maturin's famous Melmoth: "The famous Melmoth, which will live for a long time in Baudelaire's memory and which, along with the *Night Thoughts* of Young, is probably the most vivifying of the sources from which Lautréamont's powerful inspiration has drunk." (*Limites*, p. 208)

Breton is not alone in experiencing this attraction for haunted places, for the whole surrealist tradition has, by anticipation, paid tribute to it. Does not the immense prestige that Sade has among the surrealists come, in part, from the fact that he has taken up once more, under a new form perfectly acceptable to atheism, the theme of the castle of horrors, in which men are raised to the level of demonic spirits?

In this connection, Breton makes a striking social psychoanalysis of the myth of the castle in the gothic novel:

> The ruins appear charged suddenly with meaning to the extent that they are the visual expression of the disintegration of the feudal period; the ghost which haunts them marks, with a peculiar intensity, the fear that the powers of the past may return; the tunnels are the image of the slow, dark and perilous progress of the human individual toward the light; the stormy night is but the transposition of the almost unremitting noise of cannon. (*Limites*, p. 209)

In other words, he considers this myth as "symptomatic of the profound social disturbance which took hold of Europe at the end of the eighteenth century."

It would be wrong, however, to limit oneself to this aspect of the question; Breton is too sensitive to the complexity of events and their meaning to reduce everything to a single interpretation. On the preceding page, he points out himself the perspectives which could lead to another orientation: "It is only on the brink of the fantastic at the point where human reason loses control, that the deepest emotion of the being is most likely to be translated." (*Limites*, p. 208) Social upheavals permit the consciousness to have a sudden glimpse of the deep fissures that accompany them.

We shall bring out further on the essential place that automatic writing has in surrealism, but it is important to note immediately that its appearance in modern literature is closely tied to the genesis of the gothic novel. Breton himself points out that the first of these, *The Castle of Otranto*, written by Walpole in 1764, was set down automatically; this was formally sworn to by the author (*Limites*,

p. 211). This fact is all the more meaningful in that, for Breton, automatic writing is not simply a superficial phenomenon affecting language, it is linked to the mediumistic, even the spiritist idea, in spite of Breton's hostility to the notion of spirits and spirit-literature in general. Once again there remains a basic ambiguity that resists all attempts at elucidation. One sees, in any case, that the source of the gothic novels is not that of ordinary literature, but the quasi-mediumistic activity of quasi-haunted human minds.

It is curious to note in speaking of these so-called "gothic" novels, that William James qualifies as "gothic" psychology (*Point*, p. 225) Myers' research on the subliminal world and the automatism of mediums. This is more than an overlapping of vocabulary. Breton states, in this regard, that he owes even more to Myers than to Freud; it is remarkable that no one has ever drawn attention to so important and significant a fact.

Breton asks himself this question:

> Are there places predestined to the carrying out of the particular form of mediumistic activity which in such a case manifests itself? Yes, there must exist observatories of the interior heavens; I mean ready-made observatories, in the exterior world, naturally. That would be, one might say from the surrealist point of view, where castles come in. (*Limites*, p. 211)

He notes with interest that Lewis spent his youth in a very old manor-house, and that Huysmans situated in an abandoned castle the work which Breton considers his masterpiece, *En Rade.* "My own research," he adds, "trying to discover the place most favorable to the reception of the great annunciatory waves, immobilised me as well—at least theoretically—in a sort of chateau that was able now to beat only one of its wings". (*Limites*, p. 212. Cf. "Il y aura une fois" in *Révolver*, p. 9, and the first *Manifeste*, p. 32.)

He evokes nostalgically the old castles of Aquitaine and of Montségur, linked to the Cathares (*Arcane*, p. 81), Mélusine's castle at Lusignan (*ibid.*, p. 86), and the old novels of chivalry, full of curious castles (*ibid.*, p. 100)—no doubt the source of his liking for the castle in *L'Histoire de l'oeil*,[13] and for Julien Gracq's novel, *Le Château d'Argol*, "in which probably for the first time, surrealism looks back freely in order to measure itself against the great perceptive experiences of the past, and to evaluate from an emotional as well as a clairvoyant angle the extent of its conquest." (*Situation*, p. 5) His manifest taste for the manor-house of Ango and the Chateau of Saint-Germain-en-Laye, of which the photographs are included in *Nadja* (pp. 26 and 40) and for such other remarkable fragments of the past as the Porte Saint-Denis (*Nadja*, p. 40) and the Tour Saint-Jacques (*Amour*, p. 69) is a light flowing from the same secret sources.

What gives these castles their mythical value is that they are outstanding as the setting of ghostly apparitions, the burning witnesses of an incredible afterlife. Even more than the well-known chasm by which ancient Aeneas went down into the underworld, are they the domain in which stones and night crack to give passage to men once like us, men at present gone down into that other world in which they are prey to unimaginable torments, and yet on the path of the great metamorphosis.

More than by the raised drawbridges of former times, the haunted castles are today defended by time, which has literally profaned them. Their value lies much less in their material ruins than in the electric conductors of their myths which lead the human spirit into the deepest parts of its own labyrinth. Where now is to be found the realm where the phantoms will show themselves? It is this passionate quest for a new castle of the Grail—a black Grail—wherever it may be, that in Breton's opinion gave so much importance to the German expressionists' film, *Nosferatu le vampire*. This is the basis of the frightening and fascinating glow emanating from the sentence: "As soon as they reached the other side of the bridge, ghosts came to meet them." (*Vases*, p. 50 and *Peinture*, p. 43)

Even if the bridge leading to the domain of the phantoms has been destroyed, and if free communication no longer exists, Breton, in exploring the center of Paris by the dim light of his unconscious, is nevertheless attempting to disengage the material foundations of this fantastic region from engulfing time. *Nadja's* spellbinding power lies in the double movement by which Breton puts himself forward as a kind of phantom at the same time that he consecrates as a myth in stone the polygon stretching from the Tuileries and the Tour Saint-Jacques in the direction of Porte Saint-Denis as far as the heaps of strange objects in the flea market near Porte Saint-Ouen.

It is in this neighborhood that this strange story from the early days of surrealism took place: "Louis Aragon remembers, as I do, being one evening in a café in Place Pigalle with Chirico, when a child came in to sell flowers. Chirico, sitting with his back to the door, had not seen him come in; it was Aragon, struck by the strange demeanor of the boy, who asked if this might not be a ghost. Without turning around, Chirico took out a pocket mirror and, having taken a long look at the child, said that it was a ghost indeed." (*Peinture*, p. 43)

This took place in the same epoch in which Aragon was presenting in his *Paysan de Paris* a mythical evocation of the Passage des Panoramas and of the Buttes-Chaumont park. Chirico in his turn was discovering the mystery of Versailles where "each angle of the palace, each column, each window had a soul which was an enigma." (cf. *Peinture*, p. 46) It was the time of supposedly objective ghosts, but now that time has passed. Furthermore, surrealism had to overcome this childhood illness by the strength of its self-criticism. What direction, then, would a new route toward the phantoms take, if not into the abyss that Breton had opened in the very depths of his being? Once this abyss was opened, other similar ones showed themselves. Let Breton ask Nadja the key question: "Who are you?" and she, moved by the same sentiment as the poet, answers unhesitatingly: "I am the wandering soul." (*Nadja*, p. 92) Rare are those persons capable of this unusual grasp of themselves, revelatory of their own mystery. Phantoms are concealed, not by ruins, but by man himself. Ruins are the dark mirror where he projects the spectres which haunt him in his deepest secrets. In one sense, there is a split here, a new alienation; but in another, this strange split frees him from another break-up, from another alienation.

It is the living man himself, then, who in this world becomes aware of his quality of ghost from the other world. The aim of surrealism is to awaken these phantoms everywhere, to draw up the first cohort to cross this initial barrier and to find new procedures of evocation. It was not pure fantasy on Breton's part one day to compare surrealism to an attempt to build a phantom ship. (*Manifestes*, p. 143)

To feel oneself a phantom is a mental phenomenon containing an extremely concrete meaning. It indicates the degree to which one can feel a stranger to oneself, be exiled from one's ordinary person, dragged into the underground passages of the mind, menaced by distant rumblings which betray the lava that lies beneath the floor of the labyrinth of the mind. Even the exterior world begins to be shaken by the first rumblings of a seism whose nature is unknown. Man then detects in himself a vast web of words, of images and of thoughts he cannot account for, and, in the interference between his personality and the world, a subtle network of premonitions and of magic coincidences. His mind becomes a screen receiving the projections of occult powers.

The world is not intangible. Even though it is not, as the idealists would have it, an illusion created by the mind, and even though it is the very rock of exterior objectivity, it is still not the exclusive basis of reality, in spite of contrary claims of the materialists. Besides, our awareness of it depends, not on it alone, but on the dialectical relationship between exterior matter and human awareness. Its architecture, such as we envisage it, is not then an irrefutable basic element, is not separable from the exercise of the mind that comes to grips with it. As soon as that awareness begins to hold suspect its ordinary forms of representation, it does not necessarily lose itself in irreality, but it does become more likely to discover other, no less real, faces of the cosmos. The *extravagant* forms of awareness bring man into a maze of *extravagant* worlds that normal awareness cut off.

Basically, surrealism refuses to believe in supernatural phantoms, yet it has never ceased to be haunted by their spectre and, under the light of subjectivity, tends to make them reappear. For the surrealists, such an evocation is no literary game, but the equivalent of that which to the believer is represented by the rites permitting him to enter into contact with the world of the sacred.

This new kind of psychical-tangible phantom appears in a story of Taine's that Breton relates: a man sick in bed had one day the hallucinatory vision of a wonderful creature seated at the foot of his bed in the attitude of the statue known as the *tireur d'épine*, and whose hand he could feel with his own. The man was about to engage this gracious phantom in conversation when someone brought him a bowl of broth, putting an end both to his fasting from food and, at the same time, to the apparition. "How can I hold my temper," Breton would exclaim, "at the thought of that man who would not live the most beautiful poem in the world? Damn his ill-timed hunger and that stupid broth! I assure you that I wouldn't have drunk that poison." (*Peinture*, p. 40) Those phantoms are rare who make their presence so tangibly known, at least during the time when the conditions of their apparition are respected; every effort must be made to come nearer their domain of projection. For Breton, this vision was the most beautiful of poems because the value of art lies much less in its esthetic interest than in its evocatory capacity. "The art object lies midway between the tangible and the rational," Hegel had said already. "It is a spiritual thing that appears material. Insofar as they address themselves to the imagination and the senses, art and poetry purposely create a world of shadows, of phantoms, of fictive images; and yet one cannot accuse them of being incapable of producing anything other than forms empty of all reality." (cf. *Position*, p. 122)

The general error committed in this regard is to objectivize works of art, in the pejorative sense that Beriaeff gives to that verb, and to consider them as beings in themselves, independently of the author and of the reader or spectator. A positivist, classic, and so-called realistic mentality is responsible for this error which compartmentalizes reality in an arbitrary manner, brutally opposing the work as such and man as such in the double impasse of a terminal contra-

diction. Altogether different is the dialectical conception which recognizes this opposition and tends to go beyond it. From this point
of view, the work has no existence separable from that of man,
from whom it comes, and toward whom it is directed. It is the
medium in which is mingled an indefinite interlinking of human
minds through the channels of malleable and tangible matter. It
is a screen on which the images of our phantoms are projected and
flashed back. These images are not at all fictive, in the pejorative
sense of the term; they are alive with a real life because they are
one of the modes in which our own human life manifests itself.

However, at the period when Marxism held greatest sway, Breton
allowed the idea of the phantom to die out somewhat. This is how
he could be brought to challenge "those imaginary beings born of
religious terror, escapees from the more or less troubled reason of
an Hieronymus Bosch or of a William Blake." (*Vases*, p. 60) The
motives of this condemnation were borrowed from Engels, who stated:
"The beings outside time and space, created by the clergy and
nourished by the imagination of ignorant, oppressed masses [are but]
the products of a sickly fantasy, the subterfuges of philosophic
idealism, the evil products of an evil social condition" (*Vases*, p.
59)—quite a brief explanation. Breton adds, moreover, that according
to Freud, the origin of phantoms is to be sought in those nocturnal
visitors in white night-clothes who wake up children (*Vases*, p. 64);
this explains in a much more penetrating manner the origin of certain
travesties of the supernatural, but does not go to the heart of the
problem, for other, much deeper forces are at work here.

At the same time, Breton argued that it was right to put into
a different category those strange monsters such as Dali's *Le Grand
Masturbateur*, Picasso's *Joueur de clarinette*, Duchamp's *The Bride*,
Ernst's *La Femme 100 têtes*. (*Vases*, p. 60) Such beings have always
exercised a great fascination on Breton, which is why he praises
Chirico for having painted "eternal places . . . which tend to become
haunted places (ghosts and presages)" (*Peinture*, p. 87); Dali, for
having cast upon the world absolutely new beings, full of evident
evil purpose . . . birds of prey" (*ibid.*, p. 90); Tanguy, for having

made himself master of "specters", of certain "wandering beings" (*ibid.*, p. 175), and for having gone down into that fabled region that Goethe names that of "mothers." "Human thought," he adds, "fulgurates and humbles itself in the contemplation of these divinities thanks to whom all that is possible tends unceasingly to be manifested" (*ibid.*, p. 173). From this same source comes Breton's immense admiration for Achim d'Arnim, the eminent creator of spectres and of golems. (*Point*, pp. 150-190)

One must not, however, believe that the impulse which directs surrealism toward those haunted realms where phantoms show themselves terminates in the mere recalling of the past or in purely artistic phantasies. In the first place, as we have already pointed out, these works, far from being an end in themselves, constitute the blazes (stupas or mounds of rock) on that trail leading toward the dizzying, endless heights Breton speaks of.

Automatic writing and objective chance will be examined later on, but from the very outset the importance of these two phenomena and of experiences related to them must be understood, because it is thus dually that surrealism brings to life, simultaneously within subjective human experience and at the heart of ordinary life, the active presence of an immense haunted domain. Taken in this manner, surrealism could be defined as a vast system of spectral projections and of listening posts in the dark. It can be admitted *a priori* that the nature of these apparitions is wholly psychic; however, they cannot be reduced to psychology, even as renewed by Freud. Beneath these continual whisperings, one catches the possible strain of what might be the extra-human. "Even while completely solitary," Breton tells us, "I entered into strange complicities which convince me of my illusions during those moments when I thought myself alone at the helm of the ship." (*Nadja*, p. 23)

Breton does seem to admit that, in the case of automatic writing, this feeling is caused by a certain duality of consciousness. One can also see there, as he sometimes does and notably in *L'Amour fou*, instances of subconscious communication with other human beings that cut across time and space, but it would be difficult to exclude completely the possibility of quasi-demoniacal influences. One could perhaps reduce them in the surrealist cosmology to mere impersonal mindless forces, as Breton does astrological influences. "Microbes, which are considered animals, appear above all as powers, as do the emanations of the stars." (*Pas*, p. 107)

However, even taking into account Breton's atheism and the irony with which he treated the Satanists, there remains a profound ambiguity in surrealism. For example, I do not believe that the interest surrealism exhibits in the occult sciences, in the most evil sense of that expression, has to do solely with their oddity or their poetic value. Breton and many of the surrealists have a real taste for evil for the sake of evil, incommensurate with what is necessary to their battle against religion.

In the same way, when he writes in capital letters in the *Second Manifeste:* "I desire the profound and real eclipse (occultation) of surrealism" (p. 109), it is hard to see only the expression of a refusal of purely literary glory. Why should this *occultation* take place, if not for those positive and very special reasons which will be seen further on? In reality, he is playing on the analogy of the words *occultation* and *occultisme.* If he proposes a turning aside from public attention, it is because he wants to have an "in" with the occult; so true is this that he indicates, in a footnote, how necessary it is that surrealism come to a serious recognition of the occult sciences. His cry is, "Down with those who would scatter the evil bread to the birds."

It is typical of Breton to have once proposed rebuilding the ark, with the wish that "this time, it be not the dove which returns, but the raven" (*Point*, p. 84)—not the symbol of the Holy Spirit, but that of Satan. Again, there is his interest in Uccello's painting, *The Desecration of the Host* (*Nadja*, pp. 109 and 127), and his use, in the love litanies of *L'Union libre*, of the expression: "my wife with her tongue like a wounded host."

It is he too who recalls that the morning star, shining with "a glory surpassing all the others" at the top of the seventeenth card of the tarot deck, is called Lucifer (*Arcane*, p. 106). This card gives its name to the book of which it is essentially the subject. It is here that he speaks of that "unique craftsman of darkness and evil (p. 82), that "boa," "the great Curved One," "the vanquished hypnotist who is in no way the one he is said to be." This last incident is strongly sibylline. It is clear that Breton rejects the religious conception of Satan, and yet what new form of existence will he impose on him? Towards the end of the book, he comes back to the same question:

> 'The Abbé Constant, like Victor Hugo', writes M. Viatte, 'shows us first of all the fall of that angel who, being born, refused to be a slave' and who 'falls through the darkness in a shower of suns and stars pulled down by the attraction of his glory'; but Lucifer, his intellect proscribed, gives birth to two sisters, Poetry and Liberty, and 'it is in their guise that the spirit of love will tame and save the rebellious angel . . .!
>
> It is revolt and revolt alone which creates light, light which reaches us only through poetry, love or liberty. (*Arcane*, p. 176)

What exact meaning should be given to Breton's declaration about what he names *the great transparent beings?* He writes:

> Man is perhaps not the center, the pivot of the universe. It is quite possible that there exist animals higher than he on the scale of being, as distant from him in their comportment as he from the whale or the may-fly. There is no reason why these beings should not be completely outside our system of sensory references and camouflaged under whatever shape the theory of form and the study of mimetic animals offer as possibilities. This opens the widest possible speculative field, even though man, as interpreter of his own universe, remains in somewhat the same limited condition as the child who, disturbing an anthill, conceives of its occupants as always in the same disarray. Man is witness—or victim—of such events as cyclones, or wars (about which his testimony is notoriously unreliable); why couldn't he, using a bold inductive method, undertake that vast study needed to examine the makeup and structure of such hypothetical beings, glimpsed obscurely by us through the curtain of hazard and fear. I want to point out that I am not far from the idea of Novalis who says that

'in reality, we are living as parasites of a host animal whose make-up determines ours and vice-versa,' and I am in accord with William James' query: 'Who knows if our place in nature is not as insignificant to those beings whose presence near us we ignore, as that of the cats and dogs in our homes is to us.' Even some scholars subscribe to this opinion: 'We are perhaps surrounded by beings made on man's pattern, yet different; their albumin, for example, might be dextroro-tated.[14] These are the words of Emile Duclaux, former director of the Institut Pasteur (1840-1904).

A new myth? Are we to convince these beings that they are but mirage, or allow them to show themselves? (*Manifestes*, p. 211)

This is a surprising point of view for so promethean a surrealist as Breton. Is it possible that, from the heights, invisible titans bar man's upward path, or can he count on their goodwill? In any case, who are these beings? The traces of a somewhat analogous mythology are found in the modern parascientific fiction of Wells, Rosny, and Conan Doyle, but this is not what lends it the most credibility. Breton has already given them a place higher than us, but still on the animal scale, thereby, in theory, divesting them of all properly supernatural qualities. The fact that he sees them as possibly presiding over cyclones, for instance, seems at first to reinforce this hypothesis; however, if these beings are linked as well to bellicose phenomena, to feelings of pure terror and of evil fortune, do they not then belong to an entirely different sphere, to the extra-human realm of the psychic? It is true that even the most improbable suppositions are possible in the elusive mist where these hypothetical beings hide. These disturbing creatures, however animal-like they be, could still be gifted like the human race with psychic powers, perhaps even superior to ours, and capable therefore, of acting on quite divergent levels.

It is interesting to compare these theories of Breton about cyclones with some strange lines by Strindberg:

On September 10, Paris was ravaged by a cyclone, under very strange circumstances. In a period of complete calm, it begins behind Saint-Sulpice, in the Jardin du Luxembourg, passes by the Chatelet theater and the Prefecture de Police, and finally loses strength at the Saint-Louis hospital after having gone from one end to the other of fifty meters of iron fence. It is about this cyclone, and the one in the Jardin des Plantes, that my theosophist friend asks me: "What is a cyclone? Billows of hate, waves of passion, spiritual emissions?" And he adds: "Are the Papuans conscious of their manifestations?" And by a chance which is more than chance, in a letter that crosses my friend's, I direct to him who is an initiate into Hindu mysteries this precise question: "Are the Hindu wisemen able to *produce cyclones?*" [15]

Such an hypothesis may seem absurd, especially since we can in no way determine the ultimate limits of man's direct power over nature, and it differs from that of Breton, who envisages extra-human intervention; however, the conditions basic to these two types of supposition may very well be almost, if not wholly, identical. Besides, they are not really that irreconcilable if one admits that the "great transparent beings" are able to act through the human psychism, and that the operations of black magic are possible only with the aid of those enigmatic powers called transparent or shadowy. Astrology presents an analogous case, saying that there are present in the stars strange forces capable of predetermining the physical and mental formation of man and of guiding his destiny. These are autonomous spirits which cannot be grasped directly, but which are immanent to the stellar reality of the universe and to the human psychism.

One could make remarks just as unlikely and equally as troubling about the warlike explosions that chronically ravage humanity. . . . The recourse to violence in order to have a share of gold, of women, of all the riches of the earth is a natural, quasi-animal manifestation; but in the storms of anger and irrational hate which sometimes stir mankind to the most terrible pitch of madness, there is a strange alienation of the human being, so that he becomes the victim of the darkest kind of possession. Can we not then say that he has fallen prey to hellish breeds of microbes, to savage animals of an unidentified but powerful species?

However, it is not these broad and overtheoretic perspectives, deprived as they are of particular and typical examples, which matter most here. Even if the fears emanating from nature or from the obscure unconscious of unleashed human collectivities have a secret background where one can discern the action of unsuspected forces, the latter are too closely mingled with them, too strongly disguised by them, not to seem purely gratuitous guesses, both indiscernible and unverifiable.

Breton makes allusion as well to the possible presence of the transparent beings in the sentiment of fear and in certain manifestations of objective chance. Unlike the aforementioned, which is perhaps only passing (or perhaps not), this new category of suppositions seems to have deep roots in surrealism. There are to be found a certain number of signs which are harbingers of it in Breton's work, for example, the enigmatic feeling of discomfort that the statue of Etienne Dolet causes him (*Nadja*, p. 31), or the strange fear he seems to have experienced at the sight of the skull of Rousseau's statue, or again, his pronounced taste for such upsetting works as certain of Chirico's paintings, like *L'Angoissant Voyage ou l'Egnime de la Fatalité* or Uccello's *The Descration of the Host* (cf. *Nadja*), or Duchamp's "glass", *The Bride*, as well as the gothic novels, with their ghosts and underground passages.

This is a feeling of anguish quite different from that of existentialism, it is neither abstract nor general, nor is it the paradoxical fruit of an impression of emptiness. On the contrary, it is quite concrete and proceeds from an excessive awareness of certain presences. While existential anguish comes mostly from a kind of dizziness in the face of an emptiness that suddenly opens underfoot, surrealist anguish results from a sort of terrible fascination: just as the traveler in a forest perceives in the very act of reaching for it, that what he took to be a stick is really a serpent, so the surrealist sometimes discerns in a banal, everyday object an unexpected sign of terror. It is not emptiness, but rather an excess of being, which causes his anguish. And so, far from finding life absurd because devoid of meaning, there is a sense of fatality which pierces to the depth of his being.

The most striking case of irrational fear linked to the feeling of chance is contestably the story of the house of discord belonging to Michel Henriot, a kind of evil domain, the modern transposition of the haunted places, recounted by Breton in *L'Amour fou.* In this account, according to Breton, there was at work a *local* disquieting, troubling action, even though at the time he was unaware of what place exactly he was skirting; this is a typical example of terror in its pure state. Here, at least, the hypothetical powers of the "transparent beings" enter clearly into play, making this category of phenomena of surrealism much more specific and much more troubling.

One might be surprised that Breton, in his text on the transparent beings, gives as examples of their link with chance only those drawn from manifestations of *hasard noir:* cyclones, wars, fear. Is he tempted then to see them as evilbearing, or is it only a matter of an omission in his choice of examples, an insignificant omission which does not merit being considered as deliberate? Perhaps Breton's faith in absolute revolt and his appeals to the indefinable powers of darkness lead him more or less consciously to glimpse only the presence of evil forces outside humanity. Or perhaps he is tempted to see in them powerful allies who will accept the challenge of the curse; but such accursed allies themselves are extremely disturbing: are they really capable of being allies? Are they not rather of their own choice bent on aggravating man's fate on earth? We have of course seen to what point Breton found it distasteful to enter into belief in evil spirits; he lets himself be carried to the limit without ever completely giving in to the idea. But one must ask one's self if the idea of the great transparent beings does not bring him infinitely closer to it, even though he maintains them still on the animal scale. Isn't this a way of bringing them out of their anonymity and acephalous state and of recognizing them thus newly transformed under a formidable personality?

If at first, objective chance can be seen as one of the great forces for the liberation of man, since it is the manifestation in "real" life of the magic power of the poetic spirit, it has also a hidden side that is its power for terror and servitude, even for death. Is it true that the vast network of remembrances, premonitions, and stupefying coincidences of which it is the manifestation is really placed at the disposition of man so that he can come into possession of the secret of things, so that he can guide his own destiny with incomparable lucidity and amazing power? Or does it on the contrary risk becoming, at least from time to time, the dark thread by which the transparent ones make a plaything of man, binding his destiny and leading him astray at their pleasure?

As Breton once wrote: "Using some ingenuity, it might very well be possible to provoke certain dreams in another person, if only, without his knowing it, one applies one's self to making him fall into a rather unusual system of coincidences. There would then be nothing far-fetched in claiming to have, at a distance, grave power over his life" (*Vases*, p. 166). This is perhaps only a project that no man has ever realized, but who can guarantee us that some Minotaur, the incognito ruler of the transparent beings, has not already conceived and utilized it to draw the other creatures into the labyrinth of his secret designs? In what unknown maze are we wandering in those moments when we believe we are exploring the meanderings of objective chance? In what battles do we participate all unknowing? What unimaginable creatures do we brush against in the dark corridor?

The profound feeling of *expectation* which informs all surrealist poetry with the surge of enthusiasm, and which leads Breton with marvelous passion along the complex canyons of objective chance toward the Eldorado of the wonderland, rises from the luminous zone of objective chance. But this feeling is not a lone sensation, for alongside it there remains constant the strange feeling of *peur panique*, of troubling strangeness (which Freudian analysis does not get to the bottom of); it arises from the dark zone of objective chance. If expectation is a profane form of eternal hope, does not this terror resume something of its ancient, sacred value, and does it not bring back a kind of lost memory of infernal fears through the wall of atheism, whose doors man will never manage to bolt completely?

Even in *Nadja*, at the period when Breton was completely taken up with the meaning of objective chance, before he had thought of giving it a name, he seems to have experienced with anguish this basic ambiguity of objective chance and its sometimes deep bond with the hideous powers:

> These are facts whose intrinsic value is hardly to be controlled, but which by their absolutely unexpected, violently incidental character, and the type of suspect associations of ideas that they awaken, have a way of making you pass from gossamer to the spider's web, that is to what would be the most shining and delicate thing in the world, if there were not in the corner, or in the vicinity, a spider." (p. 22)

Such anguish, such revulsion, before the phenomena that ought only to fill with delight Breton's poetic expectancy are truly remarkable. Could it be that this is not merely a question of poetic illumination or of pre-scientific exploration of indicators placed along the route leading to the supreme point? For him, it is impossible to attribute this sudden horror to a simple feeling of dismay such as a timorous explorer might feel when, having out-distanced his own courage, he suddenly finds himself in the grip of a naive distress before the vastness of the worlds he discovers. Moreover, the way in which Breton expresses himself is precise, leaving no margin for vague hypotheses. One feels a strange horror, implacably linked to the exaltation of the discovery. This same horror is repeated again later, linked also to the appearance of a monstrous insect seen in a dream (*Nadja*, p. 61).

It is known that such insects, such spiders are seen to appear also in the visions of Dostoevsky. Stavrogin, Raskolnikov, Mychkin and Hippolyte are very familiar with them, and Dostoevsky shows clearly that he knows how to make us feel what hellish powers are revealed by these signs.

This view of things places in a disturbing light the declaration Breton makes immediately after the allusion to the spider:

> It is a question of what may be purely observable facts, but which present each time all the appearances of a signal, so that in complete solitude I nevertheless enjoy strange complicities that convince me of my illusion in sometimes believing myself alone at the helm of the ship. (*Nadja*, p. 23)

It is not enough then to believe that such a statement is referring only to a possible duality in human awareness, or even to intermental human communications passing through the channels of the collective unconscious; one catches sight of much more disturbing possibilities. And it is necessary also to see things from the same confusing viewpoint when, in speaking of automatism, Breton wonders if it obeys a cosmic force, and if a conscious being is concealed within it (*Humour*, p. 181). Nor should any less importance be attached to Breton's admitting to having been dazzled by this line, taken from the mysteries of Eleusis according to Eliphas Lévi: "Osiris is a black god." He adds: "These are dark words, more brilliant than jade. Human interrogation ended, it is these which seem to me the richest, the heaviest with meaning." (*Arcane*, p. 154)

It is easy to smile at such enthusiasm! And yet one cannot escape seeing that this expression, "a black god," is a symbol which is bound to attract Breton, and which is revelatory of the basic wavering of this thought. As much as he hates God, he nevertheless wants to possess a divine life. He cannot be content with the human condition, even as improved by an endless series of five-year plans, and if what he finds attractive in the evil powers is their spirit of revolt, he still cannot consent to remain under the influence of malediction. The Eleusinian mystery all at once opens an unhoped-for way out of the situation by proposing the myth of a black god. Nothing serves better to "correct" the traditional idea of God than this associating him with the theme of the color black, attribute par excellence of the powers of hell. Now the opposition between the dove and the raven can vanish, for it is the dove itself which becomes black. God made black: here is the symbol of a "superior" synthesis of the divine and the demonic, the end of the opposition between good and evil, the fusion of God and of Satan.

As Julien Gracq has so well shown: "There is a word—a key word, a power-word—that, in what touches on 'Luciferian' attraction, polarizes negatively all the magnetic fields over which floats Breton's flag: it is the word black." [16] And he goes on to add: "It is basically only through a distant reference to sacrilege and profanation, a reference that is never completely lost from sight, that this term "noir" receives, for the surrealists, the full galvanic charge it is capable of carrying." [17]

Gracq offers as examples the terms "roman noir," "magie noire," "musée noir," "lavoir noir," "diamant noir," "dieu noir," "sang noir," to which should at least be added "humour noir." However, this myth of blackness should not be considered by itself, or isolated from the whiteness which in a complementary, antithetical but indissoluble manner is united to it, because the opposition of black and white can only be one of those antimonies which the surrealist dialectic claims to overcome. To emphasize the importance of black alone would be to warp gravely the sense of surrealism and its dialectic of metamorphosis.

Alchemic Transmutation and Poetic Metamorphosis

It is precisely this major aspiration of surrealism toward man's great metamorphosis which stirs Breton to his passion for the Great Work of alchemic transmutation. Breton's enthusiasm for "the admirable fourteenth century" (*Manifestes*, p. 163), the golden century of alchemy, the intense attraction that the Tour Saint-Jacques holds for him, linked, as he says himself, to the secret history of alchemy, derives neither from archeology nor from fantasy, but reveals the strong bond which exists between alchemy and surrealism, between alchemic transmutation and poetic metamorphosis.

When one approaches this subject, it is hard to keep from feeling impatient over the fact that for a long time this analogy between modern poetry and alchemy has been hinted at: yet, at the same time, this important question has been watered down and skirted. All too often it has been treated as a picturesque theme on superficial literary variations, bringing together a pejorative idea of alchemy with an ironic attitude toward modern poetry. In proverbial style, alchemists pass for abstractors of quintessences—without anyone's knowing what that means—and hermeticists; modern poets are treated to the same appellations so that what is considered as the obscure jumble of their ideas can be in like manner denigrated. Instead

of seeing nonsense in poetry, these ill-willed critics would do better
to point the finger at their own ingorance. But the filiation which
they rather unwittingly confirm is no illusion—far from it.

It is not by chance that Breton compares initiation into black
humor with initiation into the high-cabal (*Humour*, p. 8), it is simply
a particular example of a well-thought-out general plan:

> Consciously or not, the process of artistic discovery, even if it remains
> foreign to the whole of its metaphysical ambitions, continues never-
> theless in faithful allegiance to the form and to the very means of
> progression of high magic. All the rest is indigence, unbearable and
> revolting platitude: bill-boards and doggerel. (*Arcane*, p. 153)

It is easy to see what division he introduces into the heritage
of esoterism, how he aims to take up again its methods and even
certain of its ambitions, so as to have a share which, for all its
vagueness, is but the more efficacious. So it would be wrong to
see as a simple picturesque formula Breton's statement that "each
artist must take up again by himself the quest for the golden fleece."
("Prolégomènes" in *Manifestes*, p. 204) In fact, Eliphas Levi, one
of the occultists to whom Breton refers, says that "the fable of the
golden fleece links the hermetic tradition to the beginnings of Greece.
This solar ram, whose fleece one must win in order to become the
ruler of the world, is the figure of the Great Work." [18]

From the very origins of surrealism, Breton had said, as in *Pas
perdus:* "There is no reading after which one may not continue
to look for the philosophers' stone." (p. 98) This attraction for
alchemy is rather natural if we remember that it could be defined
in the same terms as surrealism, that is, as a kind of occultoma-
terialism. Of course, the alchemists were not materialists, but matter
is the basis of the Great Work. Their poetico-mystic aspirations rise
out of their material experiments as the flames mount from a burning
object.

Moreover, there is a very close relationship between the prime
matter of traditional alchemy and that of surrealist alchemy. The
latter often brings into its *verbal* material the evocation of those

minerals and elements that were favored by the alchemists of former times. Of course, their glossaries are not exactly identical, but in both cases, there is a preference for the use of mineral symbols such as stones and gold, for elements like water and fire. To the chemists who in the interval took them over, the surrealists relinquished the material manipulation of these elements and minerals, using from then on only their imaginary forms. Does this mean that by this evolution, this passage from the real to the imaginary, the surrealists distanced themselves from the alchemists? Even the alchemists reinforced the most material labors with a powerful aura of dreams and poetic meditations on the object of their work.

The writings of the alchemists have already a clearly presurrealist style. If surrealist poetry is markedly distant from that of the classics, the way in which it takes its place in the prolongation of that of the alchemists is equally as pronounced. To be quite convinced of this, one has only to look through the quotations given on the subject, not only by Eliphas Lévi, but also by Berthelot in his *Origines de l'alchemie*,[19] or by the Reverend Festugière in *Hermès Trismégiste*.[20] It will be sufficient here to recall an ancient text of Hermes, presented by Breton as a "first-rate esoteric text": "The raven's head disappears with the night; by day, the bird flies without wings, he vomits the rainbow, his body turns red, and he swims on his back above the pure water." (*Peinture*, p. 194) If one had come upon this sentence in the middle of surrealist texts, and had not known its origin, any difference would hardly have been noticeable. Its heterogeneity would not have leaped to the eye.

Once warned, it is possible, by having recourse to a basic analysis, to object that this sentence had an extremely precise meaning in the language of the alchemists, its incoherence being only apparent, the result of our ignorance of alchemic symbols. This would be correct. However, the same is true for Nerval and Mallarmé, and now it seems that it was so also for Rimbaud. Surrealist poetry, too, even though unpremeditated, holds nonetheless a hidden and precise meaning which we are beginning to discover.

On the other hand, however much calculation enters into the elaboration of alchemic texts, they cannot be reduced to a sort of symbolic algebra. Even today, one can still imagine what delight their author felt he derived from them, with what love he must have lingeringly caressed their strange wording. This is in no way a retroactive, anachronistic projection of a sensitivity cultivated in us by surrealism; it could not have been otherwise for the alchemists, for the incantatory value of these texts cyrstallized from within alchemy's power to captivate.

This is even truer in the pictorial realm. Breton, like Derain, marvels over those mysterious, completely irrational touches of white that enhance certain Dutch and Flemish paintings of the seventeenth century. "We know," he points out, "that the artists in question were frequent visitors to alchemical laboratories." (*Pas*, p. 107) We tend to be unaware that the seventeenth century was not only the epoch of Descartes and Boileau, but also an important century for alchemy. Eliphas Lévi writes:

> At this time there appeared Phillip Muller, Jean Thorneburg, Michael Maier, Ortelius, Poterius, Samuel Norton, the baron of Beausoleil, David de Planis-Campy, Jean Duchesne, Robert Fludd, Benjamin Mustapha, the president d'Espagnet, the Cosmopolite—who should be named first, de Nuysement, who translated and published the remarkable writings of the Cosmopolite, Jean-Baptiste Van Helmont, Eirenaeus Philalethes, Rudolph Glauber, and the wonderful shoemaker, Jacob Boehme." [21]

And Crollius, of course.

As one goes back in time, the influence of alchemy becomes much wider and more evident, as in the fifteenth century, in the work of Hieronymus Bosch. To verify this, one has only to turn to the fascinating introduction that Jacques Combe has consecrated to this painter. [22] For if surrealism renews bonds with alchemic poetry, the resemblance between the two corresponding types of painting is no less evident. Breton rightly points out that the famous "figures" of Nicholas Flamel are the astonishing precursors of surrealist paintings (*Manifestes*, p. 166). One need only look, for example, at the reproductions that Grillot de Givry gives in *Le Musée des sorciers, mages et alchimistes* [23] to be struck by the proof of this remark. The same is true of the illustrations taken from Robert Fludd and from Basil Valentin, which are to be found in the same place. One cannot help thinking of Chirico, Dali, Ernst, Masson, and even sometimes Picasso. And there is William Blake to link the two eras.

There is nothing more natural, then, than for Breton to identify the spirit of Max Ernst and that of "the great Cornelius Agrippa" (*Peinture*, p. 162), or to say of the painting of Wolfgang Paalen that "his painting has the plumage of the marvellous bird of changing colors which appears in *Les Noces Chymiques de Christian Rosenkreuz*, and which has the power to restore life." (*Peinture*, p. 100) It is not only the materials and the forms used by the two schools which resemble each other, there is also a community of more profound inspiration which unites them: the end they pursue, their essential intention. To grasp it, it is necessary to go more deeply into our present introduction to alchemy.

Let us emphasize the end of the preceding statement by Breton: *to restore life*. It is indicative of one of the secret meanings of alchemic research which, in any case, went far beyond the simplistic idea of manufacturing gold. Breton writes in his *Lettre aux voyantes:*

> Nicholas Flamel's invention of the philosophers' stone meets with little belief, for the simple reason that the great alchemist seems not to have been enriched. Apart from the religious scruples that may have kept him from making such a vulgar gain, one must ask one's self what interest he could have found in obtaining a few bits of gold, when the main motive for his action was to build up such a spiritual fortune. (*Manifestes*, p. 81)

To the extent that such a spiritual fortune is of a mystical nature, Breton rejects it; but to the extent that it represents a psychic metamorphosis, and consequently the obtaining of psychic powers, it thoroughly excites him. Besides, since the theme of extra-religious immortality is essential for Breton, he comes back again to Flamel in respect to this question, saying

I acknowledge how very close I am to admitting that a person named Paul Lucal met Flamel in Brousse at the beginning of the seventeenth century, that this same Flamel, accompanied by his wife and a son, was seen at the Opera in 1761, and that he made a brief appearance in Paris in the month of May of 1819, at which time it is said that he rented a shop in Paris at number 22, rue de Cléry. (*Manifestes*, p. 167)

It is in any case correct to say that the search for the fountain of youth figured in much of the principal research of the alchemists. In his *Dictionnaire mytho-hermétique*, Dom Pernety points out that, in fact, this expression designates

the perfect elixir of the magistery of the Hermetic Philosophers, because they say that this elixir is a vital balm and a universal remedy that preserves the health and even, so to speak, renews the youth of those who use it, by renewing their energies and by conserving their strength beyond the normal limits of human life.[24]

The alchemists were not, as one is too easily lead to suppose, just the forerunners of the chemists; even more were they wise men, in the double sense of magicians and of mystics. The discovery of the philosophers' stone was prepared for not only by prescientific formulae, but also by the moral requirement of a special purity, as Breton reminds us (*Manifestes*, p. 175), and in addition by continual meditation on a *gnosis*. It was meant to lead less to the possession of material advantages than to a more intimate contact with the divinity in the act of penetrating the mysteries of religion. Grillot de Givry writes:

The attentive reader of any book on alchemy will not fail to notice an important point, that is the identification which the adepts invariably affirm as existing between the creation of the Cosmos and the operation by which they accomplish the Great Work.[25]

Their manipulations have then, in their eyes, a kind of liturgical and sacramental value. It is hard for us to understand this, in today's laicized world where many Christians themselves no longer have any idea of what constitutes a liturgical, sacramental act, because the living idea of symbolism has been lost. If its existence has become an incomprehensible fact, evidently characteristic of religious mentality, in a properly religious liturgy, then how could similar ideas possibly enter into a consideration of work with metals, this having become purely profane and industrial in our times; it seems incredible that it could have been so closely bound up with a mystique as to have been accorded the importance of a sacred ritual.

However, for the alchemists, as for the ancients and the "primitives," it is the opposite which was unimaginable. For all of them, the sacred was as living as fire. It was not a world apart, but was the global sphere into which earth itself was integrated. For the alchemists, the metals were placed under the influence of gods such as Mercury, Venus, and Mars. They were linked to planets which corresponded to them and which were themselves the seat of "supernatural" forces—whence the alchemists derived, in the course of their operations, an intense emotion that was due to the sensation of participating intimately in the supernatural. This emotion was quite different from that which a modern scientist might experience, for the latter's enthusiasm is aroused only by the hope of physical discoveries, while for the alchemist, it means entrance into "supernatural" mysteries. His "contemplation" of metallic bodies was comparable, not to the medical examination of a human body, but to a loving contemplation. (This is no way excludes the interpretations which economic materialism and psychoanalysis might give to the aspects of these phenomena. There could be a whole study devoted to the history of metals in the life of the human race, made from these three points of view.) Perhaps in this way it can be better understood how the aim of the Great Work was much less the making of gold than the accession of the alchemist to an interior metamorphosis, to which end these exterior operations helped him in an almost sacramental fashion. Going beyond any alchemic theory, they aided him to acquire that "interior gold," as a particularly meaningful image names it, and which in our day a Claudel has made his own.

Why is it, then, that the expression "philosophers' stone" is so misunderstood? We fix upon the word "stone" and consider the adjective that qualifies it as an unimportant curiosity; but it means precisely what it says: that this is no ordinary stone, but the stone of wisdom. Our minds are clouded by the fact that we no longer think of philosophy except under the form of university dissertations, and it is hard for us to come back to its original sense of the possession of mysteries. The philosophers' stone has no more place in these dead and cold monuments to learning than have the stones a jeweler works with. The white pebble the Apocalypse speaks of is a much closer analogy—though analogous only on the symbolic level; however, in the eyes of the alchemists, this stone is what will change the leaden spirit into gold. What comes immediately to mind is the metamorphosis of man into a creature of light, that most grandiose myth of surrealist hopes.

If, to the reader's surprise, we did not speak earlier of the fact that Rimbaud, one of the great forerunners of surrealism, was already a proponent of "the alchemy of the word," it is because only now is it possible to grasp fully what is meant and to appreciate Breton's commentary: "The alchemy of the word: this phrase that one hears today being used carelessly must be understood literally." (*Manifestes*, p. 163)

But he adds at once:

> Even if the chapter of *Une Saison en enfer* which these words designate does not measure up to their expectancy, it is nevertheless true that it can be authentically read as an outline of the difficult activity which today only surrealism is carrying on.

Further on (p. 167), he adds the clarification:

> The alchemy of the word: it is equally regrettable that "word" is taken in a rather restrictive sense; moreover, Rimbaud seems to realize that "worn-out poetic ideas" have too much importance in this alchemy. The cabalists, for example, see the word as nothing more or less than the image in which the human soul is created; it is known to have been traced back to the point at which it is the prime example of the cause of causes.

It is easier to understand these reservations when one knows to what extent the research of the alchemists went beyond a mere specialized working with metals; the work of the poets also must go beyond the stage of mere esthetic and scientific experimentation in language. Thus the *travaux exquis* of a Valéry constitute poetic alchemy only on a very secondary level, and the same is perhaps true of that part of Mallarmé's work which consists of occasional poetry. Now, with the study made by J. Gengoux,[26] it would seem that Breton's reservations about Rimbaud, based on pure intuition, have been solidly justified from the same point of view.

In order to make any attempt comparable to alchemy's, it is not enough for modern poetry to produce texts of great beauty, embellished with mysterious obscurity, nor is it sufficient to mime to perfection man's future transfiguration, as in the case especially in the work of Eluard. It must attempt to make man really penetrate the cosmic mysteries (which is already the aim of the Great Work), it must be a magical action, must try to arrive at magical efficacy, must begin to actualize the metamorphosis, must begin the aurification of the being by developing the luminous link of clairvoyance into the unexplored depths of man and of the universe.

This is why surrealism places more store in automatic writing than in any other process, however esthetic it may be. It sees there much more than a release of the floodgates of the unconscious for Freudian analysis; it sees it as a *message* (it matters little that the messenger cannot be named), as a chosen instrument by which objective chance, that is, the cosmic mystery, seen as a kind of *anima mundi*, begins to reveal itself to man. Seen this way, it is absurd to compare the esthetic beauty of Eluard's poems with that of Breton's for the latter have as their essential object not beauty but revelation. It is just as absurd to judge the value of automatic writing without taking into account the essential bond which unites it to objective chance, as whose mode of verbal manifestation it is intended, nothing more. Breton reminds us of this strong meaning of the word "verbal": the emission by man of a fragment of the cosmic Word.

It is in this setting at least that one ought to understand what Breton means when he states:

> I ask that special notice be given the fact that surrealist research presents a remarkable similarity of aim with alchemic research: the philosophers' stone is nothing more than that which will permit the human imagination to take a startling revenge on all things. (*Manifestes*, p. 165)

According to surrealism, this revenge will be obtained because the imagination, working through automatic writing in an apparently subjective and arbitrary manner, discovers on the contrary how closely bound it is to exterior necessity, and discovers within itself premonitory or telepathic powers. This idea is based on cases like that of the "night of the sunflower," [27] but it is probable that this belief is founded on a number of recent experiences, at least in the realm of the telepathic. (cf. *infra*, Chap. VII) That is, in any case, what Breton is inviting us to believe when he concludes that surrealism gives itself over with an intense hope to certain practices of mental alchemy (*Manifestes*, p. 175).

My own thoughts were already leading me in this direction when I had occasion to read Berthelot's study on the *Origines de l'alchimie*, and I must confess how much clearer they became when I read that the Greek word signifying "poetry" had been used by the writer of an alchemical papyrus to designate the operation of transmutation itself.[28] What an enlightenment! We know that the word "poetry" comes from the Greek verb which means "to make." But it designates an ordinary fabrication only for those who reduce it to verbal jewelry. For those who have kept a sense of poetic mystery, poetry is a "sacred action." It exceeds the ordinary human scale of action. Like alchemy, it wishes to associate itself to the mystery of the "primordial creation"; that is (cf. Grillot de Givry), to accomplish the Great Work at the heart of the microcosm.

This shows how much the material operation of transmutation took on, in the eyes of the alchemists, a "poetic," a sacro-magical value. But modern poetry is no less enlightened. It too represents an effort at transmutation, this time of language; its detractors do not know how correct they are when they qualify it as alchemy. It too claims to work an interior metamorphosis through an exterior transmutation. In the case of surrealism, the conjunction of automatic writing and objective chance and the foreshadowing of clairvoyance and man's future glorification, announce the effort toward the metamorphosis of man and of the universe.

Alchemy, then, is poetry in the strongest sense of the word, and surrealism is truly an alchemic transmutation. Both have as their goal the metamorphosis of man and of the cosmos through the transmutation of matter, mineral or verbal. Putting off for a moment a consideration of whether the means are really adequate to the end desired, we see that both these enterprises are situated along the road leading to the recuperation of the lost powers and, finally, the conquest of the supreme point.

It is interesting to note, in this regard, that the alchemists gave to the mysterious prime matter, destined by election to engender the philosophers' stone of the Great Work, an incredible number of different names, 497 of them, if we are to credit the list given by Dom Pernety in his *Dictionnaire mytho-hermétique.*[29] This alone is proof of the excitement aroused in the alchemists by the contemplation of the object of their art, but it is even more important to note that these names belong to the most contradictory categories, as though the alchemists had perceived, or wanted others to perceive, in the aim of their research the unity of contradictories, the supreme point. They called this enigmatic matter Lamb and dragon, Jehovah and nature, male and female, head and sperm, Adam and Eve, father and son, summer and winter, heaven and earth, life and death, sun and sea, gold and feces, good and evil, light and shadow, spirit and matter, cock and hen, water and fire, root of metals and meeting of spirits, king and servant.

The unity of all things would then be already contained in the origin of all, already inscribed in matter; and the mission of the Great Work would be only to actualize it, to reveal it to man so as to place it in his possession. All this would once again affirm, more clearly than ever, the alchemists' intention of taking hold of all opposing natural forces in order to accomplish man's great metamorphosis.

It is this myth of the metamorphosis of man, stripping himself of his miserable aspect to put on a glorious body by a transmutation analogous to that of the alchemists' mystical lead turned into mystical gold, that inspires most of the essential themes of surrealist symbolism including, naturally, Breton's. Although it is not possible to go into the analysis of it here, we should at least indicate some important declarations. There is, notably, a fine mythic expression in the *Second Manifeste,* where Breton exclaims:

> It is clear that surrealism has no interest in attaching a great deal of importance to what is happening alongside it under the pretext of art or even of anti-art, of philosophy or of antiphilosophy, in a word of all which has not as its end the destruction of the being, the total absorption of the being into a blind and brilliant interior, which is no more the soul of ice than of fire. (*Manifestes*, p. 92)

Breton saw perfectly well that his desire for the transfiguration of existence and his ambition of possessing the forbidden world were compatible only with a mental metamorphosis. This represents, moreover, an implicit condemnation of all the activity which was being produced contrary to the vital aims of surrealism itself "under the pretext of art, or even of anti-art," of poetry or of anti-poetry, even among many of the surrealists. The fact remains that the nature of the metamorphosis is clearly indicated here: the consciousness which wants to break with a banal existence, to blind itself to all of this and to cross over into the unknown, must of necessity withdraw beyond the sources of exterior sensation, into an empty and translucid space on the way to the supreme point.

The idea of "total absorption" and of a "blind and brilliant interior" evidently complete the declaration by which Breton demands that it become finally impossible to distinguish a flame from an animal or from a stone (*Manifestes*, p. 111). However, it seems to me that this demand has to do only with methodology, and touches on a merely provisional phase. Later, Breton will write: "Man's great enemy is opacity." (*Arcane*, p. 52) This is an idea which constantly underlies Breton's thought and which, under a slightly more abstract form that is seen here from the position of the obstacle, translates his call for the vitrification of the being. This total absorption and this blinding, as well as the darkening which we will see further on confirmed to be the indispensable moment of revelation through automatism, must not be considered absolute and unchangeable objectives. This would be to understand poorly the essentially dialectical nature of surrealism, and to wander far off the mark of the supreme point which calls man to overcome the antimony of light and dark as well as all the others.

The surrealist must plunge provisionally into this abnegation and this will to blot out the exterior world the way an explorer must first wander off every known course before penetrating into the heart of unexplored territories. Afterwards, he puts them in communication with the whole of the known world, for otherwise he would only become lost without having been able to transmit any message to the rest of men. But this is a task which comes only at the end. It is this same dialectical necessity which obliges the mystic to cross through analogous zones in which he "dies to the world" and in which, differently from Nietzsche, he traverses the night of the "death of God."

One must not interpret Breton's thought in a purely subjective sense, for it is not only the human spirit enclosed in its individual subjectivity which is called to become transparent to the light of the midnight sun of dreams or ecstasy, it is nature itself which must open the unexplored depths of its nocturnal self and their secret links with the diurnal side. Thus it is man's entire life which is called to be brightened little by little by an unusual and transverberant light. Breton turns one day to "the praise of the crystal" and exclaims: "The house I live in, my life, my writing: my dream is that these have from afar the same appearance that cubes of rock salt offer close up." (*Amour*, p. 19) He dreams of inhabiting a house of glass.

"There," he says, "I lie at night on a glass bed with sheets of glass where *who I am* will sooner or later appear to me engraved by a diamond." (*Nadja*, p. 20)

It would be naive to take such wishes literally. It goes without saying that there is no real house of glass, nor an "I" of the kind inscribed on an identification card. This mythical place of crystal is evidently the one where the mystery of the human person will be revealed in all its mystery and where man will come into possession of his supra-natural self. It is not, however, correct, to place myth and reality in categorical opposition, for what is concerned here is the metamorphosis of a real man leading a real life in a city of stone; it is this hard reality itself that is called to vitrification. How can this be possible?

This is where we touch again on the theme of castles and of ruins, linked not only to that of phantoms, but also to that of alchemy. More precisely, the vistas of the surrealist alchemy of metamorphosis reach out to include even the myth of phantoms, for they too are witnesses (imaginary, but having worth on the level of imagination) of the desire for metamorphosis since they call to mind the possibilities for the migration of the human being at other levels of reality.

In any case, the theme of ruins is caught up by the same attraction into the very orbit which bestows on it the fascination it exercises. This is easy to believe if one notices the extreme importance for Breton of certain Parisian ruins which acted with magnetic attraction on his favorite wanderings:

> Yielding to the attraction which the Saint-Denis neighborhood has for so many years exercised on me, an attraction which I explain to myself by the isolation of the two city gates one finds there, and which must owe their touching look to the fact that once they were part of the wall of Paris; because of this, these vessels, drawn as if by centrifugal force into the city, have a look of being completely lost, which, for me, they share only with the inspired Tour Saint-Jacques. (*Vases*, p. 116)

There is an essential attraction here which determines not only the course of Breton's reveries, but his very steps as well. If it sometimes happens that Breton hesitates about the value of the Porte Saint-Denis, if at a certain time he takes objection to the possibility of an (occult) attraction on its part, it is perhaps because he fears that the poetic potential of "this very beautiful and very useless gate" (*Nadja*, p. 38) could be reduced to the superficial prestige of archeology. On the other hand, the attraction of the Tour Saint-Jacques seems to him much surer and much more potent because of "the rather strange circumstances which attended its erection and to which we know is linked the millenial dream of the transmutation of metals." (*Amour*, p. 70)

It is curious to note that in the link between the portal and the tower there is incarnated in the center of Paris an essential theme of Chirico's painting whose divinatory and transfigurative atmosphere is evident. Perhaps the relative mythical weakness of the Porte Saint-Denis comes from its having the form of a gateway, which makes of it a feminine symbol, awakening only an idea of passage, while the tower is a masculine symbol, a point of departure or of arrival but not of passing through, a prototype of the initial creative power.

It is in any case in this section of Paris, as real as it is mythical, that Breton often wandered in quest of the unhoped-for and in which took place the strange adventures of "the night of the sunflower". By these phenomena of divination were marked the first states of the nocturnal transparence of life which must radiate not only in the depth of the human heart, but also in daily objective events.

The radiation that Prague has for Breton comes from the same source of masked light, the city appearing to him with "all its uniquely bristling towers, like the magical capital of old Europe" (*Position*, p. 121); Prague, one of whose most famous sites is the "Street of the Alchemists" (*Humour*, p. 208).

No less remarkable is the strange nimbus cast around a curious construction seen by Breton in Bohemia and of which he writes: "A starry chateau, built of the philosophers' stone, opens on the side of the abyss." (*Amour*, p. 142) This alliance of the myth of the star and the philosophers' stone with that of the castle which we find a second time confirms the strict relationship which unites Breton's most secret subjectivity with the exterior decor of the chateau. The "brilliant interior" does not indicate a mere subjective state, any more than it does an object or a place: it signifies the point of fusion at which being annihilates itself, which in this case means casting off its miserable and strictly limited form in order to take on the pure transparency of the formless and to penetrate the background of nature with its light. These themes of storm, of phosphorescence, of convulsive trembling that the fantastic is able to breathe into the being to the point of making it lose all control, all these phenomena with which the myth of the chateau is bound up: are they not ideally suited to precipitate man to that point of hoped-for fusion at which the phenomenon of metamorphosis seems to come about? Within these privileged enclosures, the past is more than a memory, for it offers itself to be reconquered. Man is going perhaps victoriously to remount the course of time toward the secret engulfed places. Breton dreams:

> I am in the vestibule of a chateau, a dim lantern in my hand; on shining suits of armor, one after the other, I cast its light. Don't think that this is the ruse of some evil-doer here. One of these suits of armor seems almost my size; if only I could put it on and so find something of the mind of a man of the fourteenth century. (*Point*, p. 7)

This enigmatic recuperation of the consciousness is reversible in the direction of the future as well and leads Breton to prolong his musings in that sense:

> I am in the vestibule of a chateau, a dim lantern in my hand; on the shining suits of armor, one after the other, I cast its light. Later on, in this same vestibule, who knows, someone, without thinking, will put on mine. From pedestal to pedestal the great mute colloquy will go on. (*Point*, p. 8)

The act of putting on the armor contains here a magical sense, like that of the slough of snakes in folklore, and the use of ritual vestments symbolic of rebirth or resurrection. It signifies the possibility of a

kind of immorality through the communication of being from generation to generation. We should, however, guard against being led
to see anything very precise here, such as, for example, a belief
in reincarnation, first of all because we are dealing with a poetic
text to which it would be wrong to ascribe a dogmatic sense and
also because, once again, it is the way of surrealism to approach
such ideas as closely as possible without ever giving them free entry
into the city, so to speak, and by remaining in continual ambiguity
towards them.

It is nevertheless evident that it is this close relationship between
castles and the myth of metamorphosis which incites Breton more
or less consciously to evoke the silhouette of castles in his poems,
as the geometric point of the interlacings of his myths. (cf. *Poisson*,
pp. 135-141, 156; *Révolver*, pp. 31, 101; *Amour*, p. 20; *Arcane*,
p. 39)

Finally, it is one of the most ancient of castles, perhaps a monstrous
prototype of the haunted castle as well as of the sadistic castle,
which he evokes by merely pronouncing the fabled names of Crete
and Theseus, at the beginning of the *Discours sur le peu de réalité*.
He modifies in an extraordinary manner the barbarous lair where
the Minotaur laid in wait when he imagines himself as a new Theseus,
enclosed in "a labyrinth of crystal" (*Point*, p. 6). This is the picture
of the "brilliant interior" developed to the dimensions of an immense
citadel of clairvoyance.

However, in fact, the labyrinth of existence remains for a long
time opaque and torturous. It represents the oppressing reality of
the earth and of the demonic underworld powers. Its thousand bends
enclose a cruel and superhuman secret incarnated by the legendary
monster born of a coupling that is at the same time both bestial
and "divine." If in the eyes of the surrealists it today has so much
prestige, it is because it expresses the essential antimony of surrealism
divided between the celestial and demonic magnetisms. Breton does
not declare any the less strongly the primacy of the celestial principal
when he calls for the illumination and transparency of the labyrinth:

does this not also indicate implicitly the putting to death of the Minotaur, the intelligence of the darkness?

This is why, much as we have valued the quite correct remarks of Julien Gracq on the importance of black in Breton's symbolic scheme as a sign of recourse to the powers of darkness, it is still impossible to make of it the backdrop of surrealist tragedy and to play down the even greater importance for surrealism of the symbols of crystal and light. If the dove of the ark is replaced by the raven, that is, if the white sign is meant to be chased off by the black, in the inverse situations where the black sign had been given first, it is invited to relinquish its place to the white. Breton himself speaks of "an entirely white artificial fly" (*Point*, p. 12). Concerning Picasso, he mentions also "shining flies, completely new, the way Picasso would make them." One could quibble and claim that nowhere is it indicated that they had become white; they are however clothed in that unusual brightness, in a aura which is no longer opaque black, but a shining forth of daylight. There is no question here of a mere game of switching colors; this is the expression of the continual possibility of the exchange of colors, a dialectic virtuality of continual mutations between the opposite qualities.

The epithet "black", even if it stands alone in an image, cannot be taken as completely isolated, as if it did not enter into composition with any other color and as if it signified a total ascendency over the dark powers. The expression "black god" is a typical example. Eliphas Lévi, to whom Breton refers in several instances, and who furnished Breton with this expression, gives this precision: "Satan is not a black god, he is the negation of God." [30] Satan, as such, is not a god, even a black one; he is a mere creature and the enemy of God. The term "god" always bears in itself something celestial, and so something pure and luminous, even if by being united to a contrary quality, black, it assumes a confusing and contradictory quality. The expression "black god" is not then purely Luciferian. It designates as God having reintegrated in himself the evil powers, or else Satan reintegrated into the divine, which comes to the same thing. . . . In any case, it implies a dialectical movement, a process of metamorphosis that brings the idea of God and that of Satan out of their traditional conception.

This fact has consequences which are prolonged into Breton's whole symbolic scheme. One can discover there a symbolic power centered on black, but it is not found in its pure form. One finds also a much more abundant symbolism—white, luminous, solar, crystalline—which outlines in filigree in his poetry the same myth of man transformed into a being of crystal and light as is found in the work of many other modern poets: a triumphant image which, through the magic of poetry, brings us into almost sensitive contact with the eternal transfiguration of the whole man, body and soul. But it is perhaps peculiar to Breton to associate almost continually to this dazzling myth the counter-color black. This could be an esthetic corrective designed to heighten the gleam of the gold, but it is in this way also that Breton brings into his poetry the presence of lead and the black matter of the alchemists which is to be the object of the marvellous transmutation. More deeply still, in this spontaneous association of the principal of the shadows and the principal of the light, there is the permanent desire of a total reconciliation of these two principals, the outlined dream of a fusion of the divine and the satanic, the dream of a victorious transfiguration of a humanity become capable of transcending by itself the opposition of all foreign powers.

We shall soon see, moreover, how these influences of esoterism continue in surrealism to inspire its research into automatic writing and objective chance, and how they attempt to clear a path for the process of the transmutation of man and of the universe.

THREE

Disintegration and Reintegration

of the Mind

The mission of surrealism is to predict humanity's entry into the dazzling zone of marvels. Its aim is to use poetry and the other arts, as well as all of life itself, to prefigure the coming of that incredible kingdom. Surrealism, though, is not content just to predict and prefigure; it is a praxis which hopes to lead humanity in an effective manner toward the goal it has caught sight of. Its prefigurations cannot be static, but must themselves be the first breaking with the established order, fissures through which wells up the shining light of future splendor.

Black magic and alchemy are immensely inspiring themes for the recuperation of the lost powers that will lead to the conquest of the supreme point, well-suited to urging the mind forward in the exploration of its unknown zones, but their conventions and techniques seem to the surrealists to be, at least in some senses, outdated, and new ways of access must be found.

The new alchemy invented by surrealism has taken man himself as its prime matter, for although the philosophers' stone does not yet exist in material form, it does already exist in the human mind which conceived of it and even now seems to see it in the poetic reveries. It is the brilliant interior, the bed of diamond in a house of glass, the crystal labyrinth of a singular island, the burning center from which springs a night of lightning flashes which are the fulgurating images of the metamorphosis. The metamorphosis is there, impossible to situate or to grasp, but present in our inner heavens, the first star rising on the horizon.

Astonishment is sometimes the reaction to the fact that surrealism does not confine itself to this positive aspect of poetry; this only shows a miscomprehension of the former and a misguided love of the latter. To confine oneself to the positive aspect means necessarily to accept the limits of that aspect, poetry's place in exile outside our life, and to keep ourselves shut up within the present condition of humanity. To get beyond it—and this is what surrealism is struggling for—one must desire that that far-off light expand until it encompasses the whole universe. How could this be possible unless the universe burnt away all its dross and shattered all its limits in order to become a pure sphere of solar crystal? The negative tasks of poetry are no less important, then, than the positive; both are indissolubly linked to each other by the dialectic of the real. The *sine qua non* of man's reintegration to the supreme point of the cosmos is his previous and total disintegration from the present human condition.

The Spirit of Negation

A chasm separates us from that world which Dali called the "longed-for land of treasure." To enter that land without crossing over the chasm is impossible. This is, of course, the perpetual dialectic of existence: winter must be journeyed through before spring is found once more; the sea or the mountains, before a new land is entered; death, before the empyrean. It is true that in its moments of exaltation, surrealism likes to believe that it is possible to reach the empyrean without passing through death, but it does not avoid the necessity of crossing a zone of peril and destruction which is a kind of ersatz death, in the same way that the great mystics entered into a mystical marriage only after having experienced while alive anguish as terrible as that of death. This is perhaps what Breton is evoking when he writes: "One crosses in trembling what the occultists call dangerous landscapes." (*Manifestes*, p. 66)

The "I" of the poet—in a singular fashion, of the surrealist poet—tends toward the supreme point. What does this mean, if not the desire to become the Whole by imposing on it one's own domination? But how can the Whole be attained without first crushing the self? How is it possible not to break the shell that encloses the egg?

Given this, how could poetry not be above all a negative power, contrary to the belief of the over-pacific reader peacefully settled before his hearth to savor the beauty of some poems? In front of familiar calm of the glowing ashes of his fireplace, he savors these other glowing and burning embers whose reflection is cast on him by the poet's book. He forgets that these embers of poetry have appeared only because there was first a roaring fire of which the poet was both the matter and the source of combustion. This is forgotten as well by all the fine scholars who think poems can be written the way one writes a composition set for a school examination. Poetry is no bed of roses.

There are, of course, in these poetic embers positive, even prophetic, visions which arise spontaneously from them as from the seer's coffee grounds or from the old mossy wall of da Vinci, but it is precisely in the tearing apart of the usual vision of existence that these visions are engendered, in the crushing of habitual ways of thinking and of feeling. It is, therefore, only an amazing lack of understanding of human nature, a monstrous insensibility, that could lead anyone to believe that this tearing apart could take place in the heart of the poet without that heart's being terribly affected by it, without the poet's life being overturned. Or rather, how could anyone suppose that such visions could be born in the heart and intellect of the poet without the prior overturning of his feelings? Is not this interior destruction the greatest common denominator of all poetic minds, to which the divergence of poetic forms takes merely second place?

How could poetry arouse in us the evocation of a radical metamorphosis of life if a profound breaking away in the heart had not already undone our bonds with the normal universe and opened within us a fissure through which we could hear the call of another life? The greatest scope must be accorded this saying of Spenlé's, written about romantic irony: "There can be no creation without previous chaos." [1] This principle does not apply uniquely to literary creation as such, but to the very life of the poet in the throes of creation.

There is a remarkable duality here, and yet no heterogeneity. This is a dialectical contradiction whose two terms are matching parts of the whole of poetry, rigorously complementary. As long as this is not grasped, nothing can be understood of the essential link that modern poetry posits between anguish and enthusiasm, between genius and madness, between the horrible and the marvelous. Lightning flashes only from the midst of the blackest clouds.

When Edgar Allan Poe declares in the *The Poetic Principle* [2] that the spirit of negation plays a primordial role in poetic creation, he is pointing out a major fact, and comes quite close to revealing to us the obscure essence of poetry. He stops short halfway, however, seeming to see there nothing more than an artificial process of composition. If this were so, though, one would never get very far, for such a machine would produce nothing. For it to be efficacious, it must be charged with a living experience—meaning that this spirit of negation must act first of all in the poet himself.

This expression must therefore be taken in its most serious sense, for it is indicative here of an intense and truly experienced sentiment of the vanity and vacuity of all things, that state in which we discover a certain analogy with the "dryness" of the mystics. It is indeed a feeling of nothingness, of nausea, as Sartre has demonstrated, a spirit of revolt and of destruction; but it is also what guarantees the possibility of afterwards reaching new life powers.

The illumination itself is the breaking open of appearances, with the difference that this is a blindingly brilliant breaking apart, rather than being dark and hopeless. It represents the second moment, that in which the despair-inspiring breaking open seems changed into a shining egress.

Words escape the poet in the instant in which he wants to witness to this state which, defiant of all structure, defies that of language as well. It is then easy to understand why Eluard and Breton could define the poem as "a *débâcle* of the intellect" [3] and lyricism as "the development of a protestation." [4]

Poems are really disorientation maps. They violently cast a gleam of irrationality, a disintegrating and subversive light over the breadth of this world, a light which bursts upon the poet and is reflected on the reader. The point of a poem is not to gather together a museum of poetic expressions that one has only to admire passively, but to put into circulation mental explosives destined to blow up the walls of habit and inertia. Thus, Breton's insistence on the capital role of negativity in poetry:

> Note the case that she (poetry) makes of the possible, and this love of the unlikely. What is, what could be: how insufficient that seems to poetry. Nature, she denies your reign; things, what do your properties matter to her? She knows no rest until the whole universe has passed under her negativist hand. (*Point*, p. 22)

Disintegration and Reintegration

The key word, that of disintegration, was used by Breton personally when he wrote of Picasso that "it is with Picasso that will be obtained with implacable lucidity the sum of all these needs and of all these experiences of disintegration." (*Point*, p. 196)

If surrealism tends to work toward total disintegration, it is not in order to end at pure nothingness, but for the sake of advancing toward the point which is the synthesis in act of all antimonies. How can one overcome all contradictions without first abandoning oneself to them completely?

This disintegration is not final; in contrast to what took place in dadaism, it is not a goal but rather a preparatory stage. It is moreover possible that it be a continually repeated phase, permitting an indefinite renewal. It is indeed difficult to conceive of the supreme point as an immobile axis of references. It must be seen rather as the highest point of an indefinitely ascending spiral destined to surmount an ever-rising sea of ever broader and stronger opposition. In any given moment, it resumes all the antagonisms existing in that instant, but from this very synthesis there come forth new life developments so that new oppositions, more powerful than the preceding, are created; yet it overcomes them as well and so on, indefinitely. Even in this perspective, humanity, holding the position of supreme point, would be radiantly sovereign, because instead of having to submit to the blows of the antagonisms no longer at its level, it would find itself drawn out of all suffering and servitude because it would be borne above such conflicts like a ship which dominates the waves.

The sole excuse for those who, from the exterior, see nothing but the destructive side of surrealism is that on the inside, too many surrealists themselves have put the accent only on devastation. Thus, when disorder of the senses is preached, the characteristic adjective added by Rimbaud is almost always omitted; what he recommends is a *"raisonné dérèglement des sens,"* and that changes everything. It shows that disorder is not the only point in question. It develops while bound to its opposite, at all times canalized, controlled by reason, oriented towards its goal which is clairvoyance.

Breton's position in this regard is the same as Rimbaud's. When he recommends, for the application of Rimbaud's precept, the systematic practice of hallucination, he stresses that it is proper to lead it back "without any possible ambiguity to the *moi*" (*Point*, p. 244). Doesn't this make of it a directed hallucination? The same is true elsewhere, when he is lauding Dali's critical-paranoic method; for if critical, the implication is once more that it is controlled. Or again, Breton's giving himself over to exercises in the simulation of mental disorders. (cf. *L'Immaculée Conception)* In like manner, when speaking of exercises in hallucination, he states:

> One can work systematically, safe from any delirium, at making the distinction between subjective and objective lose its necessity and its value. (*Point*, p. 250)

Also, when comparing automatic writing as it is practiced by the surrealists with that of the mediums, he brings them into strong opposition:

> Contrary to what spiritism proposes, that is, the dissociation of the psychological personality of the medium, surrealism proposes nothing less than the unification of that personality. (*Point,* p. 240)

And if, at first, the practice of automatism seems purely disorientating, even for the surrealists, Breton shows that the final result is quite different:

> The practice of psychic automatism in every domain has been found to enlarge considerably the field of the immediately arbitrary. This is just the point: that which is arbitrary has, upon examination, tended violently to deny its own arbitrariness. (*Position,* p. 145)

Breton justifies this statement by showing what close ties seem to him to exist between objective humor and objective chance; those texts seemingly the most subjective become occasionally the most revelatory of the directive lines of exterior necessity—an idea whose most famous example is the premonitory poem of the *Nuit du tournesol.* We shall comment at length on these problems.

Even if one objects to the value of this interpretation which tends to reintegrate the most subjective mental phenomena into the deepest innervation of the body of cosmic objectivity, it would remain at least certain that the texts seemingly most arbitrary admit of systematic analysis, allowing us to discover in them an internal structure revelatory of the person. In spite of Benda's [5] theories, it is a fact that there is a profound coherence at the base of surrealist poetry, if only it be looked at in the right way.

The Negative Capability

It is necessary to stress, however, that in the surrealist climate, one must, when treading in the domain of poetry, more than anywhere else, appeal to what Keats has magnificently named "the negative capability," [6] that is, "man's ability to know how to exist in the midst of uncertainties, of mysteries and doubts, without the irritating desire of getting back at any cost to the land of facts and of reason." [7]

It is evident that the spirit of negation, the disordering of the senses, objective humor, the techniques of surprise and of disintegration could not represent truly creative values for the man who did not in some degree possess this gift of negative capability.

Common sense protects us from excesses of the reasoning faculty, but we have no less need—indeed, quite the contrary—of a sure sense of balance when we venture out into the irrational, far from ordinary experience and from what is reasonable. At such a time we make use of something like that kind of flair which singles out the real from the false in everything that is the object of empirical knowledge. We have to sharpen it to its keenest in order to explore chaos, the unlikely, the blinding light of ecstasy.

In *Les Abeilles d'Aristée*, W. Weidlé rightly insisted on this point when he wrote:

> The negative capability is the gift of remaining faithful to an intuitive certitude which reason rejects and which common sense does not admit; of keeping to a mode of thought which can only seem unreasonable and illogical, but which from a more profound point of view can reveal itself as superior to reason and transcending the logic of conceptual thought. For the poet and for the artist, this gift is more essential, more rudimentary than anything which can be called a feeling for the beautiful.[8]

This negative capability is a guide for the poet there where the spirit of negation throws him off course; it allows him to discern, in this overwhelming and changing reality, that which has real value of being and of poetry, without its becoming more definable and comprehensible. It is, in a word, a power of divination. Obviously, it is opposed to ordinary common sense; it is just as much opposed, though, to sheer delirium. We could perhaps call it dialecticalised common sense. I mean by this common sense that has escaped the flat, short-sighted conceptions of which it is generally the subject, to become capable of grasping the contradictory unfolding of existence and yet no longer to let itself be misled or put off by it.

The negative capability conducts the poet as well through the tumultuous rapids of the creative flux of poetry as through the phases of despair and disorder which have their source in the very life of the poet. The whole of surrealist activity is contained in this balance between the spirit of negation and the negative capability, between the forces of disintegration and of reintegration. Given these principles, we have now to see how surrealism makes them work.

Disordering of the Senses and Voluntary Hallucination

Let us look first at Rimbaud's text in the *Lettre du voyant:*

> The poet makes himself a seer by a long, immense and reasoned disordering of all the senses. He searches for every form of love, of suffering, of madness in his own being; he exhausts every poison.[9]

It is essential, then, to break out of the normal structures of sensation; it is the logical corollary of this orientation which he explains in *Alchimie du Verbe:*

> I accustomed myself to simple hallucinations: I would see quite clearly a mosque instead of a factory, a school of drummers made up of angels, carriages on the roads of heaven, a drawing-room in the depths of a lake; monsters, mysteries; a vaudeville billboard set terrors in my path.[10]

These rules of experiences have become an essential law for the surrealist. For if the images of surrealist poetry are in continual rupture with the normal order imposed by reality, this disordering of poetic images is no artificial process—except of course for the imitator—but rather the direct projection of the disordering of the sensations into the life and imagination of the poet.

Breton insists:

> Let it be understood that this is no mere regrouping of words nor a capricious regrouping of visual images, but the recreation of a state which need in no way envy mental alienation. (*Manifestes*, p. 166)

Poetry need feel no envy, not because it heeds the limits of insanity (loss of judgment) but because, without losing its lucidity, it incorporates insanity's privileges. It moves among directed hallucinations: "In the final analysis, everything depends on our power of voluntary hallucination." (*Point,* p. 90) The adjective "voluntary" has the same essential corrective value as the adjective "reasoned" in the Rimbaud statement. Surrealism is not sheer delirium, but exploration of that delirium, which is something quite different.

It is from this that Breton takes the idea that surrealism must produce "a fundamental crisis of the object" (*Position,* p. 125). It is not the intention as such which must be seen as producing the delirium; the appearance which we habitually accord to objects is not so absolute as we like to believe. It merely corresponds to the level we occupy on the scale of sizes; science demonstrates this to us ever more clearly, and not only science:

> Poets and artists, theologians, psychologists, the mentally ill and psychiatrists have always been looking for a valid line of demarcation which will permit the imaginary object to be isolated from the real one—it being taken for granted that the first can easily disappear from the field of consciousness and its place taken by the second, while subjectively their properties are seen as interchangeable. (*Point,* p. 247)

In other words, it is a question of taking a second look at the real relationship between so-called normal perceptions and the others. The ordinary bases of the feeling of reality become suspect and are open to revision. This is what lies at the bottom of the question Proust asks himself when, at the moment of setting foot on the Guermantes' "stone," he staggers at the same moment on an uneven pavingstone of Saint Mark's Square in Venice.[11] Does the degree of reality depend, for example, on the degree of actuality?

It is noteworthy that Proust is not the victim of his hallucination; he dominates it along with the "present reality," not to the point of being able to arbitrate their conflict, but even so to the point of knowing that the question presents itself. He stands balanced, come what may, at the point of junction, at the confluence of the two zones of reality which meet in him. As for himself, Breton, as he writes in the *Nuit du tournesol,* believes himself to be standing in that mysterious region where the future is preformed in the heart of the present. In any case, what is most important to him is to dominate the antagonism of these different ways of apprehending the diverse levels of the real. This is what he has in mind when he touches again on the processes of insanity:

> The greatest benefit which surrealism had up to now derived from this type of operation is to have succeeded in dialectically reconciling these two terms which, for the adult person are violently opposed: perception and representation; to have thrown a bridge across the abyss separating them. (*Position*, p. 164)

The only objection one could pose here is that if surrealism aims for this reconciliation, it is far from having brought it fully about. The essential is that at least it aims to succeed. When Breton states that perception and representation are but "the products of the dissociation of a unique, original faculty" (*Point*, p. 250), it is not to deplore its loss but rather to incite us to regain it.

As he reached the conclusion of his *Alchimie du verbe*, Rimbaud could say: "I end, convinced that the disorder of my mind is sacred." [12] He was affirming his belief in the revelatory power of what passed for hallucination in the eyes of the profane. He meant that he was leaving behind the categories of the profane and was becoming capable of reading the hieroglyphics that mysterious powers inscribe in the deepest regions of the mind.

If Breton attaches so much value to automatic writing, it is because to him it seems the primordial source of the manifestation of those sacred hieroglyphics capable of imposing themselves with hallucinatory force. Before any other interpretation, this ability to overthrow reality holds his impassioned interest:

> Practiced with any fervor at all, automatic writing leads straight to visual hallucination; this had been my personal experience, and a look at the *Alchimie du verbe* will show that Rimbaud before me had the same experience. (*Point*, p. 248)

Indeed, some of those strange pilgrimages, mentioned earlier, which Breton made through Paris would be hardly understandable if one were unaware that, at the moment of undertaking them, André Breton was steeped in that quite special atmosphere emanating from the practice of automatic writing. To the eye these wanderings have hardly any sense; they can be explained only by a certain interior climate in which the mind feels itself apt to discover the unexpected character dissimulated under the most banal of appearances, even in the business districts. For, in spite of the pronouncements of certain writers who know little about surrealism, one of the surest signs of automatic writing is that it frees itself from mere literature in order to come to grips with life. It brings about a profound change in sensitivity and fosters quasi-hallucinations which may seem revelatory. Witness this example given by Breton, about a walk taken in the company of Soupault, with whom he co-authored the first collection of automatic texts, *Les Champs magnétiques:*

> The words *Wood and Coal*, spread across the last page of *Champs magnétiques*, have a special meaning for me in that, during an entire Sunday that I spent walking with Soupault, they were able to exercise a strange prospective talent in regard to those shops that they designate. It seems that I was able to say, no matter what street we took, at what point on the left or on the right one of these shops would appear. Each time, it was verified. I was warned and guided, not by the hallucinatory image of the words in question, but rather by those little circles of wood represented in cross-section, crudely painted in little piles on the storefront on either side of the door, all the same color with one sector darker. (*Nadja*, p. 33)

This link with the revelatory phenomena of objective chance would suffice to show that the automatic writing of surrealism has not a purely dispersive aim, for if it breaks down our habitual comportment and the usual structure of the world, it is in order to recompose them on another level where a more profound grasp of reality is at work.

Often, however, these planes of recomposition are inexplorable at the moment when man is immersing himself in automatism. So, for example, when Breton was writing the poem entitled *Tournesol*, it seemed quite incomprehensible and disappointing to him; years were to pass before he suddenly discovered its meaning—an incident confirming the importance of the negative capability without which he might not have been able to tolerate this state of things. While waiting for the phase of recomposition to begin, it is necessary to orient oneself systematically toward a veritable dislocation of the landscape:

> As an aid to the systematic disordering of the senses, that disordering recommended by Rimbaud and constantly kept before our mind by the surrealists, I deem that one must not hesitate—and such an undertaking may very well have this consequence—to uproot [dépayser] the senses. (*Position*, p. 138)

It is evident that this is the source of his attraction to the curious experiments of the psychologists of Marburg:

> According to the masters of this school (Kiesow, Jaensch),[13] unusual abilities could be cultivated in children, enabling them to alter a given object by gazing at it fixedly. (*Point*, p. 249)

He writes along the same lines, speaking of the collages of Max Ernst: "Surreality would be, moreover, in function of our dépaysement from everything" (*Point*, p. 82)—a desire which will lead us "into another world, known or knowable, in which, for example, a hatchet can be taken for a sunset." (*Point*, p. 83)

Automatic writing is not alone in possessing the power to introduce us into the field of voluntary hallucinations; painting also can play that role. If Breton can make special reference to the quest for hallucinations undertaken by Rimbaud, Ernst quotes Leonardo da Vinci as his authority:

> In my opinion, it is not to be scorned (writes da Vinci in his *Treatise on Paintings*)[14], when you recall certain aspects that you have stopped to look at in spots on walls, in the ashes on the hearth, in clouds or in streams. If you look at them carefully, you will discover wonderful things there that the mind of the painter can draw profit from for the composition of battles of animals or men, of landscapes or of monsters, of devils and other fantastic things that will bring you honor.

Ernst himself continues:

> On the tenth of August, 1925, an unbearable visual obsession led me to discover the technical means that in great part, allowed me to put this lesson of Leonardo's into practice. Beginning with a

childhood memory (related earlier), during which a panel of false mahogany situated in front of my bed had played the role of poetic provocateur during a vision between sleep and waking, and finding myself at a rainy time in a seaside inn, I was struck by the obsession exercised on my irritated vision by the board, its grooves accentuated by a thousand washings. I decided to delve into the symbolism of this obsession, and to help my *meditative and hallucinatory faculties*, I made a series of designs from the boards by placing on them at random pieces of paper which I then rubbed with a piece of lead. Looking carefully at the designs thus obtained, the dark parts and the others in soft penumbra, I was surprised at the sudden intensification of my *optical* faculties and by the *hallucinating* succession of contradictory images. . . .

My curiosity aroused and amazed, I began to investigate indiscriminately by the same method all kinds of materials coming into my visual field: leaves and their veining, the ragged edges of a piece of burlap, the brush-strokes of a "modern" painting, thread unwound from the spool, etc. My eyes saw then human heads, different animals, a battle that ended in a kiss (the bride of the wind), rocks, the sea and the rain, earthquakes, the sphinx in his stable, small tables around the earth, Caesar's palette, false positions, a shawl with frost-flowers, the pampas.[15]

Ernst points out himself that this is a procedure which in painting is the analogy of automatic writing.[6] He adds that he has always forced himself to "restrain more and more [his] active participation in the coming into being of a painting so as to give in this way more scope to the active role of the hallucinatory faculties of the mind." [17]

The procedure which we have just seen used by the painter, rubbing with lead the strange surface irregularities through a piece of drawing paper placed against the graining of an old floor or against any of the unevenly-surfaced objects lying about him is precisely what he has called "rubbings" *(frottage)*. Summing up the spirit of the undertaking, the word indicates that the process is based "on nothing other than the *intensification of the irritabilities of the faculties of the mind* by appropriate technical means." [18]

But it is not da Vinci alone to whom he could make reference; there is also, and more directly, Edgar Allan Poe. It is indeed striking to read in *Berenice*, an essentially hallucinatory and spectral story, lines by Poe that Ernst had only to adopt—consciously or not—in order to define the nature of his experiment. To describe the disease afflicting his hero, Poe has, already used the words,

> *a morbid irritability of [those] properties of the mind* . . . that nervous intensity of interest, with which, in my case, *the powers of meditation* (not to speak technically) busied and buried themselves, in the contemplation of even the most ordinary objects of the universe.[19]

These expressions are remarkably similar to those which Max Ernst will use, but the facts indicated by Poe are also strikingly analogous. For example, his hero remains "absorbed, for the better part of a summer's day, in a quaint shadow falling aslant upon the tapestry or upon the floor." [20] This apparently harmless sight, or that of the embers of a fire, or a word repeated over and over until it has lost all its meaning served to support, not a vague revery, but an hallucinatory valorization: "In my case, the primary object was *invariably frivolous,* although assuming, through the medium of my distempered vision, a refracted and unreal importance." [21]

What importance is there in knowing if there was on the part of Ernst deliberate borrowing, a remembrance, or just coincidence? What is important is this convergence toward the same end, which is sufficient to demonstrate that research in this direction is in no way misguided, but instead underlines a permanent orientation. Besides the particular interest marked by Ernst in this area, there is the passage from an impression of hallucinatory values to a technical application destined to bring them systematically to light.

It is in an allied sense that the critical-paranoiac method invented by Dali is employed, "a spontaneous method of irrational knowledged based on the critical and systematic objectivation of associations and delirious interpretations." (*Peinture*, p. 144) Attention should be paid in passing to the association of the adjective "critical" with the term paranoia. Again it is a question, not of pure delirium, but of its association with a conscious element.

In the same way, the choice of paranoia from among the other pathological forms is strongly suggestive because of its hallucinatory properties. We will not of course attempt to give a scientific definition of paranoia, having no competence to distinguish between the different schools of psychiatric thought, but we can at least out of preference retain the definition given by Jaspers:

> The sick persons (paranoiacs) are no longer in control of the progression of their mental images. Finally all kinds of sensory illusions (frequent hearing of voices, visual pseudo-illusions, synesthetic sensations) complete the picture. At the same time, numerous features of the neurasthenic complex are encountered. And yet, no pronounced psychosis develops. The sick persons always have their bearings, are deliberate, accessible, often able to work.[22]

It is this dubiousness cast by hallucination on the limits of the real which surrealism hopes to avail itself of. But such doubt is not the only important trait of paranoia. A second passage from Jaspers points out another:

> Many things which take place in the immediate surroundings of these sick persons attract their attention and arouse unpleasant, barely comprehensible reactions in them. This fact worries and upsets them. Sometimes, everything seems "too much" to them; conversations ring "with too much vehemence in their ears." Sometimes even a very ordinary noise or happening is enough to irritate them. They always have the impression that someone is deliberately doing this to them.[23]

In brief, it is what is called interpretive delirium.[24] It is not surprising then, given this additional reason, that Breton could state that the domain of objective chance "is perfectly joined to that which Dali consecrated to the investigation of critical-paranoiac activity." (*Position*, p. 146)

The paranoiac tends to incarnate the mysterious "someone" in a person whom he blames rather arbitrarily as the one responsible for these signs and misfortunes. Objective chance could also be taken as a sort of interpretive delirium since it tends to pay no attention to the apparent absence of relationship between certain processes of exterior necessity and certain impulses of the subconscious. It assigns to them an intention and a weight that ordinary common sense rejects, meanwhile maintaining this "someone" in complete indetermination like an impersonal force of nature. Moreover, it claims to be open to collective and objective verification.

We should not be unduly surprised by the importance attached to hallucination. Not only da Vinci and Poe bear witness to its value, but many others, among whom Breton names the famous astronomer W. Herschel and even the eminently practical James Watt:

> With all his attention, in a dark room, Watt contemplates the future steam engine, the *coming* steam engine. What is not yet will be. (*Point*, p. 219)

This same idea is taken up again in 1947 by *Cause*, the surrealist manifesto: "Surrealism is what will be."

Objective Humor and Black Humor

The idea of objective humor is already found in Hegel, at the end of a remarkable passage defining the destiny of post-romantic art:

> Romantic art was characterized from the outset by a deeper separation, by a more radical withdrawing into its own inwardness, given the imperfect correspondence between the mind and objective reality, that inwardness then was seen to be indifferent to such reality. Such an opposition had finally, in evolving to bring the full interest of romantic art to bear either on accidental outwardness or on a no less accidental subjectivity. But when this concentration of interest on the objective reality and on its subjective representation brought about, in line with the principle of romanticism, the penetration of the soul into the object, and when on the other hand, humor attacked the object and the form given it by the subjective reflex, a settling into the object itself took place, a kind of *objective* humor. But this penetration into the inwardness of the object could be only partial

and show itself only under the form of a *lied* or as part of some larger whole, because by extending and prolonging itself within the objective reality, it would of necessity have to finish in the actions and justifiable changes of fortune of a concrete representation.[25]

It is immediately obvious that the insertion here of this text casts light on our analysis. The encounter between accidental exteriority and a no less accidental subjectivity is exactly what we have seen in studying the phenomena mentioned by Breton, da Vinci, Poe, Ernst, and Dali. The passage from Hegel is curiously prophetic and reserved: prophetic because so applicable to developments in art which took place so long afterwards, and yet reserved, because it allows a strange doubt to hover over the meaning of the last phrase: does it fear a return to classical pseudo-objectivity, or does it catch a glimpse of another penetration of the real which would be the equivalent of objective chance, but which it considered to be non-existent in that era?

Whichever it be, Breton, in taking up the idea again, refurbished it completely. Hegel's idea was forgotten, drowned in a sea of philosophy; Breton took from it a clear line of action and new enlightenment.

Objective humor, he says, is the

> synthesis of the imitation of nature under its accidental forms, on the one hand, and of humor, on the other—humor seen as the paradoxical triumph of the principle of pleasure over actual conditions. (*Limites*, p. 205. Cf. *Position*, p. 143)

Objective humor has its origins in England with Swift and Lewis Carroll, in France with Jarry, Vaché, Roussel, Duchamp, Rigaut.

> The whole futurist movement, the whole dadaist movement can claim it as their essential factor. (*Position*, p. 143)

Relying on this principle, Breton makes a very revealing analysis of the modern evolution of art and poetry:

> I am sorry not to be able to insist more here on the remarkable oscillation between these two poles (one the imitation of an accidental exterior aspect, humor the other) which has for a century characterized

all artistic activity. On the one hand, imitation of those aspects of life designedly the most down to earth (naturalism) and the most fleeting in nature (impressionism), of the object considered as volume and matter (cubism) and of the object in motion (futurism); on the other hand, humor, breaking out especially in troubled periods and witnessing to the overpowering need on the part of the artist to dominate the accidental when it tends to impose itself objectively: early symbolism with Lautréamont and Rimbaud, corresponding to the war of 1870; predadaism (Roussel, Duchamp, Cravan) and dadaism (Vaché, Tzara) corresponding to that of 1914. (*Misère de la poésie*, p. 14)

It goes without saying that, for Breton, it cannot be a question of merely discovering new perspectives on aesthetic problems. He is not one to be satisfied with the *lied* or any other lyric equivalent; he pays attention to such phenomena only in the measure that they act as signals indicating the way to penetration into the secret strata of reality. We have already mentioned it in regard to automatic writing, hallucination, the techniques of *frottage* and critical-paranoia, but here we find him anxious to stress once again what remains for him the center of the picture:

Objective humor, objective chance: these are, properly speaking the two poles between which surrealism believes it can make its longest sparks leap. (*Limites*, p. 206)

The domain of objective chance, he explains.

is perfectly joined to Dali's investigation of critical-paranoiac activity. It is moreover the area in which take place those manifestations so exalting for the mind; there filters in a light so close to being able to pass for that of revelation that objective humor shatters itself, until the new order, against its abrupt walls. Today's poetry finds itself faced with this essential contradiction, and it is the resulting need to resolve this contradiction which is the secret of its movement. (*Position*, p. 146)

Indeed, it is one of the essential aspects of the drama of this poetry that, in giving itself up to disintegration and hallucination, it is certain only in rare instances of having crossed over the threshold of ordinary existence and reached the revelations of objective chance. Either this wait will be compensated and poetry will be wholly justified, or else this wait is in vain and poetry will remain forever shattered, carried by its own élan against the abrupt and, in this case, impassable walls. For poetry, it is a matter of life and death, of the wonderland or the abyss; there is no middle ground.

In spite of this state of crisis noted by Breton, he cannot consent to surrealism's giving way; and so, returning once more to the question, he states:

> that the black sphinx of objective humor cannot fail to meet along the dusty road, the road of the future, the white sphinx of objective chance, and that all human creation after that will be the fruit of their embrace. (*Humour*, p. 11)

While waiting for a real road to open up, we need to see how objective humor begins to open a crack in the block of massive reality into which we are incorporated by our day-to-day life. Marco Ristitch, a former Yugoslavian surrealist, has made a wonderful analysis of this point:

> In essence, humor is an intuitive and implicit critique of the conventional mental mechanism, a force which extracts a fact or a group of facts from their routine setting and tosses them into a whirl of unexpected and surreal relationships. Through a melange of the real and the fantastic that goes beyond the limits of ordinary reason and rational logic, humor and humor alone gives a new grotesqueness to what surrounds it, a hallucinatory *character* of non-existence, or at least a dubious and worthless objectivity, a laughable importance, side by side with an *exceptional, ephemeral but total super-meaning (sur-sens).*
> In contact with poetry, humor is the extreme expression of a convulsive inadaptation.[26]

This humor is not a recreation; it is a veritable vacuum-producing machine. Pushed to the extreme, it has occasionally tragic consequences, as Ristitch spells out: "To see humor as a vital attitude is untenable. Jacques Vaché killed himself, Jacques Rigaut killed himself." [27]

The effect of humor is to provoke in the mind a state of radical hostility toward the outside world. This type of derangement of the senses takes root in a feeling which strikes subjectivity at its deepest point, the feeling of the hopeless inadequacy of man and of existence, the unthinkableness of banality itself. But the greatest paradox of this humor is that in the very midst of being shattered, the insignificant, or presumed to be so, suddenly takes on an incredible set of meanings; this is where objective chance comes in.

Objective humor is a negative force, a screen interposed between the consciousness and the established order of this world whose attractions it counters with opacity. It tends to destroy all the habits born of this attraction which tied it down, it frees the consciousness from their pull and permits it to undergo the magnetization of the fields of attraction of the unconscious. It is a vacuum-producing machine, or perhaps rather a kind of internal breakwater which reverses the course of what Bergson calls the *élan vital;* Janet, contact with reality; and Freud, the course of the libido; despite their extreme differences, it carries them all away together in another direction.

Objective humor is the black source of poetry.

Some years later, on the threshold of the war of 1939, when Breton gathers together the selections that make up his wonderful anthology of humor, his thoughts on this topic have undergone a certain evolution, which is witnessed to by the fact that he no longer speaks of objective humor, but of black humor. He does not define the relationship between the two ideas, but that it is a close one seems evident from the evocation in this work of the perhaps transitional "black sphinx of objective humor". This change in terminology is probably indicative of a desire to mark a greater distance between this humor and a certain kind of chance which can only roughly be called objective, for the former is often powerless, shattered, against the latter. Perhaps it is also a sign of the fact that the influence of Hegelian interpretations of this point is growing dimmer and that Breton is turning more and more to Freud for the elucidation of the nature of this humor. There is in any case a deep continuity between the two experiences; Breton depicts in each the same general atmosphere and calls on more or less the same family of precursors.

Black humor has nothing in common with Rabelesian good humor, nor with Voltaire's intellectual wit (*Humour,* p. 15), nor with the red humor that marks the robust health of the masses, nor with the rose humor of elegance. It must not be mistaken for the sickly smile of the man who laughs unwillingly, in spite of himself; for if the laugh of black humor is also unwilling, it claims that this is not in spite of itself, but because it wishes to be unwilling. It is beyond all bad conscience, because it *wants* that bad conscience. It is the laugh of the man who, seeing himself crushed, laughs because he is crushed. It is a laugh of defiance. Yet it has nothing to do with the defiance of the Stoics, nor with the smile with which the Buddhist faces annihilation. The property of that laugh is that its motive is kept secret, unconscious. It refuses to reveal to us whether this is a completely absurd laughter seeking in the exaltation of absurdity a way of making itself heroically vanish, or whether it is aware of an unjustifiable and indestructible energy in itself that cannot be crushed, whatever be the apparent triumph of the machine that crushes it. It is in the suspense of that ambiguity that it makes a final gasp and in that same moment refuses to admit defeat.

Black humor is an insulting laugh that comes from the depths of the being in revolt to provoke and defy public opinion and the cosmic fates.

This is true for the spirit of "sinister mystification" of Sade, for that of Swift, "inventor of the fierce and funereal joke" or of De Quincey, prodigal in his praise of assassination considered as one of the fine arts and nevertheless animated by a "deep compassion for human weakness," for O. Henry, writing touching letters to his little girl and freely vowing his sympathy for "outlawed rascals," for Gide imagining Lafcadio, for Lichtenberg, the author of aphorisms full of a fierce irony, even for Lacenaire the assassin who, on the eve of his death, jokes about "the dead who pester him, the phrenologists and anatomists lying in wait for him; he owns to having brief attacks of melancholy that amuse him. At night, through the bars, he wants to play peek-a-boo with the guard."

This is also the case for Grabbe, with his "need to scandalize"; for Borel, with "his frenetic style"; for Edgar Allan Poe, with "his tragic dark coquetterie, discreet and anxious," with the conflict which brings into confrontation within him "exceptional powers of logic, high intelligence, and the mists of alcoholism"; for Baudelaire, with his "need to disconcert, to revolt, to stupefy" and whose "last words, interrupting a silence of several months, were to ask, as though nothing were the matter, that one pass him the mustard"; for Villiers de l'Isle-Adam of whom Huysmans wrote: "In Villiers' temperament, there was a streak of dark bantering and fierce teasing; these were not the paradoxical mystifications of an Edgar Poe, but a lugubrious scoffing, such as threw Swift into a rage"; for Huysmans speaking of his own "black humor"; for Tristan Corbière who "nails a dried toad on the chimneypiece. 'Here, catch, here's my heart!', hurling at a woman, along with these words, a bloody sheep's heart"; for Vaché, with his desire to devote himself to the disservice of others; for Germain Nouveau and that "machinery for intellectual subversion that he, from the outset, along with Cros, Rimbaud, and even Verlaine, had helped to perfect"; for Jarry, who on the eve of death, asked by Doctor Saltas to tell him "what would give him the greatest pleasure," asked for a tooth-pick.

However, these same men who so disdainfully announced their revolt were pitifully crushed by the social and cosmic machine: Sade spent the greater part of his life in prison, Grabbe died exhausted by alcoholism, Borel of poverty, and Cros came to no better end; Swift, before the end, went through ten years of intellectual waning, Baudelaire died aphasic, Nietzsche insane, Lacenaire by the guillotine; Nouveau and Villiers lived in squalor; Vaché, Rigaut, and perhaps Cravan also committed suicide. (For all the above quotations and references, cf. *Humour,* passim.)

It goes without saying that, seen from within black humor, these tragedies prove nothing against it; on the contrary, it boasts of nothing so much as that which crushes it. This is basically the reasoning of Kirillov, claiming that by killing himself, he will proclaim his liberty.[28] How are we to understand this attitude? Breton bases himself here on a remarkable analysis that Freud makes of humor in general:

> 'Humor', writes the founder of psychoanalysis, 'has in it not only something liberating, analogous to the witty and the comic, but also something sublime and elevated, traits not found on these other two levels where pleasure is acquired by intellectual activity. This sublimity clearly has to do with the triumph of narcissism, with the invulnerability of the ego affirming its victory. The ego refuses to let itself be approached, to allow suffering to be imposed on it by external realities, refuses to admit that it can be touched by the traumatisms of the outside world; moreover, it lets it be known that these can even become for it occasions of pleasure.'
>
> Freud gives a rough example, but one that will suffice, that of the condemned man who, led to the gallows one Monday, shouts: 'What a way to begin a week!' (*Humour*, pp. 12-13)

Freud's definition is given for humor in general, but fits black humor even more closely, in which case it is all the more surprising. How can the word sublime be used when black humor is a bitter sneer, appearing often under grotesque forms? How can one speak of the invulnerability of the ego affirming its victory when the humorist is crushed by the social machine and the annihilation of death? and yet Freud is correct. The strange comportment of black humor is not spontaneously generated. It exists in the physical world as much as in the mental; nor is it without its own internal logic. If man engages in behaviour which is in fact so delusive, it is because he has denied all possibility of the hope which he consents to acknowledge within himself, and because he has found in the taste of black humor a kind of horribly exquisite compensation. There is for him no other way out but to glorify his own despair and to hole up like a criminal in the dead end where he is at bay.

By laughing at the world and at society, he can suspend their emotional power over his own subjectivity. By laughing at his own despair, he sinks ever deeper into it, because he halts the flow of even his most intimate emotions. In other words, he withdraws from his surroundings, alienating himself from the world, from society and from his ordinary self. If he laughs at himself, it is because he treats himself as a stranger. Through this personality split, he abandons to the world, to society and to the flesh that part of himself which is irretrievably committed, and withdraws into his alter ego, that spirit sovereignly free in its visions, that other, that mental phantom that takes the point of view of Sirius, from which he can with ironic detachment pass judgment on the world and on himself.

By a kind of Luciferian asceticism, he comes to identify himself with this phantom and to transfer to it all his emotional powers. Thus this ghost, rather than remaining suspended in a heaven of pure idea where it could be destroyed by a demonstration of its absurdity, takes root in the depths of the feelings.

Freud presented this other self under a striking form which Breton sums up in the following matter:

> According to him the secret of the humoristic attitude rests in the capability of certain persons, in cases of extreme urgency, to remove the psychic accent from the ego and to transfer it to the super-ego, the latter to be thought of genetically as the inheritor of the parental guidance. The *moi* is held severely in check, and continues to be treated as the parents—or the father—formerly treated the child. (*Humour*, p. 13)

Granted that the super-ego is molded in great part through the influence of the parents, either by imitation or by opposition; but it certainly cannot be reduced to this influence alone, except in the eyes of those afflicted with a reduction complex. It is precisely this strictly personal basis of the super-ego that is most important in black humor. It is a sudden upward thrust, like the skyscrapers of New York, carrying man far above the ordinary level of life. The skyscraper image is, of course, too constructed; the black humorist is not moved by a planned idea, but by an irrational instinct. Threatened on every side, he is borne up by the overwhelming desire to save at least the most intimate part of his ego; he is like the desperate aviator in an adventure novel who, as a last resort, cuts the ropes which hold the gondola and clutches the upper part as it leaps into the air. But this leap takes place in total darkness, in the denial that there exists an earth on which it is possible to come down; and yet, the darkness is so thick that it is still impossible to state that there does not exist an unpredictable hope.

It is this idea of the super-ego, though not understood in its strictly Freudian sense, that Breton uses as the starting-point for his investigation of black humor. He writes:

> Nietzsche's whole undertaking tends to strengthen the super-ego through the growth and broadening of the ego (pessimism presented as a source of good will; death as a form of liberty, sexual love as the ideal realization of the union of contradictories: to become nothing in order to become). This is nothing other than bestowing on man the power which he has bestowed on the name of God. It is possible for the ego to dissolve at this temperature. (*Je est un autre,*' says Rimbaud, and there seems to be no reason why, for Nietzsche, this could not be a series of *"autres,"* chosen on the whim of the moment and designated by name). (*Humour,* p. 97)

Death as a form of liberty! So we have made no mistake in recalling Kirillov's challenge. It is striking also, in this explanation of black humor, to come upon the sentence which we cited in reference to the supreme point, the one in which Breton points out that Nietzsche's main idea is to get back the power which man "lent" to God. Kirillov, too, dreamed of becoming omnipotent!

But the reference to Rimbaud and the idea of those "others" suggested by Nietzsche's philosophy brings us back to the interpretation which we outlined above. We have here a clear expression of the desire for a doubling of the personality, for that ghostly alter ego, for that alibi which can be opposed to the draconian laws of life, the unquenchable desire to become *other,* indefinitely other, through all the cycles of death and nothingness, until there are no more limits and divine omnipotence is equalled—without however ceasing to be *called by name.*

I did not want to bring up this latter expression, to whose scope Breton attaches no further precisions; yet there is in it at the least the root of an immense expectation that contains a secret, undefinable hope in the very midst of the vision of death. It is from this perspective that it is easier to explain how death can be considered as the highest affirmation of liberty.

Breton has opened similar perspectives in reference to Lautréamont; his work seems to Breton "the expression of a total revelation which seems to go beyond human limits." (*Humour*, p. 100)

> With Lautréamont, not just the style, but the word undergoes a fundamental crisis, marks a new beginning. There are no more limits by which words enter into relationship with other words, things with other things. A principle of perpetual mutation has taken over both things and ideas, leading them to a total deliverance which also implies that of man. In this regard, Lautréamont's language is at one and the same time a solvent and a germinative plasma without equal. (*Humour*, pp. 100-101)

Here, thanks to a metamorphosis brought about by revolt, is a new form for the idea of man's salvation. Man goes forward, detaching himself from his ego, toward a triumphant migration into the super-ego, while at the same time the world goes through mutation until reaching a state of deliverance that liberates man.

This, however, can be admitted as immediately valid only in the measure that one feels obliged to continue doing without the "principle of reality." (*Humour*, p. 157; cf. *ibid.*, p. 90) Thus man rediscovers childhood's incredible liberty from reality and, black as this humor may be, it is still possible to taste, hidden under the fearsome outer wrappings, the phosphorescent honey of the wonderland, the magic food of all desires. We find ourselves all at once led away from Swift and Sade, through a little hidden door, into the land of marvels where Lewis Carroll brought Alice:

> The mind, placed in the presence of all kinds of difficulties, finds an ideal escape in the absurd. Accommodating oneself to the absurd reopens for man the mysterious kingdom inhabited by children. (*Humour*, pp. 7-8)

It is toward this supreme reintegration, in the eyes of the surrealists, that this grim disintegration is to bring us. Breton writes:

> We already have a more or less obscure sense of a hierarchy that
> the integral possession of humor would assure to man in the highest
> degree; it is in the measure of this possession that any global definition
> of humor escapes us now and will no doubt continue for a long
> time to escape us. (*Humour*, p. 8)

Black humor, which Breton presents on the same page as being analogous to high magic, is indeed a modern form of initiation into magic; it is that lightning-bolt that seems to bear man from the depths of nihilism to the incomprehensible summit of omnipotence, from disintegration to reintegration, from the dark prime matter to the gold of enchantment. It is an essential probess of mental alchemy.

The Technique of Surprise and Stretching of the Image

It is often seen as astonishing that surrealist texts are impregnated with a singular strangeness, full of amazing contradictions, or that they seem incomprehensible because of their complete dislocation of images. These are taken to be sheer mystification, or a technique even more arbitrary than those mocked at by the surrealists themselves. This astonishment shows a deep lack of understanding of surrealism. The strange, the baroque, the marvelous, the preposterous, the horrible, the unrecognizable, the disordered are not added ornaments, but the very stuff of surrealist poetry. They are not introduced by virtue of a preconceived intellectual or aesthetic system, but by virtue of the exigencies of the poetic spirit. It is the manifestation in writing, or in painting, of that will to disintegration that we have analyzed in other areas.

Poetry is unable to give a "healthy" image of the world, or to examine it in a "balanced" way. The images that poetry projects have to be wild or ecstatic or ironic, overwhelmed or overwhelming. Poetic expression is the result of an explosive mixture of the subjective and the objective; in no way can it represent objective reality in a stable manner, in conformity with ordinary laws. When the poet enters the realm of metamorphoses, I mean those regions and moments in which the overwhelming and illuminative action of poetry takes place, he is unfailingly assailed by the impetuous attacks of waves of irrational images which leave a deep impression on him and plunge him ever further into the stormy depths of poetry.

It is the unusual alone which produces the poetic image. Ecstasy and poetic creation can be born only of the rupture of habitudes. It is easy to understand, then, what Breton wrote of Chirico: "He could paint only surprised." (*Nadja*, p. 14) Haven't we seen that Ernst and Dali painted only when in the grasp of hallucinatory images which had taken them unawares?

A work like Proust's is born also from the strange surprise caused in him by the unforeseeable emotion brought on by flash-events, *événements-silex*, such as the paving-stone of the Guermantes, from which flashed out all at once the lightning of poetry. The difference between Proust and the surrealist lies in the fact that he worked to romanticize his wonder and to integrate it into the description of his worldly wanderings, something the surrealists couldn't have cared about less.

Briefly then, since poetry is born only of a stupefying ecstasy, a poem can do nothing else but project the reflection of this surprise and this being caught off-guard, under pain of being untrue to itself. This is the source of the idea that it might be possible to meet poetry half-way by having recourse to a systematic technique of surprise. Moreover, this applies to more than not only poetry, for it is a law of the imagination which has been brought to light, and the surrealists have found allies in a quarter unforeseen by their detractors. Breton writes:

> It is not I, but M. Juvet, who writes in 1933 in *La structure des nouvelles théories physiques:* 'It is in the surprise created by a new image or a new association of images that we must see the most important element in the progress of the physical sciences, for it is astonishment which arouses the always rather cold logic and obliges it to establish new links. . . .' 'Surprise for its own sake must be sought unconditionally.' (*Amour*, p. 122)

If poetic illumination projects groups of surprising images which deeply disturb the poet and commit him even more to the poetic state, it is possible to reverse the process and to start cold by the systematic production of astounding images which will fully engage the poet in the poetic domain.

This is no more arbitrary than digging a well to make a stream flow where one was never known to exist. Besides, we know what preliminary resources surrealism has at its disposal to make certain that the departure is not from zero. To begin with nothing in hand might be the case for a grocer or a notary, but this could hardly be the case for the surrealist.

One might object that a certain number of incomparably strange texts, such as Kafka's, have been arrived at with no dislocation of imagery, but this proves only that everything is not reducible to a single technique. Kafka uses other means to obtain the dislocation of reality.

As for surrealism, we know that its most urgent desire is to bring together, in one burst of light, the most diametrically opposed realities. Little wonder, then, that Breton has accorded the greatest importance to the famous law defined by Reverdy:

> The image is a pure creation of the mind. It cannot be born of a comparison, but arises from the bringing together of two more or less distant realities.
>
> The more distant and exact the relationships of the two realities thus brought into contact, the stronger will be the image, the more emotive power and poetic reality it will have. (cf. *Manifestes*, p. 38)

This is no predetermined doctrine, but a remarkable codification of the results of modern poetical experience from Rimbaud onward.

Breton takes into account the example of certain dadaists in this regard; he says, for instance, that

> Picabia was the first to understand that all words without exception could be used in proximity, and that their poetic value was enhanced the more they seemed at first gratuitous or irritating. (*Humour*, p. 189)

It is very interesting to compare these two texts, because all the wavering in surrealist research comes from the problem of knowing if the adjective "gratuitous" is just another way of saying "distant" or if it is substituted for this idea in such a way as to eliminate it altogether. The precision contained in the words "at first" could lead one to think that the gratuitousness is only a provisional appearance due to extreme separation, while not excluding the possibility of finding some later justification, as in the case of Lautréamont's well-known lines:

> Beautiful as the chance encounter on a dissection table of a sewing machine and an umbrella.

We know, of course, that beneath this baroque and apparently incoherent collection, psychoanalysis has been able to identify the symbols of the bed, of femininity, and of virility. It must be noted that the mystery of poetry does not evaporate, like that of the detective novel, upon the discovery of the secret meaning of events that up to a certain point had been incomprehensible. The pleasure of comprehension is partially substituted for that of mystery. In part only, for the symbol has a proper value and beauty that cannot be entirely reduced to what psychoanalysis discovers in it. Even after exegesis, it maintains, among other things, the mystery of this identification within an armorial panoply of instruments and of human flesh, so that the discovery of a fresh area of comprehension is seconded by the joy of discovering at the same time a new area of mystery which is adjacent to it. The more enigmas one resolves, the more one discovers new ones.

It is on the basis of this thought of Lautréamont's that Ernst defined the primordial law of the structure of surrealist images:

> The joining of two apparently unjoinable realities on a plane which in appearance is unsuitable to them. (cf. *Position*, p. 160)

In certain cases, this image-stretching comes uniquely from the suppression of a certain number of verbal intermediaries, that is, from an extraordinarily elliptical style:

> The value of speech (and even more, of writing) seemed to me to lie in its ability to shorten in a striking manner the account (since

account there was) of a small number of facts, poetic or otherwise, of which I made myself the focus. I imagined that this was how Rimbaud worked. (*Manifestes*, p. 36)

It seems now, in the light of the research done by J. Gengoux, that this first interpretation of Breton's regarding Rimbaud could not have been more exact. That Breton later changed his mind may have kept him from an exact definition of Rimbaud's poetry; but on the other hand, and more importantly, his penetration into the discovery of new poetic worlds became all the deeper, and the originality and fecundity of surrealism became all the more evident.

He found this early interpretation he had given of Rimbaud to be insufficient. The too concentrated mode of action that it calls for prevented the total unleashing of the unconscious which Breton expected would bring about the salvation of poetry. Reverdy's art as well seemed to him too systematic.

It is at this point that he discovered automatic writing, through the welling up of a sibylline sentence that took shape in him, independently of any premeditation, and that seemed to "knock at the window." (*Manifestes*, p. 39) On that day, automatism struck the rock of the unconscious and opened wide the floodgates of the conscious to a tide of stupefying and explosive images.

There exist, in addition, other techniques of surprise, based on the stretching of words, notably that of Roussel. This consists in dismembering ready-made sentences taken from some rather tame source, such as old nursery rhymes, and then of finding a series of more or less coherent words that can be phonetically superimposed on them. Thus Roussel, using the words of the song *"J'ai du bon tabac dans my tabatière,"* transforms them into *"Jade/tube/onde/aubade en mat (object mat) a basse tierce."* [29] He then took the disconnected words obtained in this way as real *equations of facts*, in Breton's expression (*Humour*, p. 181), equations that were to be solved by discovering the story behind these words that represented only peaks rising from the sea of the unconscious.

Roussel had a further technique for detecting these peaks of sunken worlds: "I would choose a word, and then link it to another by the preposition *à*." [30] Breton explains:

> The preposition in question would really seem to be, poetically speaking, the surest and most rapid vehicle of the image. Let me add that it is enough to link in this manner any substantive to any other, and there will immediately arise a whole world of new representations. (*Amour*, pp. 116-117)

However outrageous these procedures may seem, it is a fact that Roussel used them in a masterful manner to pierce through the shadows of the unconscious and bring wonderful realms to light. It is also remarkable that these techniques of Roussel's had quite identical antecedents in the "phonetic cabbal." [31]

Surrealism is the most powerful mental explosive ever invented. One can say, with no abuse of terms, that in the domain of language and of images, and even of sensations, it leads to the most fantastic chain of disintegration. It makes the mind jump the facile rails of habit and gives it freedom to move in every direction in the mental worlds: up, down, forwards, backwards, the wrong way, all in total liberty. This heading in the wrong direction was already characteristic of Dada. One will perhaps remember how it frightened Hitler, as he himself admitted in his *Principles of Action*. It is rather regrettable, for if he had applied this treatment to his delusions of grandeur, he might have been able to free himself of them, and what seemed to him so unreasonable might have restored his reason.

In any case, it is characteristic of surrealism to draw from these gymnastics (which Dada tended to take too much as only a game) a method that will allow it entry into forbidden worlds. If, along the way, these exercises in disintegration leave only unrecognizable verbal wrecks or, on the contrary, strange masterpieces, this is not what matters most. What counts is not whether the road of the explorers is strewn with commemorative markers or with debris: it is the fact that a trail has been blazed in the wilderness.

All these techniques are far from being perfected. We are at the stage of continually renewed experiments. It is perhaps because of the very perfection of its beauty that Eluard's poetry sometimes falls short of being surrealist, because the latter does not hesitate to refuse all perfection and beauty as soon as they seem fallacious achievements, a dimming of power, an impure touching up of the autorevelation of the human mystery. It can happen, however, that by another excess the surrealist spirit becomes satisfied with its own insatisfaction, and begins to feed voluptuously on the bitter fruits of black humor, as others savor the insipid fruits of academicism. This is to fall back, in spite of a new decor and new sensations, into an old trap; it is to sacrifice movement to static contemplation. The great temptation of the surrealists is, in fact, the useless redoing of incendiary texts, the way others content themselves indefinitely with sugar-coating things.

The problem is then to know how to use these mental explosives. Like rockets, they can be used for fireworks, for war, or for thrusting fantastic engines above earth's atmosphere. Similarly, the rockets of surrealism can be used for the amusement of highbrows, for purposes of devastating subversion, or else for the opening up of new worlds.

FOUR

Automatic Writing

It used to be held childish to believe that there might exist somewhere beyond us men made so as to walk on their head or to carry their head backwards in relation to the way men in this world are constructed. Now people say that to practice automatic writing is to stand common sense on its head. It is made the butt of abuse by all the adversaries of surrealism, but this is hardly surprising, since the whole idea of automatic writing is apt to baffle the mind formed in the classical tradition.

Here is how Breton, in a passage from the first *Manifeste*, describes the practice:

> After you have settled down in a place as conducive as possible to the turning inward of the mind upon itself, have someone bring you what you need to write with. Place yourself in the most passive or receptive state possible. . . . Write quickly and without any preconceived subject—so quickly as not to retain or be tempted to reread what you write. The first sentence will come of itself, so true is it that at every second a phrase foreign to our conscious thought presents itself, asking only to be exteriorised. (*Manifestes*, p. 51)

Such a method seems to defy all the laws of literature and even of common sense; not only does it exclude all premeditation but also any conscious control of what is written. It calls upon nothing but an unusual impulse emanating from the unconscious. How could

101

one see it for anything else but an absurd challenge of all the most elementary rules of thought? If, moreover, one consents to glance hastily and distractedly at texts inspired by automatism, the immediate impression is of a strange language that is apparently devoid of meaning.

Yet it is a fact that automatic writing has played an important role in surrealism, a role so essential that one can say it is the discovery of automatic writing that gave birth to the movement; it is the axis of the surrealist experience. Indeed, from a pragmatic point of view, Breton could find no better way to define surrealism than in reference to the practice of automatic writing:

> Surrealism, n. Pure psychic automatism by means of which it is proposed to express verbally, in writing or in some other manner, the real functioning of thought. Dictation given by the thought in the absence of all rational control, and divorced from all aesthetic or moral preoccupation. (*Manifestes*, p. 45)

It is important to remember that Breton placed an immense hope in this strange message from the unconscious. Even at a time when he has to ask himself some painful questions about the weaknesses of automatism, he still persists in declaring:

> . . . I expect no further revelation except from this source. I have never ceased to be convinced that nothing said or done has value if it is not obedient to the magical dictation. (*Pas*, p. 150)

Let us leave vain polemics to one side and instead look to see what can be the basis of such hope, what are the psychic sources of automatic writing, what are its historical origins and what special problems it poses.

The Psychic Sources of Automatic Writing

In general, automatic writing is looked on as a superficial, unruly tangle of unrelated words, odd bits of memory, the residue of thought and extravagant imaginings, a totally meaningless mass. Such a prejudice is quite comprehensible on the part of those persons to whom an Occidental education has given the habit of rejecting without examination most of the words and images arising from the subconscious. They are even less capable of picking out the main themes which organize them.

Freud used the term *repression* to designate this reflex; the word unfortunately presents the phenomenon in question as a sort of juridical and moral entity when, in fact, it is only a question of conditioned reflex set up by education and the social and practical necessities of life. Thus, in Western man, the stream of words and images rising out of the subconscious breaks against a heavy screen of spontaneous and often unconscious criticism.

It is moreover correct to say that if this system of dikes and locks is imprudently broken down in consequence of a psychic trauma or the inordinate use of surrealism, the consciousness runs a strong risk of being submerged by an ocean of dreams, obsessions, and madness. The exploration of "terrae incognitae" is always difficult and perilous.

But no one has the right to conclude that automatic writing does not make sense. Everything existing in man has a human sense. Automatic writing is not the product of chance, a word used all too conveniently to cover up what we don't know; it is rather by its nature a human fruit, a direct expression of human reality.

Spontaneous generation exists no more in the realm of the mind than in the physical world. Every word, every image used by our consciousness comes from an immense reservoir which Freud calls the unconscious, but which it would be more precise to call the subconscious, as Myers did. They are recorded by the consciousness, in the same way that it perceives the sounds and sights of the exterior world. The consciousness does not create them, but only recognizes their projection onto its luminous screen, for they are pre-existent to this perception. It is true that internal images are set in opposition to external ones under the pretext that the latter alone carry importance, because they are rooted in a stable and universal substratum, because they form a point of convergence and a bedrock of contact for all the senses, because they are flashed on a quasi-permanent background of light, because of the urgency of the instincts and of social pressures; in short, because they possess the criterion of stable efficacity.

The internal image comes, on the contrary, from a world wholly invisible where there seems to exist only the solitary screen of the individual consciousness on which this image flashes and can disappear in an instant. On this basis it seems right, then, to relegate this invisible world to the rank of the chimeric. Or else, this world's very existence is unguessed at, and the internal image is thought to exist only on the luminous screen of the awareness where it shows itself. In other words, following a constant inclination of the mind, what is not seen is held to be nonexistent, and what is only a mode of appearing is held to be a mode of creation *ex nihilo*. It is like believing that the stars exist only on cloudless nights. However—let us repeat this important point which is always being forgotten—there is no "spontaneous generation" in this area, there is no creation *ex nihilo* by the human mind, for nothing exists uncaused in the mind.

It is remarkable that those who forget this are in general those who term themselves most rational-minded, most positive. Do they think that the reason is too frail to bear the existence of a world other than the visible and tangible one? By what right do they bestow on it an absolute power of creation?

Be this as it may, no one can hope to escape these facts of mental reality. The most lucid mind can venture only a secondary elaboration of the fundamentals of the subconscious. Some, imagining the contrary to be true, point to, for example, the well-known text in which Poe claims to have invented out of whole cloth his poem, *The Raven;* however, even given Poe's reckonings, his creative activity could no more eliminate the cooperation and the initiative of his subconscious than it could the presence of the exterior world, as the excellent studies of Marie Bonaparte and Denis Marion have so well shown.

It can, of course, be objected that it is sometimes possible, by an effort of the memory, to retrace and bring to light throughout every conscious instant and in every phase of poetic creation the web of images that lead to the ultimate poetic creation. This is correct, but in no way does away with the fact that the subconscious is the sole supplier of poetic images and of their organic shape. To maintain the opposite is equivalent to claiming that the images of a film are emitted, not by the projector, but by the sequence of these images on the screen.

Just as it has a cause, and because it has a cause, automatic writing has a meaning. It is a verbal tide that flows, urged on by unknown interior inclinations and motivating forces, that in itself gives it meaning. A trickle of water that flows has a meaning simply because it flows. It is the same for this living spring that bubbles up from the depths of the word-images which are in suspension there in the subconscious. And since this is not only a question of a natural fact, but also of human fact, having meaning is having significance in terms of man's destiny, be this significance minor or major, hidden or evident. The major discovery of automatic writing is precisely that these verbal pools are not stagnant, as supposed. Even before understanding what might be the possible interest of words which in this way rise to the surface, one is confronted with this astonishing basic fact: these words flow from a source. Before the consciousness grasps them, they rise of themselves to its surface. In the deep shadows of the unconscious, there are mental inclines along which the words tumble in marvelous torrents, shimmering with the reflections of their images, revealing the vast orographic and hydrographic system existing on the dark side of the mind, ceaselessly feeding the other side, the watershed that is turned to the light.

Automatic writing is not the result of any far-fetched imagining; it is only the extreme application of an absolutely general phenomenon.

In appearance, the bright light of the sun shines unrivalled everywhere; however, in broad daylight, among the thousands who walk along and who benefit from it, using it for their enjoyment or their work, there are other thousands who close it out of their vision, who are unaware of it: scholars, lovers, soldiers, businessmen, dreamers, maniacs, mystics. Without the eyelids of the body being closed, interior lids shut out the fires of the sun while the eye of the spirit fills with a light that is no longer material. A mysterious midnight sun burns in broad daylight, stronger than the daytime sun, on the bridge of Les Invalides, in the métro, in the fields of the Beauce, in the Egyptian desert, on ships far out in the Pacific, everywhere in the world that there are men lost in meditation.

This is the unshakable law of thought. Observe yourself in the street, at the instant when you cease to reflect, and you will notice that just before, you were not present to what was taking place around you. If you became aware of something external, it was at this very moment that there occurred a break in the train of thought. To be aware of the mind's darkening while it is taking place is impossible, at least at the present stage of psychic development in the West. Only the fact of the return to awareness recalls the existence of the outside world, with its becoming again present, its oppressive contact is renewed.

In this state of darkness reigns a nocturnal light which is no other than the light of the image. Photographers are not the only ones to use darkrooms to develop their images by means of a developing agent. The work of the mind also takes place in an interior darkroom where the mental images are revealed as they are projected onto the screen of the consciousness.

For the vision which allows it to conceive of and interpret the world, reflective thought is dependent on the help of those ethereal, transparent, impalpable bodies which are words and images. But the mind does not create them ready-made at the moment it needs them to sustain the progression of thought. Words and images are instead held in continual suspension, at least in potential form, in the vast continents of the memory and the imagination, situated at the poles of the mind. It is from these vast regions, real but overshadowed by the sovereign fascination of full daylight, that rise up the moving clouds of verbal material in migration toward the consciousness. The most rigorous structures of artistic and scientific thought, discourse, and even the interrupted symphony of conversation cannot get along without the prior gift of these materials by the subconscious. This permanent phenomenon is the great enigma of human thought.

There is nothing surprising, then, in the fact that anyone who wishes can find within himself the automatic source of his word and images. While one can to some extent make himself their creator, they must still be received first from psychic areas at present unaccessible to direct observation. Just as the visible sun cannot make plants grow and fruit ripen in the air or on the dry rock, but only in humus rich in active seeds and nourishing elements, so the sun of the consciousness cannot of itself produce the harvests of the mind; first there must be contact with the deep soil of the subconscious with all its seed and nutrients, that is, with that living mass of words and images which will make an infinite multitude of words and images spring up and reach toward the heavens of the mind.

Through some strange prejudice, the products of automatism are often obstinately considered as the mere *residue* of the activity of the mind—and what disdain is put into the pronunciation of this word residue! One might just as well laugh at the memory as well, for being nothing more than the inert residue of past time. Our universal experience shows, however, to what point such residue is indispensable to life. A man without memory would be psychically dead; remembering nothing, he would be powerless before the present and the future, forever crushed by the incomprehensible massiveness of things and by their indefinable fluidity that leave him without the least familiar landmark. But, it will be objected, automatic writing presents only a minimal residue, while the memory is a sure and comprehensive table of reference. It too, though, contains many a lacuna, many a crack; it does not serve our will as much as we would like. Besides, this is not what is important. What is necessary, rather, is to point out that automatic writing has a completely different function, and that, however unusual, it is a certain and vital one. The same is true for dreams, of which automatic writing in some sense constitutes the diurnal face and the instrument of industrial recovery.

Whether exercised on a large scale during the phantasizing of sleep or intervening during the period of wakefulness to furnish the mind with the flood of word and images it draws on, the dream has perhaps as its essential function to affirm man's liberty in relation to things. It is at first reading paradoxical to claim that automatism in dream or in writing is above all a function of liberty, but such a contradiction is easily explained once it is recognized that this automatism is inward and subjective, allowing man in some measure to escape from exterior automatisims. This becomes forcefully manifest at the moment when such automatism proposes to our consciousness a prodigious and sometimes absurd metamorphosis in the appearances of the world. In this way, man spontaneously affirms to himself that he is capable of seeing reality differently than it appears to him at a time when the external senses place him completely under the sway of the universe. This marvelous game is also the richest, because without it, man would not have even the possibility of thinking himself capable of transforming the world, and still less would he be able to find the means for bringing about that transformation. From the dull and positive point of view, dreams and all the fantastic games of subjective automatism may seem insubstantial, or quite simply, unreal, but if one goes beyond the immediate limited point of view, he can rest assured that they instead represent other modes of coming into possession of reality. Today's unreal is often tomorrow's real.

Thus, far from being residual, the diurnal or nocturnal products of automatism show, on the contrary, all the powers of germination contained in the almost subterranean depths of the subconscious. They show human freedom of action with all its spontaneous power of autodetermination. They spread out before man the infinity of possibilities and impossibilities without which he would be nothing but a slave to the world, incapable of conceiving of any other state. This is the seed of all scientific and artistic invention, the source of man's inspiration with the idea of overcoming contradictions and of rising above his own natural condition.

It is true that there remain to be known the various attitudes of man in respect to these basic conditions for all poetic creation, and what problems the use of automatism poses. These are questions that will be examined after a brief look at the historical development of automatism in literature.

The Discovery of Automatic Writing

After the above summary, it should be clear, at least, that automatic writing was a discovery and not an invention. That is, it was not the contrived or arbitrary result of a project devised by man, but rather the recognition of a natural phenomenon, in this case, of human nature. Before it can be considered as a method of writing or rather, as we will see, a grouping of methods of writing in which is affirmed human ingenuity or lack of skill, genius or foolishness, it must be seen as the rising up from out of the darkness of the peaks of an unexplored continent.

Insofar as automatic writing, when manifest for its own sake and not for the sake of a domestication which will be turned to outward and utilitarian ends, allows thought to break out of its accustomed forms, it is one of the principal means of mental disintegration used by surrealism. But insofar as it faithfully projects the immensity of the interior worlds before the mirror of the consciousness, it becomes a procedure for the reintegration of thought, permitting it to repossess its sunken lands.

Typically modern under this double aspect, and characteristic of surrealism, automatic writing is in no way impeded by this from being also a highly primitive phenomenon of which the remotest antiquity was aware. In this we are once more confronted with the fundamentally antimonic aspect of surrealism. Automatic writing is at one and the same time very ancient and very modern; it takes its place as a clinical method of mental investigation, related to psychoanalytic research, but also as a renewal of sibylline and mediumistic manifestations, both these aspects being associated in surrealism.

It is not Breton defying Boileau or Benda, but Plato who writes:

. . . . there is also a madness which is a divine gift, and the source of the chiefest blessings granted to men. For prophecy is a madness,

and the prophetess at Delphi and the priestesses at Dodona when
out of their senses have conferred great benefits on Hellas, both in
public and private life, but when in their senses few or none.[1]

In another dialogue, he insists on this point:

For all good poets, epic as well as lyric, compose their beautiful
poems not by art, but because they are inspired and possessed. And
as the Corybantian revellers when they dance are not in their right
mind, so the lyric poets are not in their right mind when they are
composing their beautiful strains: but when falling under the power
of music and metre they are inspired and possessed. . . . For the
poet is a light and winged and holy thing, and there is no invention
in him until he has been inspired and is out of his senses, and the
mind is no longer in him.[2]

Already, Plato is pointing out poetry's profound identity with
unreason, ecstasy, and oracular power. Here already is the condemnation of poetry as invention and amusement. Here already are the
basic elements which serve as a point of departure for the surrealist
ideal, an ideal which still has, however, to be cut loose from its
mythological shrouds and to have substituted for them scientific ideas
and methods.

Rereading the declarations of so many poets who, from the time
of the Greeks credit the Muses with their inspiration, we are tempted
to smile; and yet, behind these naive personifications lies the expression of a most important truth: the poet does not invent, he discovers.
He does not make, he receives. In any case, to look on automatic
writing as one of those absurd modern ideas that educated persons
enjoy denouncing is only to prove one's deep ignorance of literary
history, for we have numberless testimonials by writers who admit
to having not invented, but to having received their works from
a mysterious inspiration—none other than the ancient name for the
manifestations of the subconscious. We will give some classic examples of this.

It is Hoffman who says: "In composing, I copy what I hear dictated
from outside me." Similarly, Nietzsche writes: "With an indescribable
certainty and clarity, something becomes visible, is heard . . . .

one does not search, one takes." Or Restif de la Bretonne: "I usually work under the influence of an automatic drunkenness." In the same way, Barbey d'Aurevilly defined his way of working as "an extra-lucid kind of somnambulism." Alphonse Daudet himself, without going so far as to admit formally to such a degree of automatism, recognizes a spontaneous process at the origin of his books: "I let the facts fall into place all by themselves in my head; my books write themselves naturally in my mind without any intervention on my part." [3]

Avowals of this type are so abundant that we must limit ourselves to only a few more samples here. James Leuba writes:

> George Eliot, however positivist she may have been as a philosopher, states that in all those of her works that she considered as best there was "another self" that took hold of her and made her feel "that her own personality was but a mere instrument through which the spirit was working." [4]

It is again Leuba who points out that Longfellow as well admitted that the *Wreck of the Hesperus* occured to him with some stanzas already complete.[5] Even the Goncourts could state:

> Fate is responsible for the good fortune that dictates an idea to you. After that, there is an unknown power, a higher will, a need to write that commands the work and guides the pen, to the point that sometimes this book which has come from your hands does not seem to have come from your inner self.[6]

The pen of the learned Ludovic Halévy gives us these lines about the very rational Diderot:

> Devaines says that when Diderot was dogged by a deadline or the printer, he always did well, that when he worked rapidly and without proofreading, nothing could disturb the clarity of his ideas or alter the charm of his style; his mistakes were born of his corrections, and the perfection that sometimes came of its own accord constantly evaded his efforts.[7]

Let us mention also Henri Ghéon, who tries one day to work on an idea for a play but comes up with nothing; then, all at once, two months later, the following scene takes place:

> I was in bed, about five in the morning, completely awake, alert
> . . . and clearheaded to the point of drunkenness, if there is no
> contradiction between those words. Everyone has experienced such
> a state, when you feel capable of thinking up the world. All at once,
> the tragedy of Saint-Maurice came into my mind, complete with all
> its characters, its intrigue, each act, each scene in order . . . yes,
> I was writing as though under the dictation of some other person.
> As it happens, many are of the opinion that it is worth more than
> all the others.[8]

Goethe himself, that most Olympian of men, has come to the
same sources. Here is how he recounts the coming into being of
certain of his poems:

> I had no picture of them, no advance idea; they fell unexpectedly
> into my mind and wanted to be set down at once, so that my impulse
> was to jot them down wherever I found myself, instinctively and
> as though in a dream. In this somnambulistic state, I often had the
> experience of finding a piece of paper lying any which way before
> me, of realizing this only when everything was written, or when there
> was no more room on the paper.[9]

All of these testimonials, then, in spite of the extreme diversity
of their authors, agree in testifying that poetic creation, or even
prose writing, can take place because of some exterior dictate, in
a state of "lucid somnambulism" in which come together full consciousness and the exaltation of inebriation. These terms, inebriation
or somnambulism and lucidity, do not clash in their association,
for it is the property of creative inspiration to be a lucid revery;
but this lucidity instead of being directed toward an examination
of the outside world is oriented toward the subjective one.

Even more precious is the testimony that Rilke has left in regard
to this type of phenomenon:

> 'I have always written very quickly,' Rilke said to me, 'in some way
> subject to a rhythm that was seeking through me its living form.
> When this movement is in us, expression becomes just a matter of
> obedience. In this way, I wrote *Cornet* in just one night, reproducing
> effortlessly the images cast by the reflection of the setting sun on

the clouds that I watched passing before my open window. Many of my *New Poems* have more or less written themselves, sometimes in a single day, in their definitive form. When I was writing *The Book of Hours*, I had the impression, so easy had it been to begin, that I might never stop writing.' [10]

The Princess von Thurn und Taxis-Hohlenlohe confirms this, using Rilke's words:

'It was a very similar night, a night of the full moon, with a rather strong breeze that set in flight the long dark clouds like narrow black ribbons passing incessantly across the luminous disk. I was standing at the window, looking at the clouds passing, very rapidly, like these, and it seemed to me that I heard a rapid murmur of words that I repeated to myself as though in a dream, not knowing what this was going to become: "Ride . . . ride without stopping." So I began to write, still as though in a dream; I wrote all night, and in the morning, the lay of Christopher Rilke was finished. [11]

The same person also tells us that

R. M. Rilke had gone to walk in the public park, alone as always. All of a sudden, he thought he saw a hand bearing on its back a cup. He saw it very clearly, and the verses which described it took shape of themselves. He was too astonished to know what was happening . . . and finished this poem as though in a dream. [12]

These details are especially interesting, for one finds in them the action of objective humor or, if you wish, of the irritability of the meditative function: the shapes that chance and the moment give the clouds become revelators forcing Rilke's subjectivity to express itself in poetry, without there entering in the least deliberation. On the other hand, the partly hallucinatory character of the latter vision is clearly underlined by the witness who reports the words of the poet. Finally, the last expression, *as though in a dream*, is essential; automatic writing is not purely mechanical, in the sense in which this term is opposed to that of sentiment or of subjectivity; it is mechanical in the sense that it is rigorously determined by forces outside the will and the intellect, and conceived in a special psychic atmosphere. This atmosphere is not a decor, but is rather a sign testifying to the fact that the subjectivity has completely entered into the automatic process; it witnesses to how deep into the unconscious it has descended.

It is fitting to end by recalling two other examples which have a special significance for surrealism, because it is Breton himself who pointed them out and who received direct inspiration from them. First of all, there is this statement by Walpole, author of the first of the gothic novels, *The Castle of Otranto:*

> Shall I even confess to you what was the origin of this romance! I waked one morning in the beginning of last June, from a dream, of which all I could recover was, that I had thought myself in an ancient castle (a very natural dream for a head filled like mine with Gothic story), and that on the uppermost banister of a great stairway I saw a gigantic hand in armour. In the evening I sat down and began to write, without knowing what I intended to say or relate. (in *Limites*, p. 211)

It is again Breton who cites this remarkable passage by Knut Hamsun, on a decisive page of the first *Manifeste:*

> I suddenly found, by chance, beautiful phrases, such as I had never written. I repeated them slowly, word for word; they were excellent, and still kept coming. I got up and took paper . . . it was as though a vein had broken inside me, one word followed the other and fell into place, adapted itself to its place, the scenes accumulated, the action flowed on, lines came to my mind; I was experiencing an immense pleasure. (*Manifestes*, p. 41)

It is clear that such declarations are the best justification for primitive surrealism. It would, however, be simplistic to suppose that Breton, duly alerted by such indications, had only then to codify them. The historical reality was much more complex and much richer.

Between the traditional automatism of inspiration and the revolutionary automatism of surrealism, there exists a great difference in level; the forces which dug out these hollows and in the same motion raised the modern imaginary worlds above the shadows are the poetic powers unleashed by Nerval, Mallarmé, Rimbaud, Lautréamont, and their successors. It is the mental earthquake brought about by their seismic poetry that raised out of the abyss the new summits of these worlds. In this way, surrealism rediscovered the automatism that would open up the interior of these lands to exploration, and would doubtless later lead to the discovery of other oceans and other regions that lay even further beyond.

By means of a limited inquiry to penetrate into the interior of pre-surrealist automatism instead of an exhaustive investigation which would have taken much too long, we have been able to give evidence that surrealism, in spite of its radically revolutionary aspect, nevertheless draws upon a very old and widespread tradition. This shows clearly that surrealism did not invent an absurd procedure, but that it draws support from a deep and undying constant of the human mind. One ought rather to be uneasy about some of these precedents; we will come back to this question a little later.

On the other hand, if we have stressed the fact that automatism in writing is a natural phenomenon in use since time immemorial, Plato himself being inspired, it would seem, by an infinitely distant tradition, this in no way signals the disappearance of surrealism's originality. Even while attempting to establish arguments against surrealism, the detractors of the movement recognize the close and indissoluble link existing between it and automatism, unprecedented in any other poetic school. Breton shows an incomparably clear awareness of the value and the role of automatism in creation, and uses it constantly, with a systematic rigor unknown before him. Before surrealism, automatism had known only a prehistory.

If one compares the discovery of the worlds of the imagination worlds unveiled by automatism to that of the regions of America, one finds that the comparison can be pushed even further. Columbus did not discover an absolutely virgin continent, for the new world was already inhabited by races who had come, it is said, from Asia, in very distant times; moreover, there have been found in Greenland and even in North America vestiges of ancient Scandinavian settlements dating back to the ninth century. This latter fact serves as a basis for claims that Columbus did not discover a new world, but only rediscovered it. However, before him, no one was aware that this was a new continent or, at least, that awareness had remained isolated and had not penetrated the universal consciousness; humanity had not situated this continent on the face of the planet and did not try to establish communication with it. Only Columbus and his followers had scientifically discovered it, that is, mapped it and opened it to everyone. In an analogous way, one can say that the distant imaginary worlds have from time immemorial been inhabited by the poets; one might add that since the German romantic movement and the second French romanticism, the means of access to them have begun to be known in certain circles, that a number of gifted persons have been responsible for raising their peaks up from out of the darkness. But these worlds have really been mapped and explored only by the surrealists. It is moreover essentially through them that the message of the great modern forerunners of poetry, the message of Nerval, of Mallarmé, of Rimbaud, of the great explorers of the fantastic has begun to be truly understood.

It should at this point be stressed that if surrealism has been able to undertake this scientific reconnaissance into the world of the marvelous, it is in part due to the compass provided by Myers and Freud. The intervention here of these seekers, one of whom studied the phenomena of what he calls the subliminal, the other symbolism and what he names the unconscious, is highly significant. Even though surrealism, which utilizes literature as its point of departure, can be seen as the simple prolongation of romanticism, it goes far beyond the ordinary limits of literature, for it proposes not so much the writing of works as giving man entrance and a firm footing in the fantastic world of marvels, and the systematizing of its analysis and scientific conquest. This is why Breton attaches so much importance to the esoteric and metaphysical perspectives opened up by mediumistic phenomena as well as by the methods of psychoanalysis.

The result is that, while it has followed the former trajectory of the poetic evolution, surrealism has not limited itself to repeating what the poets have said in every age; it has set out beyond that along new paths that lead unswervingly onward, toward the interior of the worlds of the imagination. It has adopted automatism's style of writing, but has made new use of it to explore untouched layers of the subconscious.

The ancient poets had noticed that inspiration, when dictating to them the words of their poems, revealed words and images that, cold, they would have been incapable of coming upon; but until inspiration deigned to show itself, they had to wait, powerless. Besides, they did not generally welcome anything but what insporation accorded them in the way of directly and immediately readable products. The novelty of surrealism is due to Breton's perceiving that there existed in the secret of the subconscious a permanent speech pattern that one need only be attuned to in order to record it at any time. Secondly, this form of speech merited the most careful attention at all times, even when it seemed to be most frequently discordant and hieroglyphic. It should be mentioned that, unlike writers of the Daudet-type and like the Rilke-type poets, surrealism does not look on automatism as a simple means of literary invention, but as a superior means for the revelation of the universe and of man by man.

Breton's path to the surrealist conception of automatism passed so indirectly along the lines of the traditional experience that even the citations, however striking, from Hamsun and Walpole that we have given above did not lead him to it; he saw them only as interesting post-factum verifications. He himself tells in several instances how he was first inspired by Mallarmé and Reverdy, how he passed though the experiences of symbolism, literary cubism and dadaism before arriving at the stage at which he gave life to the nation and the methods of surrealism. These prior phases were, by definition, provisional but extremely fruitful in that they created in him that decisive hiatus that enabled him to break away from all former traditions and to seek in a realm with unlimited liberty of horizon the new paths which he would then follow.

In this way he shows us how he admitted the principle of the stretching of the image which in general fashion had been formulated by Reverdy, and how he was nonetheless put off by its earlier relationship to the cubist aesthetic. For a while, he thought this stretching could be attained artificially, by shortening.

> The value of speech (and even more of writing) seemed to me to lie in its ability to shorten in a striking way the account (since account there was) of a small number of facts, poetic or otherwise, of which I made myself the focus. I imagined that this was how Rimbaud worked. (*Manifestes*, p. 36)

This was, however, only an artistic method, and artificial besides; already Breton had something quite different in mind.

For similar reasons, he rejected the futurist idea:

> One would have to be the lowest of the primates to give any attention to the futurist theory of "words in liberty", based on a childish belief in the real and independent existence of words.

> It is not enough for us to awaken words and submit them to skillful manipulation in order to make them serve the creation of a style, interesting as it might be. To point out that words constitute the prime matter of style is hardly more ingenious than presenting letters as the basis of the alphabet. Words are another thing indeed; they are perhaps *everything*. (*Point*, p. 54)

If Breton rejected the classic use of words (the putting together of a work) and their exaltation by romanticism, he holds in no less distaste, when it comes down to it, the pseudo-alchemy of cubism (the system of shortening), of dadaism (the system of chaos), and of futurism (another chaotic system). In each of these methods, in spite of their differences, he objected to the fact that they tried to turn words to an essentially objective use which he thought should remain the prerogative of prose, for prose expresses the objectivity of the universe and not the authentic bursting out of the human spirit in its uncontrolled *élan*—except in those moments when man, leaving aside all calculation, allows himself to be directed by the automatism of inspiration. At such a time, rejecting all exterior calculation, he wants only to turn his whole attention to listening to the enigmatic groupings of language preformed in the subconscious.

Words are the stuff of our mental life, even subconscious. Before being written on paper, even before forming on our lips, they first of all exist in the subconscious. Daily and tirelessly the memory stores them up, but they would remain as inert as a frozen ocean if the forces of intuition and imagination did not attract them, urging them into animation in an incessant movement, like a sea whose ebb and flow washes the shore. But the poets of the past and even of the present waited in their sheltered countryside for the tide to flow toward them up the deltas and estuaries of the imagination, at irregular intervals, while the surrealists went down to the water's edge and immersed themselves directly in the ocean of automatism where they could listen to that vast unending sound, the permanent oracle of the waves.

For them, it is no longer even a question of recording what has been called the "interior monologue", that is, the confused verbiage born of the spontaneous dialogue that takes place in man between his most common daily preoccupations and his primitive instincts, and that bears a resemblance only to the sound of the fresh water flowing in country streams and in the gutters of the city. The surrealists strike out much further, toward the interior oceans.

> Once again, all we know is that we have the gift of speech and that because of this, some great and dark thing tends imperiously to express itself through us, that each of us has been chosen and designated among a thousand others to give expression to what, in our lifetime, must have expression. It is an order that we have agreed to once and for all and that we have never had the leisure to discuss. . . . It is as though we had been condemned to it from all eternity. (*Point*, p. 56)

Far from being a monologue, surrealistic automatic writing is rather a dialogue between thinking man and that mysteriously lost part of his being which, on the other hand, communicates secretly with the whole universe. The poet is a medium, designated by who knows what dark power to be the the self-revealer of man's destiny at its most enigmatic.

It is easier to understand then how right Breton was to insist on the decisive importance of the influence of mediums on surrealism. He formally recognized that surrealistic automatism was "inherited from the mediums." (*Peinture*, p. 92) The account that he gives in *Pas perdus* of surrealism's invasion by mediumistic influences should be reread. He explains how René Crevel, having received the "beginnings of an initiation into spiritism," taught him and his friends how, by joining hands on a table in the dark, it was possible to obtain words completely free of all conscious control. He also retraces the steps of several experiments that the surrealists subsequently engaged in, without in any way admitting the spiritist dogma of communication with the dead. Writes Breton:

> It was 'the most exciting of solutions'. You can judge of this by the fact that after two weeks the most untouched, the most blasé among us were still confounded, trembling with gratitude and with fear; in a word, their reserve was broken down by this marvel. (*Pas*, p. 152)

The surrealists did not continue this type of experiment very long, no doubt out of distaste for a method too much marked by spiritism, and also because of the almost unavoidable danger of derangement inherent in this method; besides, they found other, more scientific procedures. However, the mediumistic experience did not cease to preoccupy Breton who, in situating the main thrust of surrealism, refers to it numerous times, especially in reference to non-spiritist research on the subliminal:

> We are, I believe, much more in debt than we know to what William James has quite correctly called the gothic psychology of F.W.H. Myers who, coming chronologically before Freud, is still regrettably unknown, and who, in an entirely new and exciting world, has benefited us through the admirable work of Thomas Flournoy.
>
> There is hardly any point in insisting on the fact that we have benefited at least as much by what this same William James called the solution of the (strictly psychological) Myers problem as we have by the solution of the (artistic) problem of the value of (artistic) exchange which could be applied to some form of non-directed expression or that

of the role of (moral) compensation filled by automatism; it was a matter, it is still a matter of determining the exact makeup of the subliminal. (*Point*, p. 225)

Again, it is interesting to note that Breton was excited by the case of Hélène Smith, Flournoy's famous medium (*Nadja*, p. 104; *Point*, p. 231), and that he turned his attention for a long time to the subject of the automatic mediumistic paintings of Sardou, Fernand Desmoulin, the Count de Tromelin, Madame Fibur, Machner, Petitjean, and Lesage. (*Point*, pp. 231-233) He has, more-over, no reason to be disturbed at the idea, familiar to these mediums, that they are guided by "spirits" or "genies" or "the dead"; he regards their remarkable adventures as fantastic, but not as super-natural. He considers it useful to repeat their experiments, but without forgetting to bring them back to the *moi* (*Point*, pp. 242-244). What comes out of it for him is that "the question of the exteriority of—let us use the word for the sake of simplicity—the *voice* is just not relevant". The experimenter is no longer apt to give himself over completely to an extra-human presence which displaces him so as to use him; he must on the contrary propose a meeting with himself and the recomposition of the unity of the fragments of his own being:

> Instead of the dissociation of the psychological personality of the medium proposed by spiritism, surrealism proposes nothing less than the unification of that personality. (*Point*, p. 240)

It is already clear how such a modification of the outlook on mediumism makes possible a later intervention by psychoanalysis which, in the spiritist setting, would be scandalous and unthinkable. And yet this mediumistic point of view, as it continued to subsist, wrecks the framework of Freudianism, for it clings to the idea that these phenomena are not completely reducible, that the supranormal has an exciting worth in itself. Taking a starting-point equidistant from both spiritist and scientific prejudices, surrealism enters by the route of pure chance into the unknown. From this experience with the mediums, Breton retains the idea of the "subliminal message" (*Point*, p. 241), because it is this unforeseeable and unforeseen message transmitted in confidence by the subconscious to the consciousness that he hopes above all to capture and turn to the service of clairvoyance.

Once again we come upon the chasm that the early "Who am I?" of *Nadja* opened up within the ego; now Breton wants to explore it to its depths. "Since the body has unity, we are in too much of a hurry to conclude that the soul has also when in fact we have within us several awarenesses." (*Pas*, p. 81) These are the phantoms haunting Breton; that they exist is singularly borne out by the well-known "second state" of artists (*Point*, p. 169), the split personality. . . the experience of telepathy and induced sleepwalking. . ." (*Point*, p. 170), in short, in all "those states in which there takes place a dispersion of the self within an 'exterior' object, especially common to childhood and to certain forms of delirium (*Point*, p. 170). It is easy to understand then all the importance Breton gives this remark: "The whole history of poetry since Arnim is that of liberties taken with the idea "I am", which with him begins to be lost." (*Point*, p. 170).

It is lost, but only to come together again on a higher plane and to draw into one the scattered fragments of the self. The result of this is that the whole climate of surrealist writing is quite different from that of mediumistic writing. The mediums, writes Breton,

> at least when they are particularly gifted, work by setting down letters and in a completely *mechanical* fashion: they have absolutely no idea of what they are writing or drawing, and their hand, anesthetized, is led by another hand. (*Point*, p. 230)

We have seen how, rather frequently, writers who practice automatic writing enter into a similar state of unconsciousness. It is remarkable to note that, contrary to what is popularly believed, this characteristic coexists in the surrealists with awareness and even, if willed, side by side with the projecting of the unconscious state. This is a good time at which to point out that surrealism in no way tends to sacrifice waking to dreaming, but rather to fuse them into a new and concrete synthesis.

It could be objected that Breton sometimes seems inclined to favor a purely mechanical writing equivalent to that of the mediums:

> 'Automatic' writing or better, 'mechanical' as Flournoy would have liked, or 'unconscious' as René Sudre wanted, has always seemed to me the target the surrealist poet should aim at. (*Point*, p. 240)

However, this is closely followed by the passage which states that, as opposed to spiritism, surrealism aims for the unification of the personality. Besides, mechanical writing is presented only as a goal toward which one should aim; there is no question of having to attain it. It is the search for this point of ideal tangency which characterizes surrealism at this moment; it hopes to immerse itself as deeply as possible in the uncontrollable processes of the subconscious, to throw out its net as far as possible, but still within the limits in which the consciousness will be able to take over and take lucid hold of the sunken treasures that are brought to the surface.

It is in this already remarkable domain, already quite different from both the poetic tradition and from mediumistic spiritism that there intervenes a third decisive influence: Freud. It is not now surprising for us to see that the opening revelation of surrealism in Breton's life took place in one of those moments which are essential to many poets as well as to most seers (whether mediums or not), as also, although in another way, to psychoanalysts: at those hours when the dawn of dreams is rising, hours when consciousness interferes strangely with the subconscious, when man becomes attentive to a voice which is not his daytime voice and yet which is his voice of the night.

Surrealism was officially born in the moment when Breton, turning his attention to the interference between dreams and reality, discovered there the prime source of all poetry.

> In 1919, my attention began to be held by more or less complete sentences which, in solitude, at the moment when sleep was approaching, became perceptible to the mind without its being possible to discover in them any predetermination. These syntactically correct sentences, full of remarkable images, appeared to me poetic elements

> of the highest order. At first, I did nothing beyond trying to retain
> them. (*Pas*, p. 149)

This was the first stage, that of spontaneous surrealism.

Breton became more clearly than ever aware of it in the course of an evening which was to play in his life a role of the same importance as Pascal's night of fire or Descartes' meditation stove.

> One evening before going to sleep, I became aware of a rather bizarre
> sentence, so clearly articulated that I was positive of every word,
> but nevertheless abstracted from the sound of any voice, and which
> came to me bearing no trace of relationship to events that I was
> consciously involved with at that time, an insistent sentence, one
> which kept on, I might say, knocking at the window. I took it rapidly
> into account and was getting ready to pass on when something in
> my basic makeup held me back. The sentence really amazed me.
> Unfortunately, I don't remember it exactly anymore, but it was
> something like: "There is a man cut in half by the window." In
> any case it was unequivocal, accompanied by a faint visual image
> of a man walking and cut through in the middle by a window
> perpendicular to the line of his body. No doubt it was simply the
> representation of a man leaning out the window stood on its end.
> But since the window had followed the movement of the man, I
> realized that I was dealing with a rather strange image, and I had
> the sudden idea of incorporating it into my poetic material. I might
> not have accorded it this place except that it fit into an almost
> continuous series of sentences that seemed to me no less surprising
> and gratuitous in the same degree that my empire over myself up
> to that moment seemed illusory; I no longer thought of anything
> but of putting an end to the interminable dispute taking place in
> me. (*Manifestes*, pp. 39-40)

What other dispute but that which sets in opposition daily existence and the human mystery, consciousness and the supra- or infra-conscious zones?

These unexpected meteorites rising from the depths of the subliminal into the heights of Breton's night-time sky were for him an unquestioned revelation of the royal road of surrealism. Poetry's great task is not the architecture of the classics, nor the music of the romantics, nor the elegant dissonances of cubism, nor the pure explosive play of dadaism, but this film projecting the word-images rising from the sunken worlds. In the fabric of earlier poetry, we have sometimes caught flashes of the sparks struck from these worlds and which confer on it a power of charm and incantation; surrealism though is not content with these poetic mines, it wants from them the precious metal in its pure state.

It becomes clear that the poetic work is not a construction built from the exterior according to a blueprint of art or of anti-art, it is a message to be received. Here Breton comes close to the Platonic and mediumistic tradition; he separates himself from it only in the measure in which he reinterprets the nature of the emission, seeing in it not the work of extra-human geniuses, but that of the depths of humanity.

From this initial stage in which Breton discovered at one and the same time the origin of poetry and the principle of surrealism, he passed on to the second decisive stage, in deciding to orient his effort systematically toward the production of these messages and toward their automatic capture:

> Later on, Soupault and I thought of voluntarily reproducing in ourselves the state in which they (these enigmatic messages) were formed. All that was needed was to withdraw from the outside world; in this way we were able to receive them during two months, more and more frequently, until soon they were coming with no interval and so rapidly that we had to use a system of abbreviations to be able to note everything. *Les Champs magnétiques* is nothing more than the first application of this discovery. (*Pas*, p. 149)

This is the stage at which psychoanalysis was brought into use to fill in the gaps left by the rejection of the purely mechanical methods of the mediums and to propose other methods that furnished Breton with new inspiration:

> My mind still taken up at that time with Freud, and being familiar with his methods of examination that I had had some occasion to

use with the sick during the war, I decided to obtain from myself
what one seeks to get from them, that is, a monologue that flows
as rapidly as possible, on which the critical spirit of the subject brings
no judgment to bear, which is therefore unmarred by any reticence,
and which will reproduce as exactly as possible spoken thought. It
seemed to me then, and still does—the way in which the sentence
about the man cut in two came to me will bear this out—that the
speed of thought is not superior to that of the word, and does not
necessarily present a problem either for the tongue or for the moving
pen. It is in this mood that Philippe Soupault, with whom I had
shared these first conclusions, and I set about blackening paper with
a fine disregard for, literally, what might happen. (*Manifestes*,
pp. 41-42)

Such was the origin of the experiment at the base of *Champs magnétiques*, surrealism's decisive act of independence in regard to all
other forms of literature.

Psychoanalytic confession consists in a kind of dreaming aloud
formulated without any control on the part of the person being
analyzed, in conditions of favorable darkness. The explication of
the unconscious repressed content is supposed to lead to the psychoanalytic cure. This is the idea Breton adopted, but in radically
renewed form. First, he completely threw out spoken automatism,
in spite of the experiments he and Desnos had for some time run
together, probably because of the personality disorders it tended to
provoke. This should not be seen as a strange timidity on the part
of surrealism, but rather as an additional proof that above and beyond
any disintegration, it was looking for reintegration. Besides, its aim
is not that of psychoanalysis. It is not just a matter of banishing
a complex by finding its root. Surrealism assigns no limit to its
exploration, trying to plunge ever deeper into the meanderings of
the subliminal, beyond the areas touched by the soundings of Freudianism. For such a purpose, written automatism is better than verbal,
first of all because of a special tension of the mind that accompanies
it, which more easily avoids dispersion of meaning, obtaining a more
ample flow of messages with more inner cohesion and, secondly,

because the written document remains available for interpretation, furnishing footholds for future explorers.

Only poor judgment will see in surrealism nothing but an affirmative by-product of psychoanalysis. When he needs them, Breton uses the techniques invented by Freud, but adapts them to other purposes and, if he judges necessary, revises them as he works out his experiments.

> Once more, it was just a matter of penetrating as far as possible along a path which Lautréamont and Rimbaud had opened up (the first line of the latter's poem *Promontoire* is proof positive) and which the putting into practice of certain methods of psychoanalytical investigation had made particularly beckoning. (*Point*, p. 240)

Psychoanalysis provided surrealism with a second mainstay by opening to it the means to a systematic exegesis of the texts originating in the unconscious.

> Psychoanalysis quite unexpectedly was able to give penetrable meaning to these seeming improvisations which up to that time one too easily accepted as devoid of meaning, conferring on them, quite apart from any aesthetic consideration, a value as human documents. (*Point*, p. 224)

Thus the wall separating conscious from subconscious opened to reveal the stretches of the unknown forest, and it became possible to trace a path there. But while Freud, especially in the beginning, was assigning the arbitrary limits imposed by his positivist prejudices, admitting only later and timidly the possibility of metaphysical phenomena, Breton on the contrary had the impression of striking out into a limitless world.

The absolute originality of surrealism's concept of automatic writing cannot be grasped unless one is aware that it brings together in itself these three currents: the poetic, the mediumistic, and the psychoanalytic. This is not just a haphazard mixture of various doctrines, but a strong new synthesis. In mediumism, surrealism rejects the spiritist ideas and retains only the quasi-permanent possibility of supra-normal phenomena. It liberates psychoanalysis from its narrow positivism and its specifically clinical preoccupations, while holding on to its methods of investigation. Surrealism rejects poetry's aesthetic preoccupations, its foolish waiting for inspiration and its vague mythologies, instead affirming the permanent presence of the interior message, bringing poetry to life at will, proclaiming its value even when this message presents itself as hieroglyphic and sibylline, and making of it an autorevelation of the self and its mysteries.

In other words, surrealism divests itself of incompatible doctrines that it finds meaningless and retains only the mental facts and the weapons it needs to undertake its exploration of the worlds of the imagination and to discover their horizons. The possible result of this attitude is a rather deep ambiguity about the exact meaning of surrealist research, but this ambiguity is not a hazard; it sums up the fundamental ambiguity of surrealism which in its turn faithfully mirrors the fundamental ambiguity of human existence.

After this brief outline of the psychic sources and the historical origins of automatic writing, an explanation is needed of the nature of this experiment in surrealism and the problems it poses.

Working Conditions for Automatic Writing

The facts which we have assembled on the historical origins of automatic writing and the insights we have tried to give into its psychic sources show clearly that automatic writing, far from being a simplistic idea as is frequently supposed, raises a number of theoretical and practical problems. This study in no way claims to be exhaustive, but will try to clear some paths by making a special study of the conditions in which automatic writing operates.

We have seen that the first words Breton recalls as having been produced by mental automatism came to him in a sort of dream, and he himself insists on the fact that the exercise of automatism is inseparable from a certain oneiric atmosphere. This state of dreaming characteristic of the exercise of automatism is brought out in evocative fashion by Francis Gérard, who writes:

> The exercise of automatic writing makes the subject undergo a set
> of sensations different from that brought on by any other kind of

writing. Louis Aragon and André Breton had already compared it to the effect of those drugs that play on a harp with hempen cords. It is a fact that the person who lets himself be carried along by the rapid and uninterrupted flow of automatism soon displays an absolute indifference to his surroundings, and is plunged into an agreeable drowsiness which carries him further and further from external reality, bringing down between it and him a mist which the mind finds particularly pleasant, even though certain new sensations take on there an extraordinary sharpness and clarity. In this pleasant state, the body experiences a general numbness, with its life seeming to take refuge in a shifting inebriation and in an especially direct sense of invigoration coming from a completely inward activity. The very pleasant sensation might be compared to the intoxication produced by tobacco or, even more so, by opium. The mind moves through an opaque, vaporous region, brushing against its clouds like a perfume.

If the writing is interrupted at this point, it will be seen that the eyes do not focus anymore on surrounding objects, the legs are unsteady, the body exhausted; the mind experiences vagueness and a slight pain, the attention is disoriented and frustrated and is drawn toward the objects of lesser emotional content and of cruder matter that present themselves as obstacles. A sort of floating stupor blurs lucidity at the same time that it is carried along on a crest of pure exaltation and feverish activity that has been abruptly halted and left in painful suspense.

It seems that anyone who has often given himself up to this practice is unable afterwards to detach himself from it completely. Even between sessions, he is aware of this woolly feeling and of the fog hanging between him and the sharp outside world. He voluntarily retreats into this inner haven so that a subtle poison can once more open wide the doors to a world where the mind can wander free in exultant freedom.[13]

This description is excellent in that it makes immediately apparent to anyone the changes in the perception of reality which are produced by the use of automatism; it gives a very good idea of the oneiric power of this practice. It is on the other hand reprehensible in that it presents this psychic atmosphere too gently, even evasively, and almost reassuringly. The really surrealistic use of automatism would seem much more comparable to the bitter distillations of black humor, or to the feverish exaltation of discovery in the midst of the unknown.

In any case, such a description should not make anyone leap to the conclusion that automatic writing is just a kind of dream, a waking dream recited as it takes place. There is this important difference between the ordinary dream, even waking, and automatic writing: in the first case the motivating power comes from images, while in the second it is supplied by words. Of course, it happens that words are read or spoken aloud in dreams, but only occasionally; these are momentary interventions of verbal automatism, while the basic frame and moving shuttle are supplied by the images. Sometimes, however, later analysis shows that the succession of images may have been secretly produced by words, in particular, by plays on words. This is only natural since, in the depths of the subconscious there is no completely tight separation between the two kinds of automatism. It is precisely during the dream that the attention of the dreamer is caught first of all by the images; their movement and the spell that they cast engage the whole attention of the dreamer.

Inversely, the words projected by automatic writing are unfailingly surrounded by an aura of images. They spring up endlessly from the furrow which words trace through the darkness, but in this case, it is the words that do the motivating. This is another aspect of oneirism which is directly revealed.

Automatic writing is in no way retelling of dreams. Even if a dream is itself automatic, its recounting, however unliterary, however exact it may be, will contain nothing strictly automatic; it will be only an attempted reconstruction or translation, along the lines of ordinary writing, of a prior spectacle. Moreover, being a translation, the account of a dream is faulty by definition. Thus, the surrealists used the following formula for only a brief period:

> I had come to prefer accounts of dreams; I wanted these kept stenographic, so as to avoid similar stylization. Unfortunately, this new test was dependent on memory, which is very shaky and generally unreliable. (*Pas*, p. 152)

Moreover, the difficulty could not be resolved by attempting to describe the waking dream as it was taking place, for while it might seem to a third party that there was concomitance between the dream and its retelling, this could only be a crude and deceptive approximation. There exists in the mind of the waking dreamer himself an impassable interval between the image-process and the formulation of sentences. It is not a matter of a minimal chronological difference which can be overlooked, for however infinitesimal a watch may show it to be, it manifests the discordant and unavoidable heterogeneity which the waking dreamer, pen in hand, will try in vain to overcome. The forming of images happens first, then that of words and while the first is in principle automatic, the second, because of the very fact that it represents an attempt at description, can do no more than try to adapt itself to the mode of automatism. Besides, there is hardly a reconcilable antimony between the quasi-oneiric activity of the waking dream and the literary activity of transposing it into words. The account of the dream attempts vainly to recapture the purity of its model. Worst of all is the fact that such an attempted reconstitution will certainly react on the course of the dream, interfering with its *élan* and its continuity.

In certain cases, there is admittedly perfect synchronization between the visual and verbal types of automatism, but these are exceptional cases and not permanent possibilities like the separate bringing to light of one of the other level of automatism. It is perhaps possible for this synchronization to take place in certain moments of spontaneous inspiration, perhaps possible also to arrive at it through extreme mental tension, but it is better in any case not to attempt similar experiments at the outset of automatic writing if one intends to work under rigorous conditions.

Automatic writing, then, is indeed a type of waking dream but of a special character and it is first of all a verbal, not visual, automatism.

This recourse to automatism poses new problems. Since the intellect abandons its role as sifter of information and refrains from hoarding the output of verbal automatism for use in some aesthetic or rational construction, it seems that the verbal material is bound to appear to the mind only under a disorganized and literally meaningless form. However, such is not the case at all. The words come one by one to the surface, as though dictated by an indwelling voice and are molded together in a correct syntax even when the images they present seem incoherent. Thus Breton can speak legitimately of an interior dictation.

The use of the word dictation is valid also because of the fact that it is no longer the writer who has to hunt for his words, as in other forms of writing in which man can rely only on himself, that is, on the groping of his intellect. The surrealist who writes automatically records an interior message which he consigns to paper limiting himself in what he puts down as though he were writing under foreign dictation. His sheet of paper then becomes for verbal automatism the counterpart of what the crystal ball is for the visual automatism of the seer. This is the image proposed by Breton himself:

> Within a simple crystal ball like that of the seers, a man or a woman can manage to see after a short time, if they keep themselves in a state of mental passivity, the more or less clear depiction of some object, or a happening in which the actors are perhaps recognizable. . . . The expression "Everything is written" must, it seems to me, be taken literally. Everything is written on the blank paper, and the efforts of the writers to turn it into something like a revelation or a photographic development are indeed useless. (*Point*, p. 220)

It should be noted in passing that there is no question of pure passivity in the sense of inertia, but of receptivity, which supposes a certain tension of the mind that sets itself to pick up the images or the interior words. The consciousness falls silent and makes itself deaf to anything that is not the interior murmur.

However, with the suppression of the mythological or spiritist hypothesis of the intervention of muses or extra-human genies dictating a series of words to the poet from without, what happens to this idea of dictation if there is no more dictator? From this point of view, the term dictation is misleading. It is a dangerous heritage from the terminology of the mediums. When a set of words rigorously connected one to another flashes like a comet across the con-sciousness, there is no more dictation, strictly speaking, in this occurrence than there is voluntary movement in the trajectory of a shooting star. In other words, it is correct to say that there is dictation in the sense that there takes place the setting down of unpremeditated, automatically given words; on the other hand, it should not be forgotten that no autonomic directing being is back of this process, but only a function of the human mind itself, bringing up out of the dark, with more or less force and continuity, the verbal layers of the subconscious.

It flows necessarily from this that there is no guarantee that this surge of words will be the expression of an individual and homoge-neous automatic emission. Experience has shown this. This serious difficulty did not escape Breton's attention; this is why he stated specifically that the question of the unity of the dictation was to remain the order of the day (*Point*, p. 245). Even though only a single mechanism is called into question, as soon as one directing entity is no longer in control, there is nothing to give prior and complete assurance that a telemechanical engine of this type, explor-ing the furthest reaches of the mind, can follow a perfect trajectory in a determined homogeneous area, without experiencing upsetting changes of route and wild spinning out of control. Anyone who uses automatic writing with some degree of intelligence cannot fail to notice that the internal causes of the perturbation and disruption of the subliminal message are numerous.

Breton more than once laid strong emphasis on these causes of alteration in the automatic message. After what we have pointed out about the opposition differentiating automatic writing from dreams, even waking ones, it is hardly surprising that Breton put strong stress on the often disastrous influence caused by the interven-tion of visual automatisms during the carrying out of the verbal automatism.

> An off-shoot of the inevitable pleasure triggered by the images and symbolic figures in which these abound has distracted their authors from the aloofness and indifference in which they should be keeping

themselves in regard to these (visualizations), at least during the time of production. This instinctive reaction on the part of persons attuned to the appreciation of the poetic has had the unfortunate consequence of giving the one recording immediate hold on each part of the message recorded. And so the cycle of aperceptive auto-representations, that is, of automatism, is broken. (*Point*, p. 244)

Again, he says:

The result of this was that we received, even as we were listening, an almost uninterrupted succession of visual images that broke into the murmur and, on which, to the great detriment of the latter, we could not always avoid focusing. (*Point*, p. 245)

The verbal process which engenders automatic writing will evidently contain many images, poetry being made up of the perpetual association of words and images. The danger lies in these images being too visible, for in the measure that the mind becomes too sharply aware of them, contemplation and the pleasure born of these images tend to carry off the attention and to distract it from the verbal network emerging little by little from the horizon of the subliminal. Either wonder strikes the mind with sterility, leaving it speechless as it is when confronted with the overpowering images of the external world, or it is flooded by conscious associations of ideas. In either case, the spell is broken. If Orpheus wants to get Eurydice back to the surface of the earth, he must not turn back to look at her while he is travelling through the subterranean world. Orpheus, we know, was unable to obey this law, and the poet is no less tempted to commit the same transgression.

How can anyone avoid visualizing, to a certain extent, what he says? How is one to tolerate the disorientation of passing from the auditive to the visual? (*Point*, p. 228)

Breton has to ask the question without resolving it, for at least at present, there is no technique that will allow the image of Eurydice to be kept veiled and developed only later. There is a constant risk that the sun of the awareness will "veil" it, but in the photographic sense of the term, that is, destroy it. The only possibility lies in stronger psychic conditioning. The mind must allow itself to be so strongly attracted, so rapidly borne along by the flow of automatism, that it will dash after it in breathless pursuit with no desire to go back. It must in no way seek the immediate enjoyment of its own images. There is a kind of asceticism of creation which demands that the poet be always hastening austerely forward on the path of the constantly fleeing marvelous. The least look over his shoulder, the least misstep, and he has lost his way, becoming, like Lot's wife, a pillar of salt or, like Orpheus, losing his bride twice over.

Breton concludes with a violent condemnation of all preliminary "lucidity," because it can only be fake, a turning back to self, and therefore a retreat:

> I still hold—and this is the essential—that verbal inspirations are infinitely more resistant to the eye than visual images properly so-called. This is why I have never ceased to protest against the pretended "visionary" power of the poet. No, Rimbaud and Lautréamont had no prior vision or enjoyment of what they had still to describe; they stayed in the dark antechambers of the being, listening to indistinct voices speaking, during the time that they were writing, of certain achieved or achievable things, without understanding them any better than we do, the first time that we read them. *Illumination comes afterwards.*
>
> In poetry, it is always the verbo-auditive automatism which seems to me creative in the reading of the most exalting visual images; the verbo-visual automatism has never seemed to me creative in the reading of any visual images which can be distantly compared to them. (*Point*, p. 246)

There is, in effect, a wide difference between the two kinds of automatism. Visual images are immediately reincorporated into the awareness as soon as they are perceived, while word-groups remain sibylline, that is, they do not immediately surrender their image-content to the consciousness, thus allowing the flow of the toward the conscious to be maintained.

Breton brings to our attention another no less serious cause of alteration in the automatic process; it is the fact that not even the homogeneity of the verbal automatism itself is guaranteed. It is this danger Breton indicates when he speaks of "the extreme complexity" of the "verbal impulse." (*Point*, p. 223) He returns to it later to state: "I think there is almost always complexity in imaginary sounds." (*Point*, p. 245) He was closely preoccupied by this problem, since he explains further:

> I likewise omitted to clarify the nature of the obstacles which, in most cases, compete to turn the verbal flow aside from its original direction. How can one be certain of the heterogeneity of the parts that make up this speech where so frequently there seem to reappear bits and pieces of other speeches; how can interference and lapses be prevented. (*Point*, p. 228)

We have come a long way from the simplistic conception of an unavoidably unilinear dictation, all the further since, in the case of surrealism, it is not a question of a dictation thrust upon us by its setting of itself into motion, but rather of the conscious, on its own initiative, tuning in on the subconscious.

In the case of the writers who antedate surrealism, it is more correct to speak of dictation, since the surge of the subconscious could come to light only by forcing the prejudices of the times, compelling attention by its own dynamism. The same is true of those phrases uttered on the edge of sleep, in which there is spontaneous projection of the subconscious. On the contrary, in the case of surrealist automatism, there is often less real dynamism of the subconscious and ongoing flow of automatism than there is a certain state of abandon in the consciousness which picks up at random odd bits of verbal matter floating just under the surface.

Thus, between the periods in which a single outflow takes place, there occur occasional gaps. Sometimes the flow stops, and even if this interruption lasts only for a second, there is always the fear that such a suspension may be the result of an interior disturbance and in turn lead to a breakdown in automatic writing. Even if it is just a simple deficiency, the time that it lasts may be enough to disengage the gears, so that when the automatism starts up again, it may be connected to a completely different circuit of emission. In other words, the least weakening of continuity can open the way to heterogeneity.

At other times, there is a doubling of the dictation. Ceasing to be unilinear, it allows two words to take over, or even two simultaneous series of words superimposed on each other, and forced into competition, since the simultaneous recording of two emissions is a practical impossibility. The risk here is to opt arbitrarily for one or other of the two when it is impossible to discern immediately which of them constitutes the prolongation of the original emission.

This is the great pitfall of automatic writing: to be unable to record the luminous path of a single comet because one finds oneself caught in a shower of shooting stars. The poet runs the risk of wandering in vain in this region in which automatism holds less sway than does chaos. This extreme dispersion of images characterizes a remarkable region that the consciousness is absolutely obliged to go through in order to leave its usual dwelling place, but this zone is not to be found at the pole of the mental nadir. It is at the circle of intersection of the diurnal and nocturnal hemispheres, a domain of luxuriant vegetation that one has to penetrate and cross from one end to the other to get to the hidden continents of the other hemisphere. The glory of dadaism is to have thrown itself headfirst into this chaotic region, but this is also its limitation.

There is not, then, a single source in the subconscious, nor a unique dictation, but instead numerous lines of force which convey the floods of images and of words and which fight for the attention of the consciousness. Thus there is always the risk that automatic writing will change its content, or direction, or field or pace; it could resemble a succession of views taken by a movie camera that was being jerked about. The great obstacle, then, is not at all the lack of interest and of meaning in the magnetic fields of the mind which it explores, but, quite to the contrary, their superabundance and the difficulty of tuning into them perfectly.

Just as there is truth in saying that the worlds of the imagination are not the exclusive prerogative of the poets, and that all men have direct access to these marvelous regions through their own subconscious, so is there also a consequent principle of equality for all men before this heritage, and so also are there manifest differences in the efficacy of their attempts to regain this heritage. Breton has often affirmed this principle of equality, as for example in this passage:

> It is proper to surrealism to have proclaimed the equality of all normal human beings before the subliminal message, to have constantly maintained that this message constitutes a common heritage of which each one has only to claim his share, and which must immediately cease to be looked upon as the prerogative of a few. (*Point*, p. 241)

The descriptive "normal" is of course here taken in a special sense; it precludes not delirium, but rather the drying up of minds fossilized by utilitarianism and rationalism.

This general asserting of rights, this desire to abolish the patent privileges of the poets, this Fourth of July of poetry is strongly typical of surrealism. It characterizes the deliberate intention of the surrealists to withdraw the worlds of the imagination from the appropriation that reserved them to the jealous profit of a lucky few, and to trigger a general invasion of the whole of human life by the marvelous. No longer were there just a few ivory towers to be built, but a whole poetic revolution to set into motion for the benefit of all humanity.

It does not remain any less true that such a revolution cannot be brought about in a moment by the abrogation of poetic privileges and the divulging of the secret of poetic inspiration. Things would be much simpler if the dictation were unilinear and compelling, if it led everyone to be able to hear, unimpeded, the deep murmuring of his being. We have seen, though, the difficulties that listening encounters in automatism. It is not enough to know the principle of the secret, one must still learn to receive the signal, one has to train oneself to plunge as deeply as possible into the subconscious, and especially to turn resolutely away from all temptation to deforming literary exploitation.

Breton himself noted how often automatic writing has been used for the most misplaced and most illegitimate of purposes:

> Many have been willing to see in it nothing but a showy new literary form, which they made haste to adapt to the needs of their little industry. (*Point*, p. 229)

> This view of artistic talent and the incredible vanity that goes along with it is, of course, not foreign to the internal and external causes of the mistrust that, in surrealism, have prevented automatic writing from keeping its promise. Even though the original idea was nothing other than grasping in its continuity the involuntary verbal representation and setting it down in written form, without bringing any kind of qualitative judgment to bear upon it, critical comparisons have not failed to call into question the more or less rich and elegant internal language of this one or that one. In this game, that detestable poetic rivalry will soon get what it deserves. (*Point*, p. 244)

Even without going as far as this vulgar denaturing of automatic poetry, there is always the danger that as the poet is writing, he allows the notion to creep into his mind that these lines may one day be published. There may result an unfortunate warping of the purity of the message. With admirable frankness, Breton accuses himself in this regard in the publication of *Champs magnétiques*. He writes, speaking of himself and Soupault:

> By listening, even out of devilment, to a voice other than that of our unconscious, we ran no less risk of compromising the essence of that self-sufficient murmur, and I believe that that is what happened. Never again afterwards, when we deafened it in our anxiety to use it for more specialized purposes, did it take us very far. (*Pas*, p. 150)

Elsewhere he writes along the same lines:

> I had recently come to the conclusion that the intrusion into this domain of conscious elements that let it be dominated by a human, literary, predetermined design, delivered it up to an ever less fruitful exploitation. I lost complete interest in it. (*Point*, p. 151)

Even though a matter of only momentary regression, this shows that for Breton the experience of automatism was subject to rather serious crises. It would be naive to see this as a sign of weakness; it is rather a solid guarantee that here was an authentic and sincere experience. From the same point of view, it is remarkable that Breton, after having written in the first *Manifeste:* "I do not believe that we will see the establishment of a surrealist stereotype" (*Manifestes*, p. 68), was not afraid, five years later, to recognize that experience had shown the opposite to be true, as this passage from the *Second Manifeste* shows:

> The appearance of an unquestionable stereotype within these texts is completely prejudicial to the kind of conversion we were hoping to bring about through them. (*Manifestes*, p. 141)

This is because, in the interval, Breton had covered the whole route separating the idea of a unilinear, imperative dictation from the experience of an automatism shot through with differing currents and continually threatened by the danger of literary deviations.

The same kind of compromise explains all the sins which have been committed against the authenticity of automatic writing.

> Others have been satisfied with the half-measures that consist of favoring the appearance of automatic language at the heart of more or less conscious developments. (*Point*, p. 229)

This explains also the "putting into circulation" of "rather numerous *pastiches* on automatic texts." (*Point*, p. 229) It is not surprising that Breton concludes harshly:

> I do not hesitate to say that the history of automatic writing in the surrealist movement is one of continuous misfortune. (*Point*, p. 226)

We must, though, admire Breton who, disdaining those on the inside who pleaded the usual excuses, made such an effort at self-criticism, without worrying about the fact that he was putting weapons in the hands of the detractors of surrealism. Besides, it was not with these arms that the rapport of the group could be overthrown, since in any account they could serve no other purpose than to betray the weaknesses in the exercise of automatism wherever they existed. By pulling up the drawbridge of aesthetics, of inauthenticity, of compromise of all sorts, they ultimately effected the radical separation of the domain of authentic automatism from the indeterminate regions of pseudo-automatism which is lost in the shifting sands of literature. The citadel remains impregnable.

However, while these forays into the poorly defended and hardly defensible regions of automatism are taking place, the battle can break out elsewhere.

After the sketch we have tried to give of the prehistory of automatism, one could really wonder about the fact that such unlikely authors as Alphonse Daudet, Henri Ghéon, and George Eliot were able to draw from the same source of inspiration. This proves that recourse to automatism, at least to some degree, is not in every case a surefire guarantee of the worth of the resulting product. This observation holds as true for the future as it did for the past, as true for the hack authors who used a primitive unformulated automatism as for the imitators of surrealism who abuse an automatism which they have falsified.

The problem posed here is so vast as to go beyond the bounds of literature, for it is striking to notice that spiritist and mediumist dictations often inflict on us no less sorry disappointments. They may, as it is said, come from the lips of another world, but for all that, they certainly aren't earth-shaking. By definition, such dictations ought to differ radically from the habitual view of things and to smash through our earthbound horizons the way a fist tears through a piece of paper stretched across a frame; but the fact is that in most of these dictations, one has to submit to an almost unlimited flow of platitudes and repetitions.

In short, the lips of darkness are not infallible, for they do not, in every case, convey the words of the spirit in its pure state, no more than the aqueduct is responsible for the quality of the water it carries. Everything depends on the source from which it flows. The question of automatism is much more complex than one might think, reflecting the psychic level at which it is formed, the richness of content at that level and the care with which the message is picked up. The facts show that as used by the second-rate writer, as with the falsely great ones and most of the mediums, the verbal automatism explores only the surface depths of the mind, staying at the same level from which come the most boring conversations or the formalism of rhetoric.

I, for my own part, would like to stress a much more subtle danger.

Breton always refused to formulate the conditions for listening (*Point*, p. 227); a justifiable reserve kept him from making any effort to indicate ways of interfering more or less successfully in the automatic process, and still more from establishing any rules. However, at least once, he felt obliged to do this in a case in which automatism itself seemed in evident danger:

> If silence threatens just because you have made a mistake, for instance a mistake of carelessness, do not hesitate to break off a line that seems too clear. After a word whose origin seems to you suspect, put any letter, an "l" for instance, and keep repeating that "l" to bring back the arbitrary by imposing this as the initial letter of the following word. (*Manifestes*, p. 52)

One can, of course, attach a perfectly valid meaning to such a rule, but he should nevertheless be on guard against a dangerous ambiguity in its presentation. Let us begin by looking at the last part, which advocates a system for the recovery of the arbitrary. But what does that arbitrariness consist of? If it were only what common sense holds to be so, there would be little difficulty; to common sense—and in this it is greatly mistaken—automatic writing seems arbitrary through and through. But here, one begins to wonder if this is not an arbitrariness directed against automatism itself. Automatism, of course, whenever it is strong enough, can profit from any bit of straw, bearing it away on its current; that arbitrary "l" can enter into its game of fantasy in the same way that the grain in a floorboard can conquer the eye of the painter; it can be the automatic advance notice of the first wisp of a mental cloud rising on the horizon. But it may also be that this straw disturbs the current, turns it in an entirely different direction toward new word associations; if this recurs, especially in any systematic fashion, the remedy may prove worse than the evil, literally hacking up the course of automatism and dispersing it in every direction. Even if this "I" which serves as an occasional needle to the thread of automatism, letting it be used to mend the torn fabric of the subconscious, is itself proposed by the automatism that seeks to tie together its broken ends, a rapid decision to put it back into use every time the thread loses tension or breaks becomes much less justifiable.

The use of the term "arbitrary" is, moreover, especially ambiguous here, opposed as it is to the idea of a too great clarity in the text, which is the motive, or one of the motives, for suspecting the authenticity of the automatism. In the latter case, it is evidently legitimate to suspect the obtaining of a too-clear line in the measure in which this is the usual indication of the appearance of some form of stereotype signaling the return to a more superficial level. We will see in a moment that it is not illogical to bring a seemingly external criterion to bear on the course of the automatism, nor a judgmental capability that the practice of pure automatism would seem in principle to exclude; but that does not mean that such interventions are without risk. Uhe danger here would be the systematic rejection of all clarity, however intense, in favor of setting up the principle of obscurity for obscurity's sake as a dogma. There are other clarities than that of the stereotype, just as there are other obscurities than that in the depths of the subconscious. We shall see also how one can hope to find a balanced standard that will permit the avoidance of oversimplified positions as well as of those that are too dialectic. In short, Breton's proposal must not be read too rapidly or understood without qualification.

One might think that at the stage of surrealism when this proposal was made—the time of the publication of the first *Manifeste*—the ambiguity it contains could come from the still insufficient confrontation between the principle of automatism and the principle of disintegration. This is one of the main questions not yet clearly resolved by surrealism; between these two principles there exists a certain antimony which can be not destructive, but dialectic, if it is able to keep a certain balance. Ideally, the problem was to be solved by the existence of the third principle, which is that of reintegration. If there is here a theoretical difficulty and an insufficient elaboration of surrealist doctrine, easily applicable by the vast complexity of the problems it takes on but cannot resolve all at once, it lies in the fact that this principle of reintegration itself has not been sufficiently clarified. It must, however, be included in the esoteric viewpoint of surrealism especially, if nowhere else, in its conception of objective chance. It is through the principle of reintegration that the apparent arbitrariness of automatic writing "tended violently to deny its own arbitrariness" (*Position*, p. 145), but as soon as this principle makes a reappearance as a supreme value, it is no longer able to surmount the wide variations of disintegration or of automatism. The question is not to rebel against the principle of disintegration, but to refuse to assign to it a systematically exclusive value, as dadaism did, for left to itself, it can no longer lead man toward the supreme point or toward the regaining of his lost powers, but only toward a shapeless or meaningless chaos.

The principle of disintegration as conceived of here seeps into the very heart of the automatism, weakening its bases and disastrously altering its message. In such a case, the poet tries to get into the magnetic fields of automatism, not to make a sincere attempt at capturing their emissions, but rather to try to record them in a style and form that fit into his already formed aesthetic conceptions. It is true that instead of taking a classical model, he plans to try to reproduce the pure explosion of images along the lines of dadaism, and so he sets out toward a region of erratic flashes that float in a mind filled with self-uncertainty, into the heart of total equivocation.

I would not, however say that in such a circumstance the poet witnesses to nothing at all. The negation of all meaning has a meaning in itself. The refusal of all choice (whether voluntary or automatic) is in itself a choice, the destruction of the face of man is in itself an act of man; just so, the most absurd poem deliberately absurd, the most horrible mixture of automatism and of calculation has a witness value in regard to the man who is responsible for it, whether he admits it or not. However, we have strayed far from automatic writing, which does not oppose negligence of attitude to classical strictness, but rather to classical strictness a greater, though differently controlled strictness.

In addition, it must be said that snap judgments have no place in the practice of automatism. It would be quite unjust to apply the principle of reintegration as a panacea for all ills, because this would only mean imposing new falsifications on automatism, outrageously simplifying its difficult handling, and by the opposite abuse, doing away with the necessary role of disintegration.

Finally, if it is necessary to be almost as careful to avoid dadaist prejudices as classical prejudices, one must take no fewer precautions against inventing new ones, however good our intentions might be. The exercise of automatism in the difficult conditions under which it appears in the midst of very diverse fields, demands an unfaltering balance between the two extreme tendencies of surrealism: disintegration and reintegration. Even though when all is said and done, we can correctly suppose that reintegration will have won out over disintegration, it would be a tremendous mistake to try to anticipate this and to tip the scales in favor of the first. This would be to fall into a trap. Reintegration cannot really triumph until after disintegration has set off its final explosions.

However, we have to go on living, living on the real level of the surrealist experience, without waiting for all problems to be solved, all the more in that no prior deductions can solve the problems of poetry and of automatism. Poetry is not a theorem to be constructed by reasoning, it is a world to be explored by automatism; if automatism—its nature and its handling—is the great problem facing poets and surrealism, this does not diminish the fact that it is the experience of automatism, or rather experimentation with it, that holds the key to the secret.

We know that automatism is the dictation of a waking dream, an infinitely complex dictation in which the poet must many times over orient himself at crossroads, avoid pitfalls, guard against the return of automatism to the stereotypes of classicism and dadaism, set himself with deliberation to listening with the greatest fidelity to what emanates from the farthest reaches of the magnetic fields of his mind. But what must he do to follow this *voie royale* of the subconscious? What landmarks can guide him, what discipline must he impose on himself to strengthen within him the sense of that perfect rigor which remains the ideal?

In this area, no simplistic answer is possible. It is authenticity, without a doubt, that is the highest law, and Breton rightly says:

> I mean that in my opinion, it will continue to be very easy to distinguish the partisans and the adversaries of this movement, according to whether they show the unique desire for the authenticity of what is produced or whether they would be content to see it in combination with something other than itself. (*Point*, p. 227)

But the whole difficulty comes from the fact that it is impossible to deduce from this principle objective rules of application. Even at the very time when Breton is protesting against the fabrication of pastiches on automatic texts, he admits that it is not "always easy to tell them from the authentic texts because of the objective absence of any standard of origin" (*Point*, p. 229).

Even more upsetting is the fact that even now, it is still not possible to formulate an objective criterion that, located within the subjectivity, could at least serve as a standard to the experimenter himself. This why we saw Breton refusing "to codify the ways of obtaining that very personal and infinitely variable dictation of which we are speaking." (*Point*, p. 223) This is also why he recognizes that

> It must be admitted that we are far from completely clarifying the conditions in which, to be fully valid, an "automatic" text of drawing must be obtained. (*Point*, p. 223)

How can we help asking then if this problem of the handling of automatism is not insoluble? If automatism is not a unique message, inevitably determined and deeply revelatory, if we have to pick our way through the maze of the verbal fields of the subliminal without possessing any definable standard, are we not doomed to wander in vain? Perhaps this time we must admit that the detractors of surrealism, in spite of the weakness of their preconceived arguments, were probably right.

To this we can reply that the exacting analysis of automatic texts is enough to show that they do have a meaning, and we can content ourselves with saying: what do we care about the philosophers who deny movement as long as the arrow flies. The result of this pragmatic argument, irritating perhaps to the pure reason but valuable to man, is that (in this case at least, as in many others) intuition resolves practically what abstract reason cannot resolve theoretically. Even if that doesn't satisfy the philosophers, it is enough to encourage the worthwhile and victorious experience of automatism to continue. There is, though, an even better response.

The best, and perhaps the only rule in this matter was formulated as early as the *Second Manifeste*, in a passage of capital importance for the understanding of automatic writing.

> The appearance of an unquestionable stereotype within these texts is completely prejudicial to the kind of conversion we were hoping to bring about through them. The fault is due to the extreme careless-ness of most of their authors, who are generally content to let their pen fill up the paper while they pay not the least attention to what is taking place in them—this duality being however easier to seize and more interesting to consider than that reflective writing—or to assemble in a more or less arbitrary manner some oneiric elements that are destined rather to showing off a picturesque style than to allowing any useful insight into their play. (*Manifestes*, p. 141)

While so many of surrealism's detractors, and its imitators as well, persist in thinking that surrealist automatism consists in simply letting the pen negligently move over the paper, Breton states here in the most formal way that automatic writing as he conceives of it has nothing in common with this kind of mental relaxation. Any clearer statement is impossible. This ought to have cut the ground from under many a brazen and irresponsible judgment. Many readers, to be sure, and not the least among them, are content to skim without taking the trouble to really read, except to sample here and there some lines that strike their fancy. Their opinion is so quickly formed!

On the other hand—and this is an even more precious indication—Breton invites us to open our eyes to what the essence of automatic writing consists in, revealing its true nature at the same time in which he prescribes what the poet's proper attitude should be: that strange duality which is its living source.

In this passage, Breton does not go into detail about what this duality consists in, but he does note that the authentic automatic experience includes, on one hand, the unfolding of what is taking place, that is, the appearance of the mental dictation; and on the other hand, the need to observe and to try to discern the play of the dreamlike elements. In other words, it means a very subtle reintroduction of the consciousness into the heart of the automatism.

This does not signify a retreat on Breton's part, a concession to the adversaries of automatism, or a distortion of the automatism. This reappearance of the consciousness does not mark a return to its old errors, letting itself be used in the literary and aesthetic adaptation of automatism which Breton so often denounced. Instead, this time, it has been assigned a completely new role. Rather than intervening from the outside to use as it wishes the concepts of automatism, it takes a position on the inside, assuring the integrity of the listening, clearing the way for the tide rising from the subconscious, giving itself up to the attraction of the deepest and strongest magnetic fields.

This conception of the role of the consciousness in automatism is hardly a concession; in the first *Manifeste*, Breton had already stressed its prime importance. Generally, though, attention was paid only to the statement in which he points out that in automatic writing the first phrase comes of itself, "so true is it that at every moment there is a phrase foreign to our conscious thought processes that needs only to be exteriorised," which evidently means that the initiative in these events belongs to automatism. This does not prevent him from adding, a little further on—and this is what went largely unnoticed:

> It is rather difficult to make a judgment about the sentence which follows; it probably participates simultaneously in our conscious activity and in the other, if we admit that the fact of having written the first occasions a minimum of perception. In any case, you ought not take it too seriously. This is what, in great part, makes for the interest of the play of surrealism. (*Manifestes*, p. 51)

In the interval, Breton had recommended, the experimenter in automatism should not try to go back and read what he had written, because of the attendant danger of falling into self-complacency or of becoming so distracted by the images as to lose the thread of the dictation. Obviously, this kind of lagging and of going back is the contrary of what ought to be the frame of mind of an explorer bent on pressing on ever deeper into the heart of unknown worlds.

Now he urges us to something else: the consciousness must not place itself outside the automatism, but neither should it, within, keep looking back. It is not meant to gaze out at the wake, but to remain forward at the pilot's post, while the winds and currents of the high seas of the subconscious carry the ship irresistibly outward.

Breton's writings have many times put the limelight on this dialectical character of automatic writing, which is neither pure unconsciousness nor even a simple chance manifestation of the subconscious, but a completely new type of cooperation between the consciousness and the subconscious. We have already noted this in commenting on the passage in which Breton warns the experimenter to regard as suspect the "line that is too clear" since it obviously supposes the intervention of the judgment. The same holds true in his assigning as a task the *voluntary* reproduction of the state in which the enigmatic sentences that precede awakening are formed (*Pas*, p. 140). A similar instance is the invitation to place oneself in the most passive state possible, while being at the same time ready to concentrate (*Manifestes*, p. 51). If there takes place a subsequent darkening of the outside world, it is not for the sake of establishing the kingdom of darkness everywhere, but rather to incite the consciousness to turn all its power of illumination onto the shores of the subconscious.

None of this has anything in common with the half-measures that Breton denounces between the use of automatism and the untimely intervention of the consciousness, for here, the consciousness is not intervening as an autonomous power, profiting by rules exterior to the subconscious; instead, it enters completely into the play of the subconscious.

The truth is that there is not, on the one hand, a purely reflexive writing (except perhaps in mathematics, and even then . . . .), and on the other, a purely unconscious writing which, in any case, would be nonsense. There are indeed two kinds of antagonistic writing, but in both of them conscious and subconscious have their role and cannot be dissociated. In ordinary writing, it is impossible for man not to delve much more than he likes to admit into the treasures of the subconscious; he is not especially free to reorganize them according to his fancy, but in any case, he submits them to external, aesthetic, utilitarian or rational controls. In automatic writing, it is unquestionably the subconscious that holds the initiative, but it is impossible for the consciousness not to interfere, or else the message of the subconscious would never be audible or transcribed. Moreover, the deep experience of automatism is almost inevitably accompanied, as Breton points out, by an unusual and remarkable development of the new functions of the consciousness.

There is nothing mechanical about automatic writing in surrealism; it can still be called automatic only insofar as this signifies that its prime motivation is the determinism of the verbal fields of the subconscious whose spontaneous dynamism is rendered explicit in the consciousness; yet this in no way detracts from the valid reaction of the consciousness which reinforces the precision and the strength of this process. The term *automatic writing* is a precise guide, but it is not a definition. As with the terms *atom* or *the sun is setting*, the concept is evident.

We can say, then, that these two kinds of writing are not opposed to each other, as would hypothetically be the case with pure consciousness and pure unconsciousness, for the two types of writing receive mutual support based on a cooperation of conscious and subconscious forces, though this differs in degree and attraction.

Similar observations could be made about waking and sleeping. The consciousness is certainly operative during dreams, since we can often recall them; as for our waking hours, unconsciousness occurs during them a thousand times a day, as the most basic manual of psychology will testify. This allows us to show that surrealism in no way wants to make sleeping philosophers of us, as has stupidly been said, but to lead us to make a new synthesis of the forces at work in us in wakefulness and in dreams. This should make it all the more clear that the automatic writing of surrealism is not in any way trying to bring about the breakdown of the consciousness, but hopes rather through this new mode of mental action to make consciousness and subconsciousness flower into a superconsciousness.

As Jules Monnerot has so well said on this point: "This is not a question of 'non-directed thought', but of 'other-directed thought.' " [14] Automatic writing is not just a simple disordering of the language, it is another way of ordering it. It is here that the degree of concentration becomes so important, requiring the mind's greatest fidelity to the solicitations of the subconscious so as to skirt the thousand pitfalls that open up before it, avoid the quagmires and let itself be oriented by the purest and deepest magnetic fields. This is not a matter of instant knowledge, especially today; it requires a long apprenticeship in the school of divination.

When automatic writing is not seen as a dictation in the absolute sense, that is, as a unique and unilinear message which may be followed ultimately by other messages but which will not return again, when it is not seen as the passing confidence of some "spirit" that must be seized in flight before it disappears forever, but as the momentary expression of a magnetic field in the subconscious that is immovably present or at least sufficiently lasting, there is nothing illogical in supposing that this magnetic field will show itself again, just as there are dreams that repeat themselves and other differing, successive ones that appear in episodes like a movie serial.

Since, moreover, the recording of the verbal automatism is rather different from the manifestations of the visual automatism during the dream (making it a double difference), there is again nothing illogical or anti-automatic in admitting that, since the first dictation can be fragmentary and can contain impurities, it is possible to do it over again, not to falsify it, but to develop it and purify it automatically, on the condition that the experimenter is able to take the same place he had before in the area of broadcast. By making a series of investigations into the same point, he may be able to obtain a more exhaustive and perhaps more authentic revelation of the constellation of images that he had only glimpsed at first. If automatic writing is a complex phenomenon demanding an usual tension of the awareness, it is only natural that it cannot obtain its objective at the first attempt and that later tentatives are both possible and necessary.

Besides, if fidelity to the first welling up of inspiration were the unbending standard of authenticity, we would come to the paradoxical conclusion of having to consider a Ghéon, a Daudet or an Eliot as the paragons of surrealism in its primitive form, at least in some parts of their work, and that is asking too much! Inversely, we would have to object to the highly valuable (from the surrealist point of view) work of Roussel, because of his recourse to infinitely complicated methods of writing, far removed from the simple dictation. If such were the case, the prodigious work of Kafka as well would fall under the same heading. Rather than rush into such hasty judgments, it would be much better to try continually to increase our awareness of the complexity of the problems arising from the lawful marriage of subconscious and conscious in automatic writing, allowing a wide range of experiments, all valid and enriching, on the sole condition that they be guaranteed by loyalty of intention and a steady refusal of any kind of compromise.

If it were possible to come up with an objective standard for this fidelity to the deepest authenticity, I would be tempted to find it in the image of the *clair-obscur.* When Breton warns the poet to beware of the line that is too clear (I am ignoring the simplistic interpretations of these words), it seems to me that he is demonstrating a very sure sense of the basic conditions of poetic revelation, where too much clarity is a sure sign of the stereotype. However, Breton no more advises obscurity for its own sake than he does disintegration for disintegration's sake. His disapproval touches only a certain kind of clarity and there is, on the contrary, another kind of clarity that excites him. What could be clearer, for example, than that famous line from *Nosferatu* that he takes such delight in: "When he reached the other side of the bridge, phantoms came to meet him."

No less clear, at first glance, are the commonplace, proverbial expressions that the surrealists often chose as titles: *Point du jour (Daybreak), Les Vases communicants (The Communicating Vessels), De derrière les fagots (At the Back of the Cupboard).*[15]

Lautréamont's clarity is often powerful, and the same holds for Roussel and Kafka. Let me call to your attention a very significant sentence by the latter:

> When I write without choosing to, a sentence like this one: 'He was looking out the window," it is already a perfect sentence.[16]

What is immediately noticeable is that, in the expression "without choosing to," he is making a passing reference to automatism. In appearance, such a sentence contains a clarity bordering on the banal, but all of Kafka's work and life show to what degree such clarity had a deeply personal meaning, how much it expresses his obsession with liberty and health, how a window could become for him the active and mythical image of all his longings. Through this sentence's grammatical coherence and conceptual precision shines, for whoever enters the universe of Kafka, one of the essential themes of his mythical constellation.

Aided by the tools forged by psychoanalysis and surrealism, by sociology and the esoteric tradition, we notice as we draw closer to the apparently most obscure poets—Rimbaud, Mallarmé, Hölderlin, and so on, down to the surrealists—that the light never ceases to penetrate them and to reveal them distinctly.

Thus, it is the reciprocal presence of the dark worlds appearing in the clarity of words or the layers of immanent brightness in the dark verbal fields which must be the criterion of the authentic value of poetic works, since this is the sign of the highest degree of cooperation in them of the conscious and the subconscious. The only difference between the two types of work is that one or another of these aspects surfaces first.

The seal of authenticity becomes, then, the regal *chiaroscuro* that reigns over all deeds of magic and over all descents into hell (here should be understood the descent of the consciousness into the hell of the subliminal), if one is to believe these lines of the *Aeneid:*

> Ibant obscuri sola sub nocte per umbram,
> Perque domos Ditis vacuas, et inania regna:
> Quale per incertam lunam sub luce maligna
> Est iter in silvis.[17]

Of course, like anything else, this *clair-obscur* can be faked, but never in a serious way, because for it to be authentic, it is not enough to juxtapose a flat and common brightness with areas of pure meaninglessness. There has to be a real encounter of the night and the day of the mind, between awareness and subconsciousness, so that the same sentences, the same verses give off simultaneously a strange storm of flames and of shadows. Their juxtaposition means nothing; what has value is their encounter, the coition of star and storm-cloud, of the conscious and the subconscious.

Such poetry resembles neither plain prose nor allegorical poetry; it is symbolic, in the most perfect meaning of this term. Platitude is a statement of fact. Allegory is the flat knowledge of a fact that one then sets about methodically hiding under a curious disguise, but which of necessity remains flat and unrevelatory. True symbolism, on the contrary, brings about the incognito appearance of that which precisely is not yet known but is beginning to reveal itself. It brings about the real conjunction of night and day by forcefully thrusting the light of day into the nocturnal zones, and the phantoms of the night into the daylight. It makes no attempt to resolve their secrets prematurely but seeks rather to exchange their enigmas. It cracks the wall which separates them and allows the two worlds to communicate. It has no resemblance to a painting. calmly bearing its two dimensions; it is a vast and almost boundless volume of space in which is accomplished the joining of antagonistic regions.

Symbolism can come only from an authentic progress of the creative spirit through the zones of light and dark of the mental spaces, and it can be recognized, once the false starts are finished, by the real setting into motion that it afterwards causes in the one contemplating it. A Jacob's ladder of poetry is built on its alternance of clearings and clouds. There is no other poetry worthy of this name.

The value of this *chiaroscuro* is revealed by the richness and power of the meanings which little by little come out of the apparently discordant and senseless weaving of poetic images, whether they show the action of the collective myths or even the strange correspondence existing between man's life and that of the universe.

We have also to stress the importance of that other criterion of true poetry, the poetic *necessity* of the style, an idea that has nothing to do with logic and syntax. It is the projection on the level of words and images of the necessity of automatism on the level of inspiration. However, we cannot hope to examine here these broad questions which do not enter into the study of automatism, and we must for the present conclude our study of them. Meanwhile, to complete what we have said about disintegration and automatism, we shall study briefly their application in the field of painting.

FIVE

Surrealist Painting

and Objects

The revolution of the mind that surrealism brought about has not only changed literature completely, it has also radically transformed the art of painting. If painting, like the phoenix, has been able to arise from its own ashes, in the very heart of that wind of flame which is the surrealist experience, desirous of life and disdainful of pure art, it is not due to its second-rate use of imitation and ornamentation, nor its borrowing of themes from classicism or even from cubism. It is not even on the strength of new principles of artistic expression, for although the surrealist painter uses them with the utmost liberty, it is to seek something else through them.

Painting as the Will to Metamorphosis

Surrealist painting is defined, not by its methods, but by the major orientation inspiring it under whatever form it assumes: the will to summon before us in visible form the prefiguration and the prelude to the great metamorphosis of man and of the universe.

Just as surrealist poetry is the oracular creation of new formulae of magic and of alchemy destined to transform and effectively bring about at least a mental transfiguration of man, so surrealist painting

156

is the projecting of spectres, the creation of pentacles, an experiment inspired by second sight. Like poetry, it becomes the great psychic adventure of modern times. Like poetry also, it depends on the dialectical cooperation of the antinomic forces of disintegration and reintegration, of liberty and automatism, of materialism and esoterism.

Surrealist painting escapes all aesthetic and technical definition. It is free to use no matter what form, no matter what method of representation. It is recognized by this one deciding feature: it is the vehicle of an intense force for radical poetic change.

Let no one say, then, that painting has been forced to serve only as illustration for books of poetry, and that there has taken place a descent into the genre of literary painting. By what principle, first of all, can anyone try to damn this type of painting? By virtue of the concept of pure painting? Must we still in the twentieth century struggle against the classical distinction between genres and even between arts? There is absolutely no reason for regarding the barriers between the arts as immovable and for confining them to a kind of artistic autarchy. On the contrary, they have to combine their resources in order to strive together toward the one supreme end: the soaring of the human mind as it divines the mysteries of the world.

What must be done is to make painting tributary, not to literary forms, but to the poetic spirit that informs all works of art before they are particularized by one or other form of expression. Painting must be set free from servitude to previously conceived aesthetic canons and from the domination of the usual forms of representation, in order to make of it a mode for the manifestation of the highest forms of human existence. The painting becomes a turntable from which the mind quits the realm of imprisoning realities and strikes out for the other unsuspected faces of the universe. It is the launching pad from which the mind lifts off out of half realities toward the total reality. We must no longer sing the praises of appearances but unveil them.

As a young Persian, visiting an exhibition of painting in Europe, said bluntly to Picabia:

"All these artists here are really beginners; they're still copying apples and melons and jelly jars." When it was pointed out to him that they were very well painted he answered: "What is beautiful is to paint well something invented; this fellow Cézanne, as you call him, has the mind of a fruit-seller." (*Pas*, p. 161)

Invention which is not the fabrication of an artificial world—there can be no artificial world, unless there is something lacking—but the revelation of a bit of the unknown, present in daily reality. Rather than imitate an immediate appearance, the painting must try to bring to light the mystery of that appearance. Thus, Breton and Derain conclude a conversation by insisting:

It is not a question of reproducing an object, but the virtue of that object, in the primitive meaning of the term. (*Pas*, p. 106)

It is in this same sense that we can understand how Chirico's painting can be called metaphysical; not because it is in any way a philosophical painting with theses (one wonders what they could have found to cling to there), but a painting that goes beyond immediate objective appearances and keeps to this road.

What is the ordinary visual field compared to the other, that one where there is distributed, in accordance with the most unpromulgated of psychic laws, that which forms the substance of the thought of a man delivered up to his genies and his personal demons. (*Point*, p. 72)

One should not, however, make the mistake of thinking that surrealism rejects *en bloc* all painting previous to it. Its condemnation of painting is directed only against a relatively recent conception dating back, at the very furthest, to the Renaissance, and which has especially ravaged more recent times: a certain separatist, positivist conception of art. The great tradition of painting is that which dates from prehistoric times and continues up through the so-called primitives of the Middle Ages and the greatest painters of the Renaissance. The falling away from it comes only later, in the era of the *salons*. Surrealism, on the contrary, attaches itself to the great tradition.

We have seen, in speaking of esoterism, how in alchemic paintings and drawings there could be found the true foreshadowing of surrealist painting, both in the unusual forms as well as in the metamorphosis-intent that is present in both. Mediumistic drawings also have great value in the eyes of the surrealists because of their automatic causality and their significance for the revelation of the subjective. We have seen that the surrealist painters are themselves considered as evokers of spectres and envoys from the powers of darkness.

In lyrical terms, Breton evokes this new Cimmeria [1] that is explored by seekers of gold armed with magical paintbrushes.

> Dali, who reigns over these distant countries, must be aware of too many and too reprehensible examples ever to let himself be dispossessed of his marvelous land of treasures. May the powers of whom he is in the world and among us the envoy forever close his eyes to the pitiable plans that envy and spite have engineered to make him construct bridges over the brilliant, unapproachable and magnetic river. Dali is perhaps the first to throw open the windows of the mind. . . . We are literally snatched up . . . yes, into a sort of interior show-window (by his figures) which, to our fright, are reflected in the air as though the latter were suddenly revealed as a simple game of mirrors that one would have only to change around slowly but surely to see an immense hole made in which there would then appear the figures, conjurable or not, which haunt a second countryside in a second zone of which everything carries the premonition. (*Point*, p. 88)

It is possible that Dali did indeed later given in to the temptation Breton speaks of, but that is irrelevant here and in no way alters the truth of the principles we are dealing with.

If we turn our attention to another great painter, Max Ernst, one of surrealism's greatest, we will see that he was admirably conscious of the esoteric significance of his work.

> One can observe two apparently irreconcilable attitudes toward "nature": that of the god Pan and the Papuan man who possess all the mysteries and who understand her by playing at union with her . . . and that of the thinking, organized Prometheus, stealer of fire,

who, guided by thought, pursues her with implacable hatred and covers her with insults. 'This monster can find pleasure only at the farthest reaches of the land.' [2]

The farthest reaches of the land; such is indeed the place of preference of the new Prometheus, avid to possess nature, not to find his pleasure in her by obeying her laws, but so he can dominate her and make her over as he wills.

The collage is a plastic type of creation favored by the surrealists. Ernst used it in an inspired way, for instance in *La Femme 100 têtes;* it is far from being a picturesque amusement. Ernst forcefully showed what profound intention governed this type of exercise:

> What is a collage?
>
> Simple hallucination, according to Rimbaud; according to Ernst, a placing under sea whiskey. It is something like the alchemy of the visual image. The miracle of the total transformation of beings or objects with or without a change in their physical or anatomical appearance. [3]

The Dialectical Movement of Surrealist Painting

It is not the way of surrealist painting to keep itself in that dry, passive state in which the subjective and the objective, china dog-like, gaze at each other like two worlds that find it impossible to come to terms. Above all else, surrealism applies itself to shedding light on and developing the dialectical movement which keeps these two worlds in a state of symbiosis, in spite of all the simplistic theories about parallelism and pure dualism.

But this dialectical force of surrealist painting renders it incomprehensible to the great mass of those who stay shut up in the old antidialectic prejudices. It will remain impossible to understand it as long as these things are considered the immutable sources of sensations, imposing themselves like an imperious dictation that the mind has only to register.

The reality is quite different:

> Things are not revealed in sensation: sensations themselves arise in the course of man's activity on things. The starting point of perception

is not an object on the one hand, and a subject opposed to it on the other, but an *interacting process* within which sensations are just as much the resultant of the active mind (the total organism) as the things acted upon. What is beheld in perception, then, depends just as much upon the perceiver as upon the antecedent cause of the perception.[4]

This conception is, moreover, the only one that can explain progressive change in perception during childhood or in the exercise of a profession; the weaver is aware of hundreds of nuances in the fabric, while his client is incapable of discerning them. A sailor recognizes the outline of a coast or a ship where the passenger sees only a smudge of smoke or a low cloud on the horizon. And how much more subtle than ours is the eye of the painter! If the sensations seem static, it is only because we are too accustomed to the level at which our own visual experience has stabilized, and we set this up as an absolute rule. However, in the most ordinary aspects of life, we ourselves can observe this moving dialectic character of our sensations in which the subjective is continually interfering with the objective:

> To see is an act; just as the hand grasps, the eye sees . . . our open eye passes over many things which in the physical sense of the word remain invisible . . .
>
> The eye which still sees what is no longer there; a star; or, on the screen, the image that has already disappeared. Which does not see what is too fast; a bullet, this smile. Which does not see what is too slow: the grass that grows, old age . . . If I loaded your arms with a sack of lead, the amazing garden through which you then walked would in all reality not exist for your suddenly petrified eyes.[5]
>
> Baudelaire wrote that, 'Mistaking a face is the result of the eclipse of the real image by the hallucination that is born of it.' [6]

Films are beginning to force us to see in this matter many facts that we refused to admit. Thus, seeing pictures projected in slow motion on the screen makes us aware that our sense of movement is not an absolute sense, but is a function of our eye's ability to record it. The film dialecticalizes our vision by making us discover worlds intermediate to our own in the reality of the same universe. If the eye were quicker, we could see the bullet coming and step aside in time. If we lived at an accelerated rhythm, we could see a flower bud, bloom and wither at a single glance, as in certain films, or the sun dash across the sky; if we went still faster, we would know the atrocious sight of a human body going from childhood to old age in the space of a day. If films can open such troubling perspectives on the possible worlds surrounding us, in virtue of what absurd decree shall painting be forbidden to attempt to lead us by its own means into similar highly eccentric experiences? Besides, who can say if this new kind of calculating with imaginaries might not mean a new grasp on the universe for man. The unexplored worlds that beckon to man are not only those locally distant worlds like the New World, the stratosphere, and perhaps tomorrow the other planets, they can also be quite near, but qualitatively inaccessible at this moment to our sensations, as was the case for the infinitely small, for the controlled acceleration of life-rhythms and for others that still remain unsuspected.

> We know today, thanks to the film, how to make a locomotive *arrive* in a painting. With the widespread use of the slow-motion and the high-speed camera and our becoming accustomed to seeing oaks spurting up and antelopes gliding, one feels an intense excitement in wondering what must be these local times one hears spoken of. (*Pas*, p. 103)

There is nothing surprising in this excitement, which cannot be reduced to a mere sense of wonder before a film clip. We have a rather naive way of banalizing the great inventions, so quickly familiar to us, which we over-valued when first they rose out of the unhoped-for. One will recall how deeply troubled men were for some time after the announcement of Einstein's theory of the relativity of space and time. It was too quickly seen as a possible way out of the framework of imprisoning reality and especially as a fallacious justification of our constant desire to escape the passage of time. We know also how Wells had built the image of a fabulous machine capable of making us the masters of time. For the moment, these dreams have ceased to fascinate us, but some new discovery will someday bring them back to life.

Nietzsche already had a presentiment of the great dialectic of the metamorphosis of appearances when he wrote this extraordinary passage:

> Were you gifted with more subtle vision, you would see all things moving; like the paper which, burning, shrinks, so everything is always shrinking and vanishing.[7]

It is only the excessive slowness of our rhythm of life which makes us believe ourselves to be definitively closed up in the labyrinth of the ordinary world. True philosophy is already that more penetrating way of seeing. Perhaps the pure theoricians feel that they have the authority to denigrate the non-conformist works of surrealism, but the latter is much more philosophic in act, for it calls into question, more strongly than does any discourse, the reality of daily appearances. It is in the facts that surrealism brings about what Breton rightly calls "a fundamental crisis of the object":

> In recent years, it is essentially the *object* that surrealism has gazed at with ever more lucid eyes. It is the very careful examination of the numerous recent speculations to which this *object* has publicly given rise (the oneiric object, the object with symbolic function, the real and the virtual object, the silent, immovable object, the phantom object, the lost object, etc.), it is this examination alone which will allow the present tendency of surrealism to be fully grasped. (*Position*, p. 125)

These lines had already appeared in a special issue of *Cahiers d'art* devoted to "The Object."[8] They were illustrated not only by properly surrealist objects, but also by scientific objects, especially mathematical ones, which fit without the slightest difficulty into the surrealist setting. This is an especially telling fact, for there is indeed a remarkable parallelism in the two fields of research. Both have as their aim the bringing to light and the exploration of that which goes unrecognized—physical science, in the objective world; and surrealism, through the subjective world.

One has only to leaf through copies of *La Nature* or of *Science et Avenir* to find in these scientific publications abundant pictorial material on a world as strange and as unfamiliar as that of surrealist paintings and sketches. For a precise example, look at the first photograph of the sound barrier, taken at a speed of a billionth of a second by the Séguin brothers in their laboratory at Levallois, or at certain photographs included in Leprince-Ringuet's work on *Les Rayons cosmiques* [9] (pl. 29-32); there is a startling analogy with, for example, certain of Ernst's visions.

The goal of surrealist painting is the projection of the secret metamorphoses of the world of objects into the perpetual exchanges between the subjective and the objective. This is why Breton is fully justified in writing:

> In this modern period and just until recently, painting, for example, busied itself almost uniquely with expressing the obvious relationships existing between external perception and the self. The expression of this relationship became ever more dissatisfying, ever more disappointing as, revolving around itself, it became more and more incapable of broadening man, of deepening his system of 'perception-awareness'. The system, as it existed then, was a closed one, in which the most promising reactionary possibilities of the artist had long since been exhausted, leaving behind nothing but an exaggerated preoccupation with the divinisation of the external object; the work of many a so-called realist painter bears this mark. Photography, moreover, by mechanizing to the extreme the plastic mode of representation, dealt the decisive blow. Unless it were to engage photography in a battle whose outcome was discouraging in advance, painting would be forced to draw back and entrench itself, safe against all attack, behind the *necessity of giving visual expression to inward perception. (Position*, p. 153)

There is, in effect, an outward representation, not in the absolute sense, but in the sense that these subjective representations find expression in symbiosis with outward representations. While routine painting tries to shy away from this part of subjectivity, surrealism tends to make it appear at the very heart of the objective representations whose essential role it is clearly aware of. What matters most to surrealism is to be able to bring out the moments and the aspects in which the secret powers of the mind are most forcefully revealed. This is the frame of reference in which we must understand this other passage:

> The only area open to the artist's exploitation became that of pure mental representation, such as it extends beyond that of true perception, without ceasing to be one with the domain of hallucination. (*Position*, p. 155)

Here will be recognized the stand on which we commented at length in regard to the dialectic between reintegration and disintegration. These same principles justify Breton's attitude toward painting and demonstrate that it is a question here of an art as distant from so-called reality as it is from so-called unreality. Surrealist painting is as far removed from "realistic" art as it is from "abstract" art, those two extremes of aberration; it is what its name magnificently indicates: surreal.

These are far from being abstract views. On the contrary, another passage of Breton's shows that this transformation in painting is inconceivable unless accompanied by a metamorphosis in sensitivity:

> The important thing is that the appeal to the mental representation (outside the physical presence of the object) supplies, as Freud said, 'sensations relating to what is taking place in the most diverse, even the deepest, parts of the psyche.' In art, the necessarily more and more systematic seeking of these sensations works to abolish the *moi* in the *soi*, making the principle of pleasure predominate in an ever more distinct way over the principle of reality. It tends to give more and more liberty to the instinctive impulses and to break down the barriers that the civilized man throws up, barriers unknown to the child and the primitive. The importance of such an attitude, given on the one hand, the abrupt changes in sensitivity that it brings about (causing considerable psychic change in the set-up of the

perception-awareness system) and, on the other, the impossibility of regression to the former state, is socially incalculable. (*Position*, p. 155)

As Breton later brings out, there is absolutely no question of in any way proclaiming an absurd negation of exterior reality, for this would not only show a distrust of the most basic common sense, it would also point to a very poor understanding of the dialectic which is based precisely on the intimate interdependence of the two worlds of the objective and the subjective. Nor is there any question of "spontaneous generation" on the part of the subjective images:

What seem the freest creations of the surrealist painters would of course never see the light of day if it were not for their drawing on the "visual left-overs" of external perception . . . The eventual ingenuity of these painters comes less from the amount of relative novelty of the materials that they work with than from the initiative they demonstrate in using these materials (*Position*, p. 156).

It is only because of this marvelously ambiguous pliability of visual images, capable of representing simultaneously the world within and the world without (for they take form at the point of intersection where man himself stands), that we can understand the meaning of what is being proposed by surrealism:

And so surrealism's whole technical effort, from its beginnings up to this day, has consisted in multiplying the means of penetration into the deepest parts of the mind. 'I say it is necessary to be clairvoyant, to make oneself clairvoyant.' All we have to do is to discover the means of applying this order of Rimbaud's. (*Position*, p. 156)

It is this rapprochement also which justifies the convergence of verbal poetry and plastic poetry in surrealism:

Actually, it is in painting that it—poetry—seems to have discovered its widest field of influence: it is so well established there that today poetry can in a large measure claim to share its most important object which is, as Hegel has said, the revelation to the consciousness of the powers of the spiritual life. At the present time, there exists no difference in the basic aim of a poem by Paul Eluard or Benjamin Péret and a canvas by Max Ernst or Miró or Tanguy. Painting, freed from the need of reproducing essentially forms taken from the outside world, can in its turn draw on the only external element that no art can do without, that is, interior representation, *the image as it is present to the mind.* (*Position*, p. 131)

To use the habitual evanescence of this type of image as an objection is vain, for this evanescence is not an unquestionable fact; it is due to the routine, but not irremediable, weakness of our attention. Besides, pictures, like poems, are no more than external aids meant to strengthen the projection of the images before our eyes.

> In this moment, nothing keeps my eyes from lingering on some plate in a book; already, that which surrounded me no longer exists. In its place there is something else since, for example, I can be present at some far-removed ceremony . . . The angle formed by the ceiling and the two walls in the etching has no difficulty in taking the place of the angle of the ceiling and the two walls here. I turn the pages and, in spite of the oppressive heat, I do not refuse to enter wholeheartedly into this winter landscape. I mingle with these winged children. 'He saw before him a lighted cave,' says a legend and, in effect, I see it too . . . The sensible difference between these beings that are evoked and those that are present carries no weight, since at every moment I make light of it. (*Peinture*, p. 21)

What Breton says here is true not only of reading, but, *a fortiori*, of verbal poetic creation as well as of pictorial; thus, he concludes:

> That is why it is impossible for me to look at a picture other than in the way I look at a window; I want to know right away what it looks out on, that is, if, from where I stand, the view is beautiful. There is nothing I like so much as that which extends as far as the eye can see. (*Peinture*, p. 21)

> What is so intensely interesting in Picasso's work, with its infinite variations, and despite his occasional failures and his sometimes pointless monstrosities, is the way in which it has, as no other, contributed to the unlimited dialecticalization of vision.

The visual faculty is there brought to its highest potential and is placed in a state of permanent revolution. . . .

A shudder runs through the dark interval separating natural things and human creation. A thrilling, untiring questioning runs back and forth between them, tending, just by the strength of the instrument placed between them to bring man forth all at once from his song, if the instrument is a guitar, or, if a mirror, the woman from her nudity. The human face in particular is seen as the eternal, the unending game of patience, the chosen place of all perturbations. The external world is only matrix to that face forever unknown, forever changing, in which, at the end, all is to be found; it is only the metaphorical world into which flow the emotions, a mold without value except as it is common to all men, formed from their daily experience. (*Humour*, p. 200)

Picasso's painting is a precision instrument whose only work is to record, outside any objective consideration for final attractiveness or unattractiveness, the dialectic movement of the mind. (*Point*, p. 197)

Such work, along with that of the other great surrealist painters, aims at nothing less than placing at our disposition an arsenal of mental telescopes that will allow us to pierce the immensities of the inward sky.

The mysterious route where fear dogs our every step, where our desire to turn back is overcome only by the false hope that we are being accompanied—this road, for fifteen years now, is swept by a powerful searchlight. For fifteen years now, Picasso, exploring this road himself, has gone far on ahead, his hands full of rays of light. Before him, no one had dared to see there. The poets did indeed speak of a country they had discovered, where there appeared to them, as natural as could be, 'a drawing-room at the bottom of a lake,' but for us that was only a virtual image. By what miracle did this man—whom I have the happiness and astonishment to know—find himself in possession of what was needed to give body to that which, until him, had remained in the domain of the highest fantasy? . . . What is there at the end of that anguishing voyage? Shall we ever really know? What matters is that the exploration continue. (*Peinture*, p. 26)

This reconnaissance into the lost lands is dangerous but entrancing, for its aim is not only to discover possibilities which will never be realized, but even more, signs of the future life of a totally free humanity. "The mind speaks to us insistently of a future continent." (*Peinture*, p. 27) This leap into the future, this discovery of infinitely distant stars from which only a glimmer of light reaches us while they wait for us to set foot on their fiery lands, cannot be made by a poetry or a painting still passive slaves of the earth which surrounds us. That is what Breton means when he states that "Beauty will be convulsive, or else it will not be." (*Nadja*, p. 215) This means that it will be emotional-dialectic, destroying-creative.

Automatism Sets the Dialectic into Motion

It would not be enough just set up the principle of the dialectic; what is above all necessary is to apply it in order to favor the movement of revelatory exchanges between the subjective and the objective. The deep forces of the human being tend spontaneously toward this, but they run up against resistance, to which Freud gave the name repression. This is not an entity in itself, but rather an abstraction designating those forces in natural and social life whose growing weight over the course of the lifetime tend ceaselessly to stabilize and deaden man's sensitivity. It is this hardening which progressively narrows childhood's field of liberty and transforms the young and flexible human sapling into a tree trunk covered with gnarled bark. Utility tends to impose itself ever more firmly, getting rid of all the forms of thought and of vision that are not in direct harmony with the demands of life, and it finally convicts of absolute inutility those phenomena of which one could have established only the relative inutility. Moreover, however grave this erroneous conviction, even more serious is the fact that sensitivity itself becomes dried up to the point at which repression becomes an unconscious and therefore almost irrestible reflex.

Direct blows of the battering ram struck against this hard wall can cause some useful shocks, and that is just what the affirmation of the dialectic principle does, but these blows by themselves are not enough. To get to the other side, there is no other way but the underground passage of automatism which, groping, tunnels under the wall for those rays of light whose source is on the other side. It is only when enough cracks have been made, when the work of sapping is far enough along, when the rays coming from the two sources of light—psychic and mental—blend all around, that the wall will crumble and the two sources of light will become only one.

If the genius of the greatest painters did not wait for the proclamation of the principle of automatism before beginning already to open deep fissures through which shines the gleam of revelation, it is precisely because genius by definition appeals to automatism as source of its inspiration. The importance of surrealism can be recognized in that it does proclaim this principle and consequently brings its application from the domain of empiricism into that of a quasi-scientific research.

We have already stressed the importance of the methods of Dali and of Ernst in this respect. The former used a very special mode of activity which he called "critical-paranoiac," "a spontaneous method of irrational knowledge based on the critical and systematic objectivization of associations and delirious interpretations." (*Position*, p. 157) The latter, as we have also seen, demonstrated the interest of optical research carried out using "the irritability of the mind" and of systematic disorientation (*Point*, p. 159), research which has been especially fruitful through the use of *frottage* and *collage*.

The fact that the first two procedures are clearly hallucinatory should be emphasized here. That of critical-paranoia consists in letting the eye be fooled as it gazes at obsessive and hallucinatory previous visions. The second, more graphically mechanical, begins rather from a still formless obsession whose procreative grain of sand is found in an object as apparently insignificant as a bit of rope or the grain of a floorboard. The painter directly interrogates this pole of disturbance of the mind by moving his pencil *capriciously* over the object so as to bring out expressive forms, revelatory of the content of his obsession.

The collage technique is quite different and risks sometimes seeming purely artificial and gratuitously wished for. But in fact, it also depends on unpremeditated research, carried out by feeling one's way, and it has the same tendency to reveal the phantoms of subjectivity. It consists in reassembling fragments of preexisting images in such a way as to form a new image answering a poetic need. Ernst perfectly defined it as leading to "the chance encounter of two distant realities on an unsuitable level" (cf. *Position*, p. 159), a formula which is the happy codification of Lautréamont's famous proposition: "Beautiful as the encounter of a sewing machine and an umbrella on a dissecting table." It also translated under a new form Reverdy's law on the poetic image. It gives us a remarkable method of triangulation which is destined, not to provide measures, but to bring to the surface unrevealed mental images.

However new, such procedures have an evocatory role that immediately recalls the methods of the seers and the metaphysicists:

> The faces of cards, coffee-dregs, the flocculation of egg-white, etc., are means of stimulating the subconscious vision. In the last two cases and in other analogous forms of divination, a grouping of particules or a tangle of diversely lighted lines offer points of concentration to the subject and induce hallucination. Myers has made a thorough study of this problem of the exteriorization of inward images. . . .
>
> In our opinion, the principle of the reversibility of the visual image must be admitted. Just as the mental image is the perception of a material image formed on the retina, so a representative mental image can create an objective image that can be localized in space on the condition that it be given real points of reference. Like Professor Ferrall, I have been able with a little practice to elicit this type of voluntary hallucination in myself. . . .
>
> The same holds true for the contemplation of reflecting surfaces: water, oil, mirrors, glass balls. . . . Nothing today is so easy to demonstrate as supernormal vision using mirrors. . . .
>
> The use of crystal provides an excellent means of receiving telepathic communications.

> By using a seashell, one can also have auditory hallucinations, related
> either to voices or to music, and which often have a premonitory
> or monitory character.[10]

These techniques, like those of surrealism, tend to project internal
images, but this does not prevent the latter from sometimes being
linked to the exterior world by hidden doors.

Since it is a question here of attaining to what it is ordinarily
impossible to see, the role of the faculty of premeditation must be
removed as far as possible, so that the appeal will be to the deep
forces of the mind, through the seeking of the unexpected and with
the aid of automatism.

> How can anyone accept being the slave of his own hand? It is
> inadmissible that drawing and painting find themselves today at the
> same point writing was at before Gutenberg. (*Peinture*, p. 113)

This proposal alone would be enough to justify fully the use of
collage. What principle of exclusivity, of arbitrary and moreover
illusory separatism of persons among themselves, like art objects
among themselves, would forbid anyone who is drawn by the irre-
sistible desire to do so, to take up some image, some bit of a drawing
or a picture or material, for the purpose of uniting them to others
torn away in the same manner from their previous support, making
out of what was borrowed from others an absolutely new and revelatory *whole* of the most personal secrets of the inspired person who
fashioned these things according to his whim? Who can say that
La Femme 100 têtes is not a profoundly original creation? It is
funny to think that those who deny this are the very ones who
are forever doing and redoing the same sunset with the same methods
they learned from their teachers and who think they are original
because a meaningless chance adds to this sunset a pine instead
of an oak and two houses instead of three.

It is most remarkable that photography also has followed in the
steps of painting: starting from the most exact reproduction of the
level of reality that we ordinarily observe, it has very quickly moved
toward the figuration of the invisible, either by the photography

of the microscopic and of stellar phenomena that escape the naked eye, or by the technique of montage which corresponds very closely to that of collage. From this point of view, it is probably photography which most boldly realizes Breton's desire to emancipate the artist from slavery to his own hand. One can hope that it will go even further, as Man Ray leads us to believe:

> The automatic camera will certainly become a reality, but this will only augment the role of the operator. Creation in photography does not consist in turning cranks or in putting a hood over your head, but depends on the contact between the subject and the operator. All that detracts from this contact is harmful. In the future we will have cameras that will be handled like musical instruments, which are held without being looked at. The best instruments, the most successful, are those that can "become part" of the human body, like the bicycle and the violin.[11]

This subtle contact between subject and operator is the one that makes the final difference between the photograph taken by a true artist and that taken, with the same instrument, by a pure mechanician. We know what new visions have been opened up by the "photographs" of a Man Ray, a Brassaï, a Raoul Ubac.

Ubac reveals for us one of his secrets, one of the ways in which he forces photography to outdistance itself dialectically, when he writes:

> An image, especially a photographic image, shows us how just an instant of reality looks. Behind the thin film that molds one aspect of things, within that image itself there exists another in the latent stage, or several others superposed in time and which are suddenly revealed by what are most often chance operations.
>
> This chance can express itself in an abrupt contraction of the image brought about by melting the wet gelatine over a stove. Technically, everything takes place outside the operator. The matter itself works to constitute a new image by destroying the old one, or to reconstitute a lost image, according to the laws set in motion by the action of water or heat on another matter. The creator's hand has only a mediatory value here. The photographs of "the back of the face,"

which represent a transmutation of the human face, as well as those of "the petrified face," were obtained in this manner.[12]

Other exciting examples of this strange kind of alchemy can be found in the different Parisian "fossils" due to Ubac: the fossil of the Eiffel Tower, the fossil of the Opera, of the Madeleine, and so forth.[13]

The future of the plastic arts lies in a continuously perfected combination of chance with a double automatism: that of the mechanical instrument and that of creative inspiration. This is the only way in which men can penetrate more deeply into the mysterious region of the "shining, unapproachable, magnetic river" of which Breton spoke with regard to Dali, to which he alludes also with regard to Picasso, saying that he makes appear before our eyes certain "shimmering, singing flecks by which the radiant river shows us that it has considered an obstacle and has just taken it in stride." (*Point*, p. 191) He points out for us the origin of this river, which is at once so known and so mysterious:

> For a long time to come, I think, men will experience the need of tracing to its true sources the magical river that flows from their eyes, and bathe in the same light and the same hallucinatory shadow the things that are and those that are not. Without ever knowing very well to whom the troubling discovery is due, they will place one of these sources very high above the summit of any mountain. The region in which condense the enchanting mists of what they do not yet know and of what they are going to live, that region will appear to them in a flash. (*Peinture*, p. 29)

No surrealist painting is the pursuit of the bizarre for the sake of the bizarre, of the meaningless for the sake of the meaningless, of the unrecognizable for the sake of the unrecognizable; it is the revelation of invisible but present worlds, a divination of future but real worlds, the already known discovery of the transfiguration of man and the universe in the up till then unrevealed regions of the future.

It is created in the continual output that takes place between the eye of the flesh and the third eye, the mental gaze, and thus shows the very paths of a migration in progress, of man attempting to come forth from the ego in order to reintegrate himself in the depths of the super-ego, which is definitively the great pole of attraction and of light. Breton says of Picasso:

> It is clear that it is the *surmoi* here that acts as a light-condenser, like armor turned inward. (*Humour*, p. 200)

In spite of the extreme differences in technique, one finds in the gigantic representations of Chirico and Dali the same immensity of perspective, the same formidable height of rampart and cliff, the same awesome and absolute daylight, the same giant stature of man, hardened into a mannequin or torn by flaying, of man undergoing the sublime torture of the great metamorphosis: it is the caterpillar man of today tearing fanatically at his shroud in order to transform himself into a dazzling butterfly, a giant phantom of light.

Surrealist Objects

There is still another way for painting to step beyond its traditional limits: it consists in introducing into the field of visual representation, spread out and fashioned by the brush, fragments of reality originally independent of plastic art; pieces of cardboard, of newspaper, even feathers and dried insects; for collage has gone as far as this amazing incorporation:

> It was in 1933 that for the first time, a natural butterfly was able to enter into the makeup of a picture, and that it was able to do it without making everything around it fall into dust, without the bewildering representations that its presence in this place could lead to bringing about any failure in the system of human representations in which it is comprised. ("Picasso" in *Point*, p. 191)

There was here, of course, a fine audacity on Picasso's part, but this representation can be understood all the better in that the bewildering representations to which Breton is alluding are not only the splendor of nature, but also those, still more mysterious, that evoke the butterfly as symbol of immortality and metamorphosis. If the usual concept of painting is shattered here and falls to dust, while a new plastic field centered on an authentic butterfly is maintained, it is to the benefit of the superior concept of *permanent invasion* which animates surrealism when it refuses to allow painting—or poetry—let themselves remain in sterile self-imprisonment, and bids them instead confront the wind in the street and the apparent impassability of nature. Not it is nature in its living forms and no longer only in its chemical extracts that are to be snatched up by the machine of plastic art. The painter seizes a leaf, for example, or a butterfly in the delicate workings of his automatisms and of his inspiration, hoping in this way one day to attract all of nature into the plastic machine and to incorporate it, live, into the human genius.

Going even further, surrealism descends into the world of three-dimensional fabrications to enter into competition with nature and with utilitarian or ornamental work, so that on every side sight, touch and all the senses will be surrounded by enigmatically human objects which serve as the first footholds on the way to the integral conquest of nature and the subversion of objectivity. This is the setting in which surrealist objects were conceived of. As early as 1917, Breton wrote:

> Our (inexplicable) tastes are rather like those of Clarisse, Paul Morand's mysterious and beautiful heroine:
> 'Little unimaginable ageless objects such as were never dreamed of, the museum of a savage child, curios from insane asylums, the collection of a consul left anemic by the tropics . . . broken mechanical toys, steam organs . . . a thousand objects destined for other uses than one might suppose.' [14] (*Pas*, p. 32)

Later, withdrawing from what the mere mention of Morand's name would suffice to cast suspicion on as only an artificial amusement, he stresses that the objects which have held his interest are those cast up on the banks of waking by the great tides of the dream:

It is to respond to a perpetual desire for verification that I decided recently to make, in the measure that it was feasible, certain of those objects that one comes across only in dreams and that seem as indefensible for utility's purposes as for pleasure's . . . I would like to put into circulation some objects of that nature, whose final fate seems to me eminently problematic and disquieting . . . There would be very carefully-made machines that had no use; there would be minute blueprints for a city that, such as we are, we would be incapable of founding, but that would, at least, outclass all present and future capitals; absurd, highly perfected robots that would do nothing like anyone else, programmed to give us a correct idea of action. (*Point*, p. 28)

Among the surrealist objects completed, I will cite particularly Duchamp's ready-mades, which were "manufactured objects promoted to the dignity of art objects by the choice of the artist" (*Position*, p. 162), the most banal object becoming suddenly charged with mystery by a systematically unreasonable use, by an unexpected situation or qualification which pulled it out of the context of reality that serves as its setting in ordinary socio-industrial reality, like the famous glass bulb filled with 50 cm.^{3} of Paris air.

Let us also cite the surrealist objects enumerated by Dali; objects whose functioning is symbolic, whose origin is automatic, such as a suspended ball, sponges, and a bowl of flour—the kind of object "which lends itself to a minimum of mechanical functioning and which is based on phantasms and representations susceptible to provocation by the realization of unconscious acts"; [15] transubstantiated objects, like limp watches, object-machines, experimental fantasies, like the rocking chair for thinking.

Belonging to a completely different order, the importance of what Breton called the found object should be stressed; it is a kind of signal of objective chance, the witness of a stupefying encounter. (*Amour*, p. 46)

Finally, going on to objects of a totally different dimension, one perceives that along with this quantitative variation, one is dealing at the same time with a considerable qualitative variation, as in the case of architecture. The qualitative change takes place at the moment when the object can no longer be taken in as a whole by sight and touch, and on the contrary envelops the human person in a sort of sacred precinct. This explains the intense interest that Breton gave to attempts like that of the mailman Cheval or to a church "made all of vegetables and of shellfish, in Barcelona" or to a certain building for which Le Corbusier planned "irrationally undulating walls." (*Position*, p. 133)

The surrealist exhibition of 1947, held in response to a similar preoccupation, seemed to surround the visitor with unusual objects and rooms that resembled places of initiation. The detail of these realizations was needlessly criticized from the aesthetic viewpoint; this was only a minor aspect of the question. It would have been more useful to criticize the magic powerlessness of its impossible references to Apollonius of Tyana, which were splendid from the poetic and mythic point of view, but inoperative, for the god Pan is dead and will not rise again. In any case, the witness given the surrealist designs by such an exhibition is the prime factor and merits our attention.

Through objects, as through painting and through poetry, as moreover through social revolution, surrealism seeks only the victorious subversion of the human condition and entrance into the wonderland where the principle of pleasure can make its empire hold sway.

SIX

Objective Chance

We have seen how surrealism adopted one of esoterism's essential principles by taking on as a goal the recuperation of the lost powers that will lead finally to the conquest of the supreme point, how it brought to light the new techniques of disintegration and automatism that lead to the discovery within human subjectivity of the presence of secret fissures through which the approach to another life is revealed. This alone would make of surrealism one of the most original and most powerful enterprises of our era.

None of this was enough, though, to make surrealism integrally itself. The spirit which animates it cannot be content with new philosophical speculation, nor even with a complete change in psychology, even though this might be from the very roots up. Surrealism can in no way accept to close itself up within the confines of subjectivity. Its very principle enjoins it to seek an active synthesis of the subjective and the objective. It is neither idealist nor intellectualist. Although it draws upon the occult, at the same time it cannot ignore the weight of matter or of social life. Its essential role is, on the contrary, to bring them into effective confrontation, to search out the ways by which the most extreme subjectivity and the most tangible objectivity can communicate.

Breton's experience and thought have never ceased making their way along the dizzying mountain path between the attraction of the

179

principle of pleasure and of the principle of reality, between the dream and material life, between the traditions of the occult and the most revolutionary doctrines of modern times. His thought, however, tends much less to lead him into discussions on the theoretical aspects of such confrontations than it does to bring to light and to interpret the most remarkable facts of an existence in which are revealed strange interferences between the subjective and the objective, between individual dreams and the events of social and material life.

Objective chance is the whole of those phenomena which manifest the invasion of daily life by the marvelous. Through them, in fact, it becomes clear that man walks in broad daylight in the midst of a network of occult forces that he need only search out and tap to be able to advance finally and victoriously, before the whole world, in the direction of the supreme point. These are the visible and verifiable presages of a new age of gold, the active prodromes of the great cosmic reintegration, the beginnings and signs of the future fusion of man and of universe in the conquest of the supreme point.

The Phenomena of Objective Chance

The feeling of expectation deeply rooted in Breton's heart is the practical source of the attention he gave to such phenomena: the expectation of marvelous and revelatory events. This feeling sometimes passes through black phases of depression, during which the mental electricity builds up, for example, in the course of "those extremely gloomy and completely idle afternoons" which Breton owns to having spent. (*Nadja*, p. 77) At such a time, he wanders aimlessly, without receiving any answer, as when he is led by a vain hope into the magic regions around the Tour Saint-Jacques and the Porte Saint-Denis.

At other times, the hope of an infinitely romantic encounter in some chance hotel seems to yield only disappointment:

> Every night, I left the door of my hotel room wide open, hoping
> to wake eventually at the side of a companion I had not chosen.
> (*Pas*, p. 12)

Taken out of context, this sentence seems to lose its specifically
surrealist meaning. It is not a question of hoping for an adventure,
in the vulgar sense of the word; what Breton was waiting for was
someone sent by destiny, a being going beyond all expectation: not
Venus, but Sibyl. Nadja, perhaps.

It is this same type of attraction that Breton and some of his
friends assigned to a mysterious girl who appeared to them in the
vicinity of Saint-Germain-des-Prés and who disappeared, leaving no
trace. (*Pas*, p. 119)

We have also recalled the anecdote of the little flower-seller whom
Chirico claimed half-humorously to identify as a ghost by studying
her with the aid of a pocket mirror. There are few accounts so
brief and so delightful. This is the height of art and the most
fascinating of lures, because we sense in it a bold attempt at forcing
the marvelous to happen in defiance of the basic laws of the principle
of reality. It is the most moving testimony that remains to us from
the early period of surrealism during which the movement came
close to getting lost in the most indefensible unreality. It was only
the fortunate later intervention of Marxism and of psychoanalysis
that saved surrealism from being more severely criticized.

With the story of Nadja, we enter into a new phase of the exploration of objective chance, one of the most important. Beginning at
this period, objective chance manifests itself more and more broadly
in the outside world, and yet it attaches itself ever more deeply
at its sources, situated in man's deepest interior night. No longer
is it a matter of the passage of a few chance comets, like the girl
near Saint-Germain or the little flower-seller whose over-imaginary
aura directly linked them in the mind of the surrealists to a fantastic
world. Nadja really lives in Paris. Her identity is known to Breton,
who sees her every day, and each of these days finds her in intimate
conversation with mystery. Her social situation is so terribly precise

that a psychiatrist would not hesitate to identify her as an insane person receiving no professional help and leading a bohemian life.

Perhaps the preceding meteors of chance would not have survived a similar verification of identity, and the woman Breton was lying there waiting for might suddenly have been revealed as being of the most common type; with Nadja, though, things were completely different. In the terms of this pedestrian identification, she nevertheless is seen to be a phantom, just as Breton feels that he is a phantom to himself. We are constrained, then, to see in her the incarnated phantom that he perceives in her, and to experience within ourselves what is phantom in our own nature.

We have already cited the astonishing question posed in the first lines of *Nadja*, where Breton, discarding Descartes' too simple question, asks himself: "Who am I?" To this he immediately responds: "Doesn't it all depend on whose company I haunt?"—suggesting that he rises up out of his deepest self like a ghost coming out of some completely unknown other world. It is from this same secret place that he speaks to Nadja, asking her: "Who are you?" She, without hesitation, finds a response equal to the question: "I am the wandering soul." (p. 92)

There is, from the very beginning of this *récit*, then, a preliminary breaking out of the bounds of the human condition. If Breton can hope to attain the supreme point, it is because he has first felt coursing through him a life which goes beyond the human condition, binding him, from that moment on, to the occult worlds. The land of election where phantoms grow like the flowers of a dream is not so much the ruins of Paris and ancient castles as the men who venture there. The projection point of the ghosts and of their strange domains is living man himself in his flesh and blood. This is the central secret which elucidates and animates the whole book.

Then, at intervals, under the subdued coloring of the magnificently austere *récit*, Breton makes appear the metaphysical abyss over which Nadja's life, his own, and ours are continuously suspended. It is the ever-felt presence of this abyss which allows every gesture depicted to cast its shadow, not on the shabby background of down-to-earth life, but against an immense firmament of darkness. Human shapes stand out against the black abyss like faintly luminous webs adrift in a high mist; in this consists that immeasurable grandeur.

This is the setting in which are revealed amazing facts of objective chance:

> It is a question of what may be purely verifiable facts, but which present each time all the appearances of a signal, so that in complete solitude I nevertheless enjoy strange complicities that convince me of my illusion in sometimes believing myself alone at the helm of the ship. (*Nadja*, p. 23)

Once more we see dawning the mysterious appeal to the powers of darkness, whether through unusual underground communication between human beings or by extra-human interventions like those of the Great Transparent Ones, and this no longer only in the poet's mind as he gives himself up to automatism in secret in his room; it is out in the street, among living beings, that these irruptions of the supranormal can show themselves.

The atmosphere of the street is indeed itself transmuted when the faculty of hallucination which spills over in the course of automatism can no longer be content with escorting the hand's movements over the blank page, but accompanies the steps of the poet who goes down into the labyrinth of the alleys and avenues to wander there as though in a foreign country. The interior automatisms are mixed then with those of the urban world and of the cosmos. In this way, lead-words such as *Wood and Coal* establish themselves like a black constellation above the facades of the houses to guide Breton and Soupault through the maze of the capital towards facades bearing the same words on the shop signs. (*Nadja*, p. 33) In full daylight, Paris is shot through by the rays of clairvoyance.

The photographs that star the book contribute forcefully to this integration of the banal into the fantastic, for they continuously join the most ordinary aspects of the capital with strange pictures by Chirico and Ernst in which reality, on the contrary, is ripped apart from top to bottom. The suit brought against this reality does not take place within reality's outskirts, but within the solid architecture of a city peopled by millions of inhabitants.

The result is that this state of "disquieting strangeness" spills over like no other into the life of the reader. This story makes man conductible to ghosts; the days that follow the taking in of such a work are charged with mental electricity. There reigns such a stormy oppressiveness that life seems to have become entirely magnetic, and that the lightning of the marvelous is about to strike at every instant. The element of the fantastic comes out of everything; it spreads from the lines and pictures of the book into your imagination and your feelings, waking there all the mysterious powers that education and self-interest had stifled. You are snatched out of your bourgeois complacency or your revolutionary presumption. You begin to wonder if all the usual certitudes on which you ordinarily count are as steady as they had seemed to you till now. You begin to recall more sharply than ever before everything bizarre in your life, all the strange and shocking things you had heard of about fatality, about coincidences. The ghost that is traced in outline on each page of *Nadja* becomes the troubling symbol of the secret self, of narcissism, of the dual personality, of nocturnal powers, of the soul, of death, of immortality, of the beyond, in short of everything you ordinarily drive from your mind. The old anxieties of childhood, its nighttime terrors, those of the primitives, all the old phantasmagorias rise up intact from the well where you thought you had forever burried them under a cover of forgetfulness and rationalizations.

During the night hours man, like the child and the primitive, faces all his fears and his feeling of the infinite; for, at night, one no longer sees the sun, that reassuring torch lit by nature, nor the lamps fabricated by the hand of man to extend the circle of his security. The world is haunted by a thousand invisible and fearful shadows, whether those of the dead, or of criminals, or those that the daylight seems to make impossible. Familiar objects have disappeared and the most unverifiable unknown is present, close against the body, within reach of the hand, that blind explorer of the mysteries

of night. On the soft and moving surface of his bed, man is cast
on the shore of the immense *mare tenebrarum*. It is this same
nocturnal ocean that Nadja evokes in full daylight, to the point
of veiling the brightness of the sun and the insolent mirages of
industry. Daily existence is seized, pale with fear, without warning,
before it has had time to readjust its stereotyped attitude, like a
sleeping woman suddenly surprised by the light of a blinding lamp.
Everything is seen in its starkest and yet most unfamiliar reality:
the sheets, the relaxed body, the hair in disarray, the face naked
as it is never seen. It does not matter whether this be a serving-girl
or a queen; it is a woman free from any bonds who appears for
a second, at the moment of wakening. The instant after, this creature
of mystery disappears within the darkness of her body; the statue
has instinctively put on its mask again.

The magic power of objective chance tends to hold back, close
to us, as though under the force of a spell, this creature of dream
and of verity. Like the enchanter who frees from a curse, Breton
knows how to pull in, even onto the shores of the flesh of a woman,
the wrecks and the echoes thrown up by the ocean of the mind's
darkness onto this farthest shore. For everyman is a ghost who,
all unaware, roams the ruins of paradise. The most disfigured, the
most soiled creature is a marvel under its veil of ashes. Whether
it knows it or not, it drinks at the spring of marvels. Let it wake
to this life of mystery and everything becomes possible, anything
can happen:

> Nadja is looking at the houses around: 'Do you see that window
> over there? It's black like the others. Look closely. In a minute,
> it's going to be lighted. It will be red.' The minute goes by. The
> window is lighted. There are, indeed, red curtains. (*Nadja*, p. 107)

Thus we enter into the domain of pure divination. However
unbelievable at first sight such events may be, they are justified
by an unusual coefficient of credibility, because they are brought
about by the inhabitual light that shines then from the nocturnal
depths of the human mind. Walking side by side, Breton and Nadja

are in some way two mental infra-red lamps that detect the mysteries accumulated under the pale gleam of the walls of the capital.

From time to time, this gleam catches on some strange objects whose apparent insignificance suddenly reveals itself as charged with meaning, as the radiograph reveals the presence of a piece of gold in a woolen stocking. In the same way, the gleaming of a mind-shattering revelation haloes with its nimbus Chirico's bobbins and artichokes, the Porte Saint-Denis, the Place Dauphine, the château of Saint-Germain-en-Laye, a fountain in the Tuileries, Negro masks and statuettes, even the strange comportment of the waiter in a café and a disquieting play. These are like new constellations rising in the sky of this sort of unknown hemisphere and whose emblem is the unforgettable painting by Max Ernst in which one sees the body of the man and the woman suspended like giant stars at the top of the firmament, commanding all the other stars. (*Nadja*, p. 174)

Unceasingly, these two strollers, avid wanderers, abandon the straight line which is the sign and the surest method of scientific acts to follow the dangerous curves of the shipwrecks or the augural flight of the birds:

> Anyone who remembers having learned to draw a straight line or a regular curve realizes that this act belongs to the order of voluntary actions. The artist or the experienced draftsman knows, however, that the fact of tracing a line or a curve falls very often in the domain of involuntary automatic actions. An action tends to become habitual, involuntary, and automatic once it has been executed for the first time. (*Point*, p. 234)

This opinion applies not only to the unthinking lines traced automatically by a designer or a writer working under a graphic impulse, but holds true also for the automatic attractions that guide a man's wandering through a city or even the spaces of a planet. We are familiar with the extreme importance of the migrations that periodically draw certain species of birds and of fish, and even certain human races, far from their habitat. It is easy to see the attraction of certain places of light or of nourishing surroundings, to figure out the role that the instinct of reproduction might have, but we are still free to think that, along with all these rational explanations, there persists a certain mystery. Not everything in this domain has been explained.

There is still a whole psychoanalysis to be done on the walks we take, especially when they lead us aimlessly on and, we think, have no fixed destination. Who knows what secret pole is drawing us on without our being aware of it? This is how Captain Hatteras became mad, walking invariably in the direction of the North Pole. In the same way, the steps of Breton and of Nadja are magnetized by the marvelous. It is this attraction that makes them walk in strange curves through Paris. Like magicians, they thus trace on the pavements of the capital an evocatory labyrinth, an incantatory circle propitious to the calling up of phantoms. These steps direct not only their legs, but also their nerves, so that the mind, as well as the body, is caught up in this eddy. On the model of this capricious spiral on the asphalt, the mind also describes an interior, ascending spiral that draws it to the top of the invisible tower from where it can gaze out over all the walls at the immense region of phantoms.

In Paris itself, then, in broad daylight, in spite of the movement of the traffic and the blind crush of the pedestrians, they perceive signals and the black hand shown in Chirico's picture:

> We arrived at the beginning of the rue de Seine, down which we turned, Nadja not wishing to follow a straight line any longer. Nadja is still very distraught, and tells me to follow a flash of light which a hand is slowly outlining against the sky. 'Always that hand.' She shows it to me really on a poster, a little further on, past the Dorbon bookstore. There is indeed, high above us, a red hand with the index finger pointing, boasting of I no longer know what. She insists absolutely on touching this hand, which she jumps for several times, finally succeeding in slapping her own against it. 'The hand of fire: it has to do with you, you know; it is you' (*Nadja*, p. 134)

The hand appears again as a theme with the unusual woman's glove that was given to the surrealist Central Office (*Nadja*, pp. 66-68 and 72) and also with the strange malformation of the hands of a former lover of Nadja's (*Nadja,* p. 83). We see how, by the conjunction of the hand in the sky, visible only for Nadja, and the poster-hand, visible for everyone, the myth of the hand works on the two levels of the real and the unreal. But doesn't this hand which traced lightning flashes in the sky recall as well the hand that guides the stars in the picture by Ernst? And Chirico's black hand? Or the gigantic hand covered with armor whose sight inspired Walpole with the terrifying story of the castle of Otranto? (cf. *Limites*) And how can we avoid thinking also of those rubber gloves that occupy a gigantic place in other of Chirico's works? Later, moreover, in the fifth issue of *Minotaure* we will see the photograph of a hand sculpted from black wood, used to illustrate one of the texts of *L'Amour fou.* In the same issue, there is also the giant hand of King-Kong, as well as a soiled hand on a steering wheel, bearing the legend "veiled-erotic," along with all the hands that illustrate Hugnet's *Rêverie du grand veneur.*

These intertwinings of the sign of hands form in themselves a sort of monstrous coat of arms of the forces incarnated in man to lead him on the ways of fate. From the hand of the giant ape to the hand of celestial fire, they designate the muddy and bestial origins of man, but also the high zones to which he feels capable of acceding by his own power. Walpole's iron hand has today become the hand of the new Vulcan, builder of robots; the hands which appear in the work of Ernst and Chirico are those which lead man into the subterranean night of sex and which are, at the same time, the indicators of fate; the hand that holds the cards is that of chance. It is once more a hand, a woman's which in the extraordinary story of *Peter Ibbetson* reveals itself as the great clairvoyant conductor through all mysteries. Working, loving, magic hands, they come and go, mysteriously detached from the body they belong to, busy, like Vulcan, Eros, and Prometheus, constructing a new cosmos around man.

But the hand of man is only a part taken for the whole. It is the entire man who engages himself in the unknown:

I plan to tell, in the margins of the *récit* which I have still to start, only the episodes that made the most impression on my life, such as I conceive of it outside its organic level, and in the very measure in which it welcomed chance events, the small and the great, within which it slipped momentarily from out of my influence, bringing me into an almost forbidden world which is one of sudden associations, of petrifying coincidences, of the reflexes proper to each individual, of chords held for a long time, as at the piano, of lightning flashes that could make one see, *really* see, if they were not even more swift than the others. . . . It is a question of what may be purely verifiable facts, but which present each time all the appearances of a signal, so that in complete solitude I nevertheless enjoy strange complicities which convince me of my illusion in sometimes believing myself alone at the helm of the ship. One would have to put these facts in hierarchical order, from the simplest to the most complex, beginning with that special indefinable movement provoked in us by the sight of very rare objects, or by our arrival in such or such a place, accompanied by the very definite feeling that something extremely serious, something essential is at stake for us. (*Nadja*, pp. 22-23-24)

This text should be reread in its entirety, for it insists in a remarkably penetrating fashion on the fundamental ambiguity of objective chance: it is divination at the very heart of the banal, of a spiritual world whose nature surrealism refuses to define.

Whether this marvelous be purely psychic or divine or Luciferian, it is in any case the marvelous with all its potential for breaking away, with all its promises of metamorphosis that surrealism hopes to take hold of. "Is it true that the beyond, all the beyond is in this life?" (*Nadja*, p. 190) By this pathetic cry, Breton signifies that in any case, he hopes for nothing less from objective chance than the breaking away from the here below, that is, from the human condition, and the regaining of the beyond, of an immanent beyond in the most hidden zones of the human being, in regions where no breaking down of continuity will separate us anymore from the supreme point.

A new phase of the objective chance experiment began during the period in which Breton was preparing *Les Vases communicants*. This time the reductive forces of psychoanalysis and Marxism function at top power and reject as impossible the properly phantomatic and occult marvelousness which was Nadja's great strength. The only marvelousness which keeps its prestige and its power of attraction is that of *desire*. The might of Vulcan, whose prophet is Marx, has eclipsed all other; Eros himself is no longer free to rule men except within the limits of the empire of Vulcan and under obedience to his laws.

It is perhaps because Eros is put in bonds ahead of time, reduced to the vague power of a captive who is respected but carefully watched, that the whole cycle of the *Vases* is nothing but a series of failures. Eros attempts continuously to manifest his magical power over existence, he flashes his divinatory signals uninterruptedly, but the routes are cut and the action comes to nothing. This fact is remarkable in itself and, in this sense, the book is unlike any other. What Casanova would be content to give an account of adventures of which one must say not merely that they have had no future, but that they have not even had a present? But even in this, there is no masochistic mulling over the failure. The signals are given almost at cross-purposes, but they are given. Consequently, something is already confirmed and conquered: the possibility for the most problematic, the most disappointing love to be a mediator of mystery, a revealer of unsuspected life forces. It reveals the secret web that connects all lives, one to another, through the communicating vessels of dreaming and waking.

After a critical exordium on the work of the different interpreters of dreams, Breton then recounts one of his own dreams, that of the tie of Nosferatu, following it by a long analysis of the dream. He seeks especially to link it detail by detail to the account of his own life at the time, so as to show how common was the thread that was binding together these two sides of his life.

Further on, and this time using the real as his base, or what is claimed to be exclusively such, he describes certain remarkable episodes of his peregrinations in Paris. He recalls the appearance in the street of a certain number of *femmes-cométes* who were particularly ephemeral, but who wrapped themselves in a long train of unusual happenings, such as the confusion of revelatory words, coincidences of names, dream phrases proffered in passing, with the result that, at this period, he lived in a strange atmosphere of interference between waking and dreaming.

The divinatory urge still exists here as in *Nadja*, but its role has been made less important, and the phenomena envisioned are less striking. Breton's very attitude impels him more than ever to attempt a new psychopathology of daily life inspired by Freud, inserted, in its turn, into a Marxist cosmology. Even in this rather restrictive setting, Breton's undertaking carries strong interest, because it attempts to demonstrate clearly how dreaming and waking incessantly mingle their waters. They do not constitute two radically separate worlds, but only the two extreme areas situated to one side and the other of the central fact which is the waking dream, that state we are never completely free from, since at the heart of our most rational and utilitarian activities, the unconscious continues to exercise a highly determining influence over us.

> Considering what has preceded, it has to be impossible not to be struck by the analogy which exists between the state I have just described as mine at that time, and the dream, such as it is generally conceived of. The basic difference in the fact that, in the one, I am lying down and sleeping, and in the other I am literally walking about in Paris, does not on either hand lead me to see quite distinct representations. It is much more significant to observe how the demands of desire searching for the object of its realization makes strange use of external things, tending to take from them only what will serve its purpose. The vain bustle of the street has become hardly more disturbing than the wrinkling of the sheets. Desire is there, cutting straight into the fabric which is not changing fast enough, then letting its sure and fragile thread run back and forth between the pieces. (*Vases*, pp. 122-123)

If Breton explores this mixture of waking and dreaming more deeply than do others, it is because, with him, it reaches such a rare degree of intensity. In this way he is able to bring out how, in this domain of the waking dream, one can find the same mechanisms that Freud had uncovered in the pure dream:

> Whether it be in reality or in dream, it—desire—is forced to make [the prime matter of the dream] pass through the same channels: condensation, displacement, substitution, retouching. (*Vases*, p. 130)

He concludes on this point which is the essential object of his musings in this book:

> It has seemed to me, and it still seems so—it is even the assumption that this whole is based on—that by examining closely the content of the most spontaneous activity of the mind, if one goes beyond the extraordinary and hardly reassuring bubbling that goes on at the surface, it is possible to bring to light a capillary tissue; knowing nothing about it, one would be hard pressed indeed to try to figure out something about mental circulation. The role of this tissue is, as we have seen, to insure the constant exchange which must take place in thought between the interior world and the exterior world, an exchange which necessitates the continuous interpretation of the activity of sleep and that of waking. (*Vases*, p. 163)

This tissue is most certainly the central domain in which take place from time to time the most outstanding phenomena of objective chance. We might be tempted to regret that, in exploring it, Breton placed himself too strictly under the laws of psychoanalysis and of Marxism. However, this fact also has its advantages, for Breton was in this way obliged to concentrate his attention to a fuller extent on the large area that remained open. Besides, we still receive the echo of some strong cries of liberty from him: what do reality and its oppressive weight matter, he shouts,

> since I have only to call sleep to my aid, have only to act as much as possible as I do in sleep, in order to get the upper hand over this reality. (*Vases*, p. 132)

I am more tempted to regret that he has not given more of the circumstances surrounding his examination of the capillary tissue. However important his theoretical observations about the interpreters of dreams and on the crisis of the *Internationale,* they enlighten us infinitely less about this capillary tissue, which remains an almost unexplored continent. It would have been wonderful if, under the title of *Vases communicants* Breton had delved deeply into the account and the exegesis of his life and his dreams, leaving Freud behind, experimentally, so that the theoretical quarrels would have fallen away of themselves, like over-ripe fruit. As for the very ortho-dox disciples of Marx, or who call themselves so, they might have hastened to see if the new discoveries about the universe of dreams were compatible with "revealed doctrine." Breton reproaches Freud for not having torn down completely the wall of private life, and for having limited the understanding of certain dreams reported in *The Interpretation of Dreams* by holding back some of the scenes of Freud's life which were to be found at the origin of these same dreams. Breton, though, on his part, neglects to depict the childhood scene from which the dream of the necktie "very likely proceeds, in part." He indicates, it is true, that this memory "would be of only secondary interest here" (*Vases,* p. 54); but are there really secondary considerations in such an area, in which one searches for the least glimmer of light to illuminate a vast sunken continent? We will not be able really to discover the role and the exact value of objective chance until the day when all the possibilities of subjec-tive interpretation have swept completely clean the surface of the dream.

But with the passage of time, Breton throws off the unbearable yoke of Marxist and psychoanalytic orthodoxies. It is the period of *L'Amour fou.* A wave of the marvelous, stronger than all the preceding ones, carries away like a tidal wave the fragile dam of economic and sexual doctrines. We find Breton in search of those quasi-oneiric objects which have always attracted him. One of them is a big spoon whose handle rests on a strange little shoe. The other, strongly suggestive of some ancient mask, is at the same time terrifyingly prosaic, for Joë Bousquet recognizes it as a war mask, the flotsam of an abortive experiment during the war of 1914. Especially striking is the fact that these objects which Breton came upon by chance in his wanderings through the junk-piles of the flea market were already inscribed in the fabric of his dreams. The discovery of the shoe-spoon was the astonishing fulfillment of a wish inspired in Breton by a phrase heard on awakening, to find an object which was, in principle, Cinderella's lost slipper. The mask fit exactly into the sculptural research of Giacometti in which Breton, at that moment, was actively participating. Breton notes the curious opposition of these objects, the mask seeming to him to express the instinct of death, and the other, that of Eros. He writes of the second object, the Cinderella spoon:

> I have no trouble understanding that it symbolized for me a unique and unknown woman, magnified and dramatized by my feeling of solitude and by my overwhelming need to abolish certain memories. (*Amour*, p. 54)

Then he discovers, shortly afterwards, that while they were busy searching, he and Giacometti had been noticed, without their seeing her, by the mysterious X who appears also in *Les Vases* and to whom is dedicated the final invocation in *Nadja*.

The second account is the famous story of the "night of the sunflower." One morning when Breton happened to stumble upon, in his memory, a line from an old poem, written automatically in 1923 under the title *Tournesol*,[1] he perceived to his great surprise that this poem, which until then he had looked down on, had a surprisingly prophetic nature, for it had prefigured, several years in advance, an event of major importance which had just taken place in his life, on the twenty-ninth of May, 1934; it is on this date that he met the woman whom for this reason he called the "all-powerful organizer of the night of the sunflower" and whom he married on the fourteenth of August following.

We can see in Breton's *récit* how he analyzes his poem line by line, linking it detail by detail to some fact connected with this overwhelming encounter. Among the most striking keywords, we can pick out especially: *With difficulty and from the corner of the eye, ball, lantern, Fourteenth of July, seem to swim.*[2] It is striking that the themes brought out by these words are not the ordinary, run-of-the-mill symbols of poetry, but themes peculiar to Breton and to the event itself. Did the same automatism preside at both .the placing of the words on paper and the unfolding of the events that took place much later?

The story based on the house of discord is no less striking. In the course of a walk along the beach in the vicinity of Lorient, but in an area of which Breton had no precise knowledge, he and his chosen companion of the *tournesol* feel a strange disharmony come between them which they cannot explain to themselves. This painful atmosphere comes down on them as they near an isolated house and disappears afterwards. When they get back, they learn that this dwelling is the one in which Michel Henriot killed his wife. Besides this, Breton notes some other curious encounters. It is known, for example, that Michel Henriot raised silver foxes; interestingly, several days before this walk, Breton and his wife had become quite enthusiastic about two novels in which foxes were the main theme: *Gone to Earth* by Mary Webb, and *Lady into Fox* by David Garnett.[3]

He remarks also a strange phenomenon of transparency during this walk. This house seems to him "to look out over a rather large enclosure leading down to the sea and bounded, it seemed to me, by a metal fence." (*Amour*, p. 152) But during a second walk taken for the purpose of verifying the places, he noticed that the reality was quite different:

> The most surprising thing was that the enclosure which had constituted the yard for the foxes was enclosed, not as I believed I saw the first day by a metal fence, but by a cement wall too high for me to see anything on the other side. (*Amour*, p. 165)

Wanting to understand, if possible, what had happened, he pulled himself up to the top of the wall where this new sight met his eyes:

> All the wire gauges were backed up against the wall which, the first time, had been facing me. It was as if on that twentieth of July—the date of the first visit—this wall had shown itself to me as transparent (*Amour,* p. 165).

It is easy to speak of illusion. That is moreover a plausible hypothesis, but it demands proof, just as does that of the absolute authenticity of the phenomenon observed by Breton. Might this have been an "evil place" as Breton is led to ask himself? or else a phenomenon of participation across time in deleterious mental influences, or even uncomprehended reminiscences gathered from divers sources like newspaper photographs, forgotten conversations, etc. All these hypotheses remain open, but a mysterious fact remains, posing an unanswered question.

Those surrealists are few and far between who have taken the trouble to bring to light such strangely revealing phenomena; however, attention should be drawn to the remarkable account given us by Pierre Mabille about the painter Brauner. One evening, during a violent quarrel between two surrealists, Brauner, who was only looking on with Mabille, was hit in the right eye by a thrown object and blinded. Some days later, Mabille realized that Brauner's painting contained strange warnings of this accident; in it, one sees numerous persons blind in one eye, or whose eye has been replaced by a horn. There is even a self-portrait of Brauner, showing him with an eye removed, the same eye which was injured in the accident.[4]

It is too little known that Goethe as well, the Olympian Goethe, was aware of similar things in his own life. It is possible that Swedenborg, the famous visionary, had an imaginary but real vision of the great fire of Stockholm; no one is surprised by it, but neither is anyone convinced. But how can anyone help but be astonished when Goethe says that he experienced in Germany where at that time he was living the sensation of a terrible cataclysm, during the very night in which Messina was ravaged by an earthquake? This is the account that Goethe's former manservant gave to Eckermann:

> 'One time he rang in the middle of the night; and when I entered his room I found he had rolled his iron bed to the window, and

was lying there, looking out upon the heavens. "Have you seen nothing in the sky?" asked he; and when I answered "No," he bade me run to the guardhouse, and ask the man on duty if he had seen nothing. I went there; the guard said he had seen nothing, and I returned with this answer to my master, who was still in the same position, lying in his bed, and gazing upon the sky. "Listen," said he; "this is an important moment; there is now an earthquake, or one is just going to take place"; then he made me sit down on the bed, and showed me by what signs he knew this.'

I asked the good old man what sort of weather it was.

'It was very cloudy,' he replied; 'very still and sultry.'

I asked if he at once believed there was an earthquake on Goethe's word.

'Yes,' said he, 'I believed it, for things always happened as he said they would.' Next day he related his observations at court, when a lady whispered to her neighbor, 'Only listen, Goethe is dreaming.' But the duke, and all the men present, believed Goethe, and the correctness of his observations was soon confirmed; for, in a few weeks, the news came that a part of Messina, on that night, had been destroyed by an earthquake.' [5]

In *Truth and Poetry*, Goethe himself tells of a personal experience of premonition caused by love. Having told how he had said good-bye to Frederica, he adds that as he rode along

I saw, not with the eyes of the body, but with those of the mind, my own figure coming towards me, on horseback, and on the same road, attired in a dress which I had never worn. . . . As soon as I shook myself out of this dream, the figure had entirely disappeared. It is strange, however, that eight years afterwards, I found myself on the very road, to pay one more visit to Frederica, in the dress of which I had dreamed, and which I wore, not from choice, but by accident. However it may be with matters of this kind generally, this strange illusion in some measure calmed me at the moment of parting. [6]

Eckermann himself tells some similar events to Goethe, who responds:

There are many such things in nature, though we do not have the right key to them. We all walk in mysteries. We do not know what is stirring in the atmosphere that surrounds us, nor how it is connected with our own spirit. So much is certain—that at times we can put out the feelers of our soul beyond its bodily limits; and a presentiment, an actual insight into the immediate future, is accorded to it.

"I have lately experienced something similar," said I. "As I was returning from a walk along the Erfurt road, about ten minutes before I reached Weimar, I had the mental impression that a person whom I had not seen, and of whom I had not even thought for a length of time, would meet me at the corner of the theatre. It troubled me to think that this person might meet me; and great was my surprise when, as I was about to turn the corner, this very person actually met me, in the same place which I had seen in my imagination ten minutes before."

"That is also very wonderful, and more than chance," said he. "As I said, we are all groping among mysteries and wonders. Besides, one soul may have a decided influence upon another, merely by means of its silent presence, of which I could relate many instances. It has often happened to me that, when I have been walking with an acquaintance, and have had a living image of something in my mind, he has at once begun to speak of that very thing. I have also known a man who, without saying a word, could suddenly silence a party engaged in cheerful conversation, by the mere power of his mind. Nay, he could also introduce a tone which would make everybody feel uncomfortable. . . . With lovers, this magnetic power is particularly strong and acts even at a distance." [7]

We can doubt the possibility of such happenings; but one should step warily here, for the fact of doubting them without completely surpressing them is enough to dull the mind to their production, condemning them to remain unknown in the limbo of the unconscious. As long as no ray of light touches and reveals them, they remain like objects hidden in the dark; but if on the contrary one takes the trouble to be attentive, there is heard in the depths of the being something like the muted sound of an immense and distant tide. In everyone's life, there are happenings on the same order which one can recall, but we shake them off as though unworthy of holding our attention, and they are lost from sight. Many events of this kind can be found also in the annals of metapsychics, and the "primitives," like the ancients, have always been attentive to them.

Breton puts special emphasis on occurrences of premonition and coincidence, without, however, diminishing the importance of cases in which reminiscence occurs, for some of these former occurrences led back to cases of disguised reminiscence. Even when we are dealing with cases of reminiscence as such, it would be absurd to challenge their interest under the pretext that they have to do only with the past, while the whole of surrealism's attention is turned to the future. It must not be forgotten that, in the domain of the supreme point, that secret source of objective chance, the past is not of less value than the future, and that the two come together into a single synthesis. The recuperation of the past is already a start toward the recuperation of the lost powers. What is sad about the past is not that it *was,* but that the passage of time separates us from it forever, it would seem. Only when man learns to remount triumphantly the course of time in order to seize, not upon the meager skeletons of memory, but upon the living flesh of glowing remembrance, only then is it true to say that he reconquers the past while at the same time grasping a new future. This is why the extraordinary reminiscences that star the work of Proust and which directed his life seem themselves to be magnificent phenomena of objective chance.

Paths and Signals of Objective Chance

As we are penetrated from every direction by electromagnetic waves which remain invisible and cannot be detected without the appropriate instrument, as we are shot through with innumerable electrical phenomena without our being aware of it, so are we also immersed from head to foot in the clouds and shafts of light of objective chance without our ordinarily being conscious of it. We are like the fairy-tale characters from a tapestry who, dreaming, forget that their matter has been woven on a loom and is only a picture placed in the tapestry.

Expectancy. It is when the personage of the tapestry thinks himself most independent that he becomes most dependent on it. Not knowing of his subjugation, he is incapable of becoming aware of his limitations, of discovering his nature, and consequently, of cutting himself free from the tapestry by utilizing his knowledge of the laws of his condition. He is alienated. If, on the contrary, he becomes aware of his real nature and of the laws of his condition, then he is grasping the lever that can free him; sooner or later, he will discover the shuttle that is weaving him, and he will be able to take hold of it to direct its movement away from the original position, to begin the immense exploration of all those former impossibles that have become possibles.

The first of prisons and the most irremediable is to believe we are free when we are not. When the presence of the prison is recognized, the walls situated, the guards measure taken, then, in spite of torment, a plan for escape can be worked out, put into execution, and will one day succeed. But imaginary liberty is a prison barred by the captive himself. In vain he dreams his pseudo-liberty and does nothing; he cannot even conceive of his having to do something in order to explore the *outside*.

Are these fictions, this stupid captive, this dreaming tapestry-character? Not at all; they are our own image. As long as we have not become aware of the powers of gold, of blood, of sex, and of the invisible encircling forces, we proclaim a derisory liberty and are incapable of setting foot on the path of real liberty.

This is why the extraordinary feeling of expectancy that shines so brightly in surrealism and especially in the thought of Breton is the golden key of liberty. It is not an idle subjective impression; it is already an interior act, it is the freeing ourselves from what binds us to the transmission belt of determinism.

In our time, there is no movement of the mind which has put more emphasis than surrealism on the thirst for liberty, for it wants totally unlimited liberty. It is not surprising then that surrealism has taken the greatest care to inform itself of the determinisms that weigh on man, so that it can measure the dimensions of the obstacle that bar the path of the great desire. Finally, no other moderns have experienced so intense a feeling of expectancy.

What is this expectancy, if not the awareness that we are chained to ordinary reality, but that limitless liberty is just at the surface of that reality, ready to come through and change everything completely, if only we could take the hand it unceasingly holds out to us through the impalpable wall of darkness that cuts us off from its presence. What other feeling could have led Breton to turn from the minor preoccupations of reasoning and to turn his attention to the interior murmur, to the echoes that are projected into the mind, forecasts of objective chance? This expectancy represents the stance of a mind become as silent and attentive as was the Sibyl to the word of the unknown. It is also the flair for negative capability which seeks to single out from among all interior whisperings that which comes from the deepest part of the abyss.

The boulevard Bonne-Nouvelle along which Breton wanders aimlessly is a waiting room open to the wind, an antechamber opening up a strange empty space in the midst of the swarming crowds:

> Without my knowing why, it is almost always in that direction that I go, it is there that my wanderings lead me, with no other deciding factor but that which tells me that it is there that *it* will happen. (*Nadja*, p. 38)

He is as attentive in the bustle of the street as he is in his bed, listening to the phrases which "knock at the window". This is a permanent attitude with Breton:

> Again today, I expect everything from my *availability (disponibilité)* alone, from my thirst for wandering out to meet whatever comes, which I am certain keeps me in mysterious communication with other available creatures, as though we had been called to sudden union. I would like my life to leave no other murmur after it but that of the lookout's song, a song to beguile the waiting time. Independently of what does or does not happen, it is the waiting that is wonderful. (*Amour*, p. 41)

This expectancy is the sixth sense that lets us perceive the signals of objective chance (*Nadja*, p. 23, cited above); it is the sentiment that prescribes the "lyric comportment" (*Amour*, p. 77) by which we cooperate in bringing to light the phenomena of objective chance. It is that indomitable hope which is able to hold as certain that, in spite of the black chasms and the great ice packs, the way to the future is sown with shining marvels and leads always to the supreme point.

Automatism. Since we have already examined automatism in detail, there is no need to repeat ourselves here. The only thing to stress is that, since automatism is a means of expression for objective chance, it cannot be used arbitrarily for so-called artistic purposes. It is an almost sacred revelation to which rules outside itself cannot be applied. It does not stand as a purely literary function on the sidelines of life, nor is it, as too many psychoanalysts suppose, a supplier of waste material. It is a revelation of life, a means by which is made manifest the communication between persons, humanity and even the universe.

The sentences spoken at the limits between waking and sleeping are not simply revelatory of individual complexes; they sometimes have—at least, according to Breton, they do—a premonitory function that goes beyond the scope of orthodox psychoanalysis. Painting also, as we have seen in the case of Brauner, is a means of projection of objective chance, and even Dali's critical-paranoiac area is tangential to it. (*Position,* p. 146) Even objective humor, which would seem to be as arbitrary as one could get, leads to the foot of the sheer walls of objective chance against which it is broken. (*Position,* p. 146) Breton, then, sees all the forms of automatism as "palpable proofs of an existence other than that which we claim to lead" (*Manifestes,* p. 149), not only because of the transfiguring visions that it calls before our imagination, but also because it helps us to see in our day-to-day life the traces of a very different existence mysteriously set into it. Our life is a palimpsest.

Dreams. Dreams are the royal road leading to the lands of objective chance. It is dreaming that already draws together most of the threads of surrealism; what is automatism if not an invasion of the dream into the waking state? And what is love, understood in the surrealist sense, if not, as we shall see, a dream-love projected into exterior reality?

This area in itself is so important for Breton that it forms in itself the essential *motif* of the first *Manifeste.* We could examine this subject in as much detail as we devoted to our study of automatic writing; like the latter, it owes its major role in surrealism to the triple influence of literary tradition, psychoanalysis, and the occult.

For a long time, dreams have enjoyed an immense prestige in literature. Delage gives abundant examples of this in his book *Le Rêve.*[8] Especially to be noted is the prime importance accorded the dream by the German romantics, as Albert Béguin has so well brought out in his great work on *L'Ame romantique et le rêve.*[9] Breton himself pointed out how the phenomena of magnetism and sleep-walking absorbed Ritter's complete attention:

> In animal magnetism, one leaves the domain of voluntary awareness and enters into that of automatic activity, in the region where the organic body acts once again like an inorganic being, thus revealing to us the secrets of both worlds at once. (*Point,* p. 158)

The German romantics, especially Jean-Paul and Novalis, insist, as will the surrealists after them, on the fact that the dream is not an isolated world on the frontiers of sleep, but a free zone communicating both with daily life and with the supra-conscious worlds. This same concept appears in Nerval's work, as well as in Butler's, as is attested by the very curious symbolic, premonitory dream he narrates at the end of *Erewhon Revisited.*

Just as Plato attributed the frenzy of inspiration to an automatism of divine or demoniac origin, in the sense that these words carried in the Greek religion, so mediums attribute their graphic impulses to "spirits"; and dreams have for a long time held a religious value for humanity. This value is well-known to the primitive man, as well as to the ancients; it is notable, for instance, in Homer and the Greek tragedians who gave to the dream an annunciatory and radical role that has been transmitted down to our own classics. Even in the Scriptures, in the Old and the New Testaments, we come upon numerous prophetic dreams. Breton, of course, violently rejected this heritage in *Les Vases communicants;* but antecedents are not gotten rid of as easily as that, not even with declarations of principle. Breton's taking this position, though, is all that was needed, in his opinion, to make the past subject to reinterpretation. from the atheistic viewpoint; nevertheless, there is retained a feeling that the dream puts man in contact with the occult worlds, however one defines them.

Here again, in spite of the shortcomings of his teachings, Freud's role is of prime importance, for he furnished completely new analytical procedures of incomparable precision for revealing the human content, especially the erotic content, of the seemingly most incomprehensible dreams.

There would be no point in insisting here on this work, which is so well-known in all its most striking aspects. However, another little-known work must be drawn to the reader's attention, one which exercised a great influence on Breton, one destined to play an important role in the exploration of dreams and the understanding of automatic writing, even if this is only by way of comparison with other works it elucidates: it is that of Hervey de Saint-Denys. This expert sinologist of the late nineteenth century wrote an extraordinary study on *Les Rêves et les moyens de les diriger.* [10] This admirable researcher who devoted years of his life to experimenting with dreams, in the very precise meaning of that word, as opposed to passively experiencing them, has brought out certain precious qualities of the dream, particularly its faculty for total recall, its ability to perceive extremely tenuous sensations (for example, the signs which precede illnesses), [11] its prospects for the abnormal extension of the possibilities of the intelligence and the imagination.

Above all, he emphasized the remarkable fact that the attention and the will can enter into the course of a dream without shattering it; he describes this tactic in the following way:

If the mind's eye sees the images of these trees, plants, and flowers, a short while ago so distinct, becoming pale and muddled, you can be sure that your sleep is fading. Allow this effect to continue, and within a few instants you will be awake.

If you prefer to try the experiment in the opposite sense, try (during the dream) to keep completely still and bring all your attention to bear on one of the small objects whose image has not yet disappeared, the leaf of a tree, for instance. This image will bit by bit regain its lost clarity, and you will see the sharpness of contours and colors returning, as though this were the image in the magic lantern that you were gradually bringing into focus. . . . The dream will have resumed its flow.[12]

This is explained, he adds, by the fact that the will to keep still in the dream acts to fix the image of the dream but acts also on the real body, immobilizing it in such a way that it can no longer break out of its numbness.

Hervey also tells how, finding himself during a dream at a crossroads, he "voluntarily" changed route, "in the interest of experimentation." This dream is quite interesting, for it allows us to understand how, even in automatic writing it is possible, without perturbing the writing for reasons exterior to it and without altering its authenticity, to direct it onto one or another of the numerous tracks that are available. Hervey repeated similar experiments several times and had several of his friends do the same. (It would appear that Jean-Paul also made similar successful attempts.) [13]

Thus, while wakefulness tends to join in the dream through automatic writing and the practice of the directed hallucination, reciprocally, through Hervey's technique, the dream tends to join in wakefulness. One can then hope to obtain in this way an ever more direct confrontation of the forces of waking and of the dream and attain a highly conscious exploration of the unconscious infrastructures of wakefulness and of the depths of the imagination. This opens up new paths to the manifestation and the understanding of the phenomena of objective chance, for the dream becomes a turntable giving access to different levels of the world; it is a system of transverse corridors, of short-circuit paths which reveal on every side the porosity of matter and of time. As Hervey, again the precursor in this respect, said:

> Do we really know all the secret communications that may exist in the world which surrounds us, among ourselves, from one to the other, as they exist between us and all that we do or do not see? [14]

Hervey's studies show that the dream is the ideal place for research into these hidden but real connections.

The dream is the geometric place in which come together the levels of psycho-physiological reality, of exterior reality and of supranormal reality. Its strangeness comes only from the fact that there are veritable collages functioning between these heterogeneous images. It delivers to us, in a sort of disorder which is, however, in itself a supplementary order and yet still an excess of complications, the film of a many-faceted and immense region. In reality, this disorder comes much less from itself than from the lack of education of our interior eye and of our awareness which does not know how to distinguish outlines, relief, meanings. In relation to the worlds of the dream, men are in the position of very small children in regard to the images of the outside world which they are still unable to class, to situate, and to interpret.

One of the serious weaknesses of Freudianism is to try to limit in advance the extent of the regions of the dream, even though in the last years of his life, Freud had begun to glimpse the immensity of this area outside the sectors of the libido; he remains, nevertheless, an explorer of genius who set out to teach us to see in our dreams human and comprehensible spectacles. Like Christopher Columbus, Freud opened up to our investigation a prodigious wild continent, a fabulous tapestry in the nth dimension where our doubles still lie enchained by the determinisms of the unconscious. On this continental base, new seekers will in their turn build a New World. Cutting through its tropical jungles, we will open up new means of penetration toward the mysteries of our own bodies, toward the mental currents that unite all mankind, and toward the cosmic mysteries themselves. Once more, man's stature will be increased by the conquest of domains that seemed forbidden him.

The greatness of Breton's work comes from its attempt to bring together into a dialectical synthesis all the modes of understanding and investigating the dream. It corrects the orderly down-to-earth spirit of Freud by the poetic spirit of the German romantics, and on the excessive fantasy and idealism of the latter imposes the control of the reductive methods of the former.

It would be absolutely false to see in Breton's interest in dreams the outcome of a desire to escape. Since his aim is to move toward the supreme point which is the active fusion of dreaming and waking, of the conscious and the unconscious, he does not promote dreams for the sake of dreams, but seeks rather the means to bring the waking state into communication with the dream, and to ensure that the flow of images and thought between the two communicating vessels is circulating freely.

> The imagination may be on the point of reclaiming its rights. If the depths of our mind conceal strange forces, capable of augmenting those on the surface or of struggling victoriously against them, it is in our interest to capture these forces first and then, if need be, submit them to the control of reason. (*Manifestes*, p. 23)

Particular attention should be paid that remarkable final conclusion: surrealism is not at all the unleashed irrationalism it is held to be, nor is it sheer rationalism; in principle, it keeps an even balance between reason and instinct or intuition, reserving the right to tip the scale in one direction or the other when in all equity this is judged to be fitting. The antimony of the rational and the mysterious is one of those toward which we ought to show the greatest respect as long as we are not really capable of surmounting it without the danger of falling into arbitrary systemizations or pointless frenzy. Besides, no one can completely bypass this antimony, because the unconscious and the consciousness see to it that the human mind continually maintain both these tendencies. It is curious, for example, to note with what grim logic the irrationalists go about demonstrating their irrationalism. It is no less symptomatic to notice how the irrational enters, at least from time to time, into the most rational structures; it would be very desirable, in this respect, to establish a psychoanalysis of philosophies.

Breton does not just open the way to a new metaphysics of the dream; what he hopes to seize are the forces of the dream. He could here adapt Marx's famous saying: the philosophers have interpreted the dream long enough, now it is time to transform it. This means exploring it, mapping it, and tapping its energies for man's benefit. Who can tell what results would be obtained, what fruits would be given by this continent that has for centuries lain fallow? Our dreams sometimes know more about us than our keenest awareness does.

> Why should I not expect more from the indication received in dreams than I do from a degree of awareness that is each day higher? Cannot the dream also be applied to the resolution of the basic questions of life? (*Manifestes*, p. 26)
>
> As soon as it is submitted to a methodical examination which will foster its full and regular expansion, we can hope that the mysteries that do not belong there will make way for the great Mystery. I believe that in the future these two so apparently contradictory states of dream and reality will be resolved into a sort of absolute reality, of *surreality*, if one may use the expression. (*Manifestes*, p. 28)

Too many of surrealism's interpreters have not kept in mind this essential perspective which Breton opened up, that is, the fusion of dreaming and waking into a superior state. This is due, first of all, to the fact that they had never paid attention to the intermediate states between dreaming and waking, automatic writing and the waking dream, those first stages of the superior state Breton hopes to attain. It is due also to the lack of dialectical feeling which is so general with the French who have a classical culture; for them, states, like things, are catalogued into distinct species which cannot overlap. They do not understand that these are more or less clearly defined currents within a single ocean, and that all types of communication, evolution, and transformation are possible among them.

Love. The Cartesian race has no better understanding of love. For them, it can be either the most unadorned sexual desire, a vague feeling, or else the marriage contract. For Breton, love is something entirely different. It is a force of destiny, like dreams or poetic inspiration. It is man's staunch ally in the fight against the human condition: "Apart from love, there is no solution." (*Point*, p. 75)

The myth of the enchanted woman is one of the major themes in Breton's thought. Nadja is not a phantom like any other, she is the silken spectre of the enchantress:

> She brings to each moment such art as to give to it the very unique illusion of the evasive Mélusine. (*Nadja*, p. 143)

This is no theatrical gimmick, but the manifestation of her secret self:

> Nadja also appeared many times in the guise of Mélusine who is, of all the mythical characters, the one to which she seemed to feel herself closest. (*Nadja*, p. 164)

This theme keeps reappearing in Breton's writings:

> Mélusine. . . . I see no one else capable of redeeming this savage era. She represents all womanhood, and at the same time, woman as she is today, woman deprived of her foundation in humanity, prisoner, if you will, of her shifting roots and yet, through them, in providential communication with the elementary forces of nature. (*Arcane*, p. 91)

Mélusine is the symbol of the child-woman, on whom time has no hold (*Arcane*, p. 94); she is

> Cleopatra on the morning of Actium and Michelet's young sorceress with the moors in her glance. . . . she is the fairy with the griffon of Gustave Moreau, and she is you. (*Arcane*, p. 95)

that is, Breton's wife. She is Esclarmonde, wrapped in an aureole of all the poetry of the "Courses of Love." *(Les États généraux)* She is Isis, the goddess who raises to life Osiris, the black god. (*Arcane*, p. 144) She is the mysterious young woman who appears on the seventeenth card of the Tarot deck, symbol of rebirth and immortality. Formed like a serpent below the waist, Mélusine is in intimate relationship with the animal forces of nature and so with the unconscious; but she has wings as well, and this puts her in communication with the superior worlds, those to which she flies and hides, according to the legend, when her husband tries wrongfully to wrest from her her secret. However, she is woman as well and belongs to our world. She is then the living synthesis of the three realms of reality. As Eliphas Lévi wrote, she is "the siren who reveals harmonies" and belongs to "the analogical alliance of contraries." [15]

This myth is not confined to an outdated folklore, though; the night of the sunflower, Cinderella's slipper-spoon, the red window all show us how, for Breton, the enchantress can still work her magic today.

The encounter with the woman loved, with the one who instantly becomes the chosen, is already a mystery, a secret of objective chance. Hofmannsthal writes magnificently:

> It is certain that along our route with its thousand detours, we walk not only in line with our acts, but also in obedience to the attraction of a mystery which seems to be waiting for us. . . . How marvelous the cry of a great bird at daybreak as he takes flight from the top of the highest pine, listened to by the unseen female. This call that goes we know not where, so full of desire and passion, this cry from the unknown male to the unknown female, makes a powerful impression. Such a meeting . . . seems to belong . . . to an order of things . . . which makes the stars move and thoughts come to fruition. [16]

In addition, there is the long and pathetic inquiry into this mystery of encounter published in the last issue of *La Révolution surréaliste*. The whole story of the night of the sunflower is also an amazing example of this intuition of Hofmannsthal's.

After the encounter, there intervenes a second no less astonishing mystery, that of communication, that fusion of hearts and minds that accompanies or even precedes carnal union. In our era in which there reigns the misconception that sees love only as a desire that is met by fulfillment, and also in which surrealism, without examination, is pronounced an inhuman doctrine, it is moving to find that, on the contrary, Breton passionately sought the meaning of true love, higher than mere sexual desire which is only one of its aspects:

> No sophism is more to be feared than that which presents the ac-complishment of the sexual act as necessarily accompanied by a falling-off in the potential for love between the two persons, a fall whose repetition will gradually lead them to a point at which they are no longer sufficient for each other. In this way, love would be exposing itself to ruin in the measure in which it sought to realize itself. . . . Juliette, if she continued to live, would not always be *more* Juliette for Romeo. (*Amour*, p. 134)

There are, of course, dark hours and perhaps evil places as well, in which love conceals its course, like certain rivers which sometimes go underground; these rivers, however much concealed by the thick-ness of the rock, do not become any less really existent. In the same way, the intermittences of the heart do not keep love from continuing in secret; the least event is sometimes enough to make it surge out of the rock or to make it rise like a secret spring in the heart of the arid desert. Once more, everything grows green.

> Those dark moments in which love grows agitated in flight and lets itself plummet to the bottom of the chasm—from which, later, it will rise in an unbroken movement—must, it seems to me, be looked at fixedly and fearlessly in the very measure in which man hopes, by conducting himself accordingly, to diminish them in the setting of his life. (*Amour*, p. 148)

"True love," Breton dares to say quite justly, "is subject to no appreciable alteration in its duration. . . .' (*Amour*, p. 75)

There is no doubt that he who is unaware of the intermittences of the heart is naive, but the person who, perceiving them, gives them absolute scope is nothing but the victim of another kind of naiveté. He is stopped by the appearance of the rock, and is unable to guess at the underground presence of the river. Or perhaps, he has never really loved. The fullness of real love is born only in the fullness of the exchange of the reciprocal gift. Without this total giving, each one places himself outside the possibility of receiving the gift of the other. In love, this is the only way to attain what Breton calls "the delirium of absolute presence." (*Amour*, p. 108)

There are, however, serious obstacles to the realization of perfect love which have to do with the demands of life in common; it is, among other reasons, to wipe out these obstacles that Breton calls for the social revolution which will break the weight with which economic necessity burdens love. It would, however, be utopian to believe that the social revolution can of itself deliver love from all its demons.

Breton seems to admit as a form of this "unique love" that he exalts a love directed successively to women who nevertheless all belong to a certain unique type, recognizable as a single poetic theme. (cf. *Amour*, p. 11)

Besides, according to Breton, there is always a deep fissure in the heart of the greatest love, a kind of fault line from which arise the noxious fumes of isolation:

> It is there, at the very bottom of the human pit, in that paradoxical region in which the fusion of two beings who have really chosen each other restores to everything the lost colors of the time of the ancient suns; it is there that solitude rages, by one of those quirks of nature which, around the craters of Alaska, makes the snow remain under the embers. (*Amour*, p. 12)

Total love is not an illusion, but it exists only by bearing up against the winds and the tides, against all the things that at every moment seek to deny it and to annihilate it. Like the sexual world, in spite of Sade and Freud, it keeps at its center an "uncrushable stone of darkness." (*Point*, p. 188)

However, it is in this very darkness, in this mystery, that woman and love are revelatory, precisely because they are mysteries, because, in broad daylight, they bring us the signs of the nocturnal world.

To the child-woman who is at the heart of *Arcane 17*, Breton declares:

> You were the very image of the secret, of one of the great secrets of nature in the moment when it delivers itself up. (*Arcane*, p. 135)

Again he writes:

> Ritter proclaimed rather mysteriously that man, a stranger on earth,
> is acclimated here below only by woman. He "delivers" only woman,
> helping her discover her purest destiny. In a way, it is the earth
> which commands through the woman. One loves only the earth and
> through woman the earth loves us in return.' That is why love and
> woman are the clearest solution to all enigmas. (*Point*, p. 189)

This is, of course, a strange way of speaking, and yet one can
perhaps understand what a succession of myths it is related to. In
all mythologies, there exists the myth of the earthmother; the earth
is the symbol of nourishing and fruitful woman, of woman who
surrounds man with her love. Let us not forget either that according
to Genesis it was woman who pulled man down to earth and that
the only paradisiac object that man could bring along into this domain
of unhappiness was precisely woman. Woman is that fragment of
paradise which has fallen from its orbit and which binds man to
the earth.

Tolstoy showed in *The Kreutzer Sonata* that man's existence on
earth would be quite different from the one we know if woman
did not exist. Is it not more for women than for themselves that
men are so tremendously avid for wealth and power? Let us remark
in passing that it is here that the Marxists should be able to see
how much influence sexual determinism and the love of liberty have
over social struggles, and that the Freudians should take note that
sexual conflicts are linked to social conflicts. No, Breton is not wrong
in saying that woman is "the cornerstone of the material universe."
(*Vases*, p. 81)

The great paradox of woman is that, while rooting man in material
reality, she is also the medium who brings him into communication
with the world of marvels. It is her love which bestows on man
that experience of *communication* compared to which homosexuality
is only a powerless mirage. It is her love which, in Breton's words,
we have seen "restore to everything the lost colors of the time of
the ancient suns," that is, of the lost time of childhood, and before
that, the colors of the time of paradise. If it shines with such sweet-

ness, hope, and light, it is because it has taken them on at what Baudelaire called "the holy source of primitive light." (*Bénédiction*)

Woman is the queen of objective chance, not only in those hours when she seems to project before her the light of love, during stupendous coincidences and the most disquieting premonitions, but also when she herself is the supreme instrument of the great remembrance, when the magic of her presence makes a ray of the light from the time of lost marvels shine in man.[17] Breton says to his wife:

> Before I knew you. . . . No, those words mean nothing; you know very well that seeing you the first time, I recognized you without the least hesitation. (*Arcane*, p. 35)

The idea of remembrance is Platonic, but no less Platonic is the idea which calls up in the form of a spectre of light the primitive Hermaphrodite. An allegory holds that

> every human being has been tossed into life in search of a being of the other sex, a sole individual made for him in every respect, to such an extent that the one without the other seems the product of the disruption, of the dislocation of a single block of light. (*Arcane*, p. 41)

It is the human being himself who was this lost sun, and it is his gleaming ego and his flesh of light that he hopes to recover in love:

> Reciprocal love alone prepared that total magnetization over which nothing can gain power and which makes the flesh into sun. (*Arcane*, p. 43)

There is nothing surprising then in Breton's preaching the idea of "earthly salvation through woman" (*Arcane*, p. 70), or in his seeing art as preparing "systematically" for the "coming" of woman "to the whole empire of the senses" (*Arcane*, p. 94). In this way alone, he says, will it one day be possible to cry out:

> The great curse is lifted; all the power for the regeneration of the world lies in human love. (*Arcane*, p. 68)

It is not just a matter of a gentler way of life or of any other "amelioration" that the reign of woman might bring to humanity, but of much more. If woman takes the light she radiates from a somewhere that existed before the time of the curse, than it is permissible to think that she possesses the secret of "eternal youth" (*Arcane*, p. 135) and that "Time has no hold on her" (*Arcane*, p. 94).

The moment in which this magic power will be confirmed in all its strength has not come, but it will come if one believes precisely in this woman who on the seventeenth arcane surrounds herself with the symbols of eternal rebirth: the rose and the butterfly, or the phoenix. Nadja already took pleasure in portraying herself "under the appearance of a butterfly" (*Nadja*, p. 165). As Christian tradition states, what one woman—Eve—has lost, another woman, the new Eve, will save. To woman always falls the great role of opening paradise: Beatrice for Dante, Aurelia for Nerval. Eloa too is redemptive, just as Mary is for Peter in that "prodigious film, a triumph of surrealist thought, *Peter Ibbetson.*" (*Amour*, p. 113)

Extrasensory communication. Love is not the only Ariadne's thread in the mazes of objective chance: friendship can be one also, and hate, perhaps, as well. There are, invisible in the air around us, many threads which bind one destiny to another. Without our being aware of it, there take place perpetual phenomena of osmosis between our minds.

A single fact would be enough to bring this to light, the surrealist game called *cadavre exquis*. It is a kind of variation on the game of *petits papiers* and consists in several persons' writing on the same piece of paper parts of a sentence, each person's contribution remaining unknown to the others. There would seem to be nothing more bland and yet it is an often surprising exercise.

Played in a really surrealist fashion, it becomes a way of applying the principle of automatism, each one writing spontaneously whthout considering what the results might be. At the same time, the principle of objective chance is being applied, because the final result can come only from the joining of these texts. It is proven by numerous examples that the sentences obtained in this way often have a strong poetic potential. More especially, they may be typical manifestations of telepathic communication.

The finest of the sentences obtained in this way is undoubtedly the one that gave this game its surrealistic name: "The exquisite cadaver will drink the new wine."

By using a variation on this method, a question and answer procedure, Breton was able, with the participation of this friends, to obtain some striking definitions:

> What is daytime?
> A woman bathing at nightfall.

> What is the army?
> Half-pay.

> What is physical love?
> It is half the pleasure.[18]

I would like to add that, with several persons, I have been able to obtain some other unstudied definitions which, under their uncalculated humor, have a wonderful precision:

> Star: pointed like a needle.
> Music: produced when a donkey brays.
> Spring-mattress: divan covered with ashes.
> Clock: chair turning in place.
> Sky: perfect sphere, red.
> Soles of the feet: dwarf crawling on all fours.

These examples are all the more convincing in that the participants were all quite ignorant of surrealism and telepathy, and were therefore innocent of preparation and technical ruses. Such experiments border on telepathy, but under a specialized form.

I was able to experiment with another form under the following circumstances. Having made arrangements with a friend who lived about a kilometer away from my home, I began to listen at the time we had agreed on, around eleven o'clock at night. The first message I received was a puppet that gesticulated like a tightrope walker. To this I then added quite uselessly the vision of a crowd of onlookers. For the next day, my partner let me know that he had sent me the image of his pendulum clock, on which he had concentrated. In another instance, I was the sender. I made a rough drawing of a sailboat, such as a child might do, on a piece of notebook paper. Then, I decided, perhaps rather naively, that the picture, schematic as it was, might not transmit too well, and so I tried to polish my drawing; laboriously, I changed the straight line that represented the sea into a series of well-defined waves. The next day, when I questioned this same partner, he said he had seen a boat setting out to sea, but it was seized by a storm as soon as it left the harbor. He then embroidered this with superfluous elements, but I knew enough to understand that the two essential elements of my transmission had been picked up by direct communication, without any outside intermediary.

Distance is of little importance in this type of experiment, at least basically, although it can lead to rather bad mix-ups in working out the time of listening. However, experimenters seem to have been able to communicate between New York and Paris. Be this as it may, there is always the possibility of such extrasensory communication between persons out of each other's sight in two different buildings, or even at the same table. We can assume then that such apparently diverse games as that of *cadavre exquis* and that of the search for oneiric objects may be due basically to the same faculty operating in the same way but under variable exterior forms.

In this type of happening, of course, allowance must be made for what might be the result of simple coincidence, in the usual sense of the term. This possibility can be dropped only when one has obtained characteristic results or if the attending details go beyond the law of probability.

It is desirable that such experiments not be conducted without a sure knowledge of the methods of interpretation of symbolism and especially of psychoanalysis. Freud clearly showed how the dream, that is, unconscious thought, transposed the images, disguising them in symbolic fashion at the very moment of emitting them. If, then, within the same mind, the fact of the images passing from one mental level to another (from the unconscious to the conscious) inflicts on it such a transformation, as the result of a kind of index of refraction must take place when the image passes from one mind into another. I see two cases of this in the examples given above: that of the clock transposed into the image of a tightrope walker, and the other of the chair turning in its place. It is probable that by examining the products of telepathic experience in the light of Freudian techniques for the interpretation of symbolism, one could obtain positive results on the basis of obvious intermental communication in cases where at first glance the result seemed on the contrary to be negative.

Folk wisdom is inspired when it says that the walls have ears, or that if someone speaks evil of you, your ears ring. While this is only true symbolically it is no less revelatory. Let no one think that the wall of private life is as impenetrable as is supposed. If our acts, our thoughts, and our dreams have unforeseen repercussions on our descendants, they have others, just as invisible and just as serious, on our contemporaries. Even the dreamer within his dream is not so isolated as he might think, for our dreams are communicating vessels, even between the most divergent, the most distant of beings. This opens up brand-new horizons in the questions of personal influence and responsibility. In the same way, we can ask ourselves if what we call the spirit of the times or the spirit of the nation are not over-abstract formulae which represent, however, the subterranean presence of currents charged with motivating images which are in mutual transpatial and transmental exchange like radio waves and cosmic rays. We are still only at the dawn of objective chance, on the threshold of an immense exploration. By means of expectancy, automatism, love, dreams, and all the modes of extrasensory communication, man is discovering great fissures in the walls which enclose him. The practice of the spirit of disintegration and of directed hallucination sets before him, on the far side of thousands of dizzying drawbridges, the entry into the focal zone of marvels, into the world of reintegration. Is this but a set of illusions, dreams, and literature? Or are these the first signs of a scientific exploration?

SEVEN

Surrealism and Knowledge

The exclusive attitude of orthodox Marxists who claim that the revolutionary movement qualifies as the one and only real praxis, in the full sense of that term, is indefensible, even if the revolutionary movement is understood as broadly as possible, the claim being made for it alone. It is vain to try to reject all the rest as being anodyne, subsidiary, superstructural, reactionary, and post-revolutionary. The modern scientific movement must at least be recognized as another praxis, one of prime importance for man's liberation.

While it is indispensable to conquer the sickness of society, it is no less necessary to combat biological disease. While it is necessary to free humanity from the yoke imposed by man on man, it is no less indispensable to free him from the yoke of the forces of nature. Of course, these two undertakings which are carried out by the same human race in the same universe and which both aim at man's total liberation overlap in many areas. Nevertheless, each has its own perspective, its specific objective and methods.

The militant revolutionary, then, does not have to be a scholar in order to be a hero of the proletariat, nor is the scholar obliged to be a Marxist in order to discover and invent. To remind anyone of such evident facts would be ridiculous if these were not all too often ignored and if it were not continually forgotten that these are the concrete mark of the autonomy of the two great praxes.

This autonomy goes so far that, even if the Marxist revolution attained its ultimate goal of the creation of a world-wide classless and stateless society, humanity would still be faced with the task of seeing through to the end the scientific conquest of the universe.

The same is true for surrealism. In spite of the social revolutionaries and the scholars who think that their undertakings have exclusive claim on the essential praxis, surrealism, in its own domain and by specific methods, has set in motion a third praxis destined to change radically human life. Through experiments in disintegration, automatism, and objective chance, it explores the new and unknown realms of existence. Under this aspect, it has a right to autonomy. It is a science of a new and irreplaceable kind. What we will try to clarify here is the nature and value of that science.

Opposition between Surrealism and Science

The surrealists rarely bothered to make any systematic comparison between their preoccupations and those of science. Considering this superficially, one might not be at all surprised, since their tasks were of such a radically different nature, surrealism being seen as no more than a school of art and literature. We know, however, that this is in no way the case, that in every way surrealism goes far beyond the ordinary limits of those schools which are attempting simply to create "things of beauty."

Surrealism is on the contrary an effort to explore and conquer the universe and, in this respect, it is related to science. At this point the temptation is to smile, under the pretext that the methods of surrealism bear very little resemblance to those of the physicists, that it shows a haughty disregard for what we call good sense, on which, in spite of Descartes, most people seem to think they have a monopoly.

For many, even today, surrealism is only a lovely poetic tapestry and at the same time a tissue of illusions. Georges Mounin, for example, finds surrealism besmirched with a capital error:

"The peremptory surrealism of the apprentice year tried to escape the censure of reality and of reason, not to flee from thought and reality but in order to seize them alive' (Hugnet, *Introduction à La Petite anthologie du surréalisme*). What it really did was introduce one more subject for confusion into a capital debate. The poetic knowledge which the surrealists engage in so deeply had absolutely nothing in common with scientific knowledge, and the reality they were trying to grasp was not the same as that which the scientists were working with. To speak, in connection with surrealism of a 'viable system of knowledge' (Hugnet) as such, to propose this as a solution to the crisis of knowledge at the beginning of the twentieth century was a pretention more ridiculous than the most ridiculous pretentions of the most extravagant scientists of the end of the nineteenth century; to believe that surrealism could supply—or *dispense* from supplying—a response to the problems raised about the quantum theories, about the idea of causality was crazier than trying to use the mystery of the Incarnation to solve an equation in organic chemistry.[1]

Further on, he concludes:

Logical, rational, scientific knowledge and poetic knowledge are no more liable to compete with each other or to eliminate each other than are the senses of smell and of sight; no more than a sky by Poussin (or Tanguy, or even Picasso) can take the place of the official weather bulletin. Surrealism thought itself anti-rationalist because it was a-rationalist. Yielding to the old impatience that wants to reduce everything to unity at any price, it believed that, since the mind is not able to take an irrational stance, it is obliged to abandon forever rational ways. In short, once again, it thought that antimonies were resolved by decreeing the annulment of one of the terms. Naville and Péret ran headlong toward the danger. Breton himself, at the conclusion of an excellent analysis, is unable to avoid it, saying that 'one can work systematically, safe from any delirium, at making the distinction between objective and subjective lose its value and its necessity' *(Message automatique)*. Automatic writing, sleep or dreams, madness, deliriums of all sorts, facts all extremely interesting in themselves present, however, the common characteristic of not validly resolving the subjective-objective antimony, but of evading it by alterations in subjectivity.[2]

Sartre makes similar criticisms, accusing surrealism of trying to "destroy objectivity" by forcing

> particular objects to disintegrate, that is, by annuling the structure of objectivity in these witness-objects.
>
> This is obviously not an operation one can try out on real existing things, already posited, with their indeformable essence. And so imaginary objects are produced, constructed in such a way that their objectivity cancels itself out. The basic outline of this method is furnished us in the false sugar lumps that Duchamp cut in fact from marble, so that they were of unexpected weight. The visitor who picked them up was meant to feel in an instantaneous flash the destruction of the objective essence of the sugar by itself; he was to have procured for him that deception of being, that uneasiness, that instability given for example by those trick objects, when the spoon suddenly melts away in the cup of tea, when the sugar (the inverse of the trick constructed by Duchamp) comes back to the surface and floats. It is hoped that, thanks to this intuition, the whole world will discover for itself a kind of radical contradiction. Surrealist painting and sculpture have no other purpose than to multiply these confined and imaginary explosions which are like the sink-drain through which the whole universe is going to empty itself.
>
> Dali's method of critical-paranoia is only a refinement of this procedure; it also boils down to an effort to 'contribute to the total discrediting of the world of reality'. Their literature will make language undergo the same fate, destroying it by telescoping words. Thus the sugar sends us back to the marble and the marble to the sugar and the limp watch by its limpness casts doubt on itself; the objective is destroyed and thrown suddenly back on the subjective, since reality is disqualified.[3]

It was necessary to give the floor here to the opposition, and rather at length, so that both sides of the debate could be fully heard. Besides, there is never any value in not letting the opposing argument appear in its full force, except for those who would rather avoid discussing it.

For the same reason, we have to admit that these arguments of Mounin and of Sartre do not lack force; in fact, they are quite convincing on certain points. It is indeed perfectly correct that it is not in the power of a painting by Picasso or an object by Duchamp to abolish the empire of objectivity, nor can any poem do this. The artist's paint brush and the writer's pen are not magic wands.

Surrealism does not then dispense physical science from pursuing its work on irreducible exterior objectivity, on that solid materiality which is its proper domain. It cannot claim to surmount here and now the antimony of the subjective and the objective, to the point of denying the objective by reincorporating it artificially in subjectivity.

We must say here that we have no difficulty in seeing that these arguments of Mounin and of Sartre are well-founded, all the more so in that this demands no concession at all on our part, since from the outset of this chapter we began by positing the autonomy of surrealism in regard to science, which carries as a corollary that of science in regard to surrealism.

This is not then simply a personal view. In the critical remarks of Mounin and of Sartre, we do not even come upon any real objections to surrealism, if we make an exception of the initial period in which surrealism, busy finding itself, sacrificed much too easily to a spirit which enthusiastically negated exterior reality in order to affirm an immediately triumphant possibility of the total metamorphosis of the world: a period long since over.

It is the whole weight of extra-human objectivity that surrealism assumes when, in 1929, Breton writes in the preface to the first *Manifeste:* "I understood that in spite of everything, life was *given.*" Thereafter, in the measure that Breton forced the further confrontation of surrealism with psychoanalysis and above all with Marxist materialism, he came up ever harder against the rock of exterior reality.

At this moment, we are far from the era in which Chirico tried, in the place Pigalle, to identify, with the aid of a pocket mirror, a ghost in the person of a little flower-seller. From then on, we are no less distant from any possibility of believing that a Picasso painting or a Duchamp object can deny the existence of the "true" world of objects and of the "real" sky that the weather bureau studies.

In the eyes of surrealists, the function of surrealist paintings and objects is something entirely different. They in no way count on them to explode objectivity in itself, they count rather on projecting through them into the exterior world the phantoms of subjectivity in order to incarnate them visibly in objectivity. Like the X-ray that does not claim to negate the existence of the epidermis and the flesh but instead merely makes the shadow of the inner bone structure appear on the outside, so surrealist painting and objects, without denying the exterior world, project the spectres of the mind to the outside. In another way, it is the same function that automatic writing exercises. It is first a question of the exploration of subjectivity; but here, once more, Sartre tries to stop us and to deny the possibility of such a mode of investigation.

> The subjective enters in indeed when we recognize that our thoughts, our emotions, our willing comes from us in the moment they appear to us and when we deem both that it is certain they belong to us and only probable that the exterior world regulates itself by them. Surrealism has taken a hatred for this humble certitude on which the stoic based his ethics . . . Automatic writing is above all else the destruction of subjectivity. When we attempt it, spasmodic clots rip through us, their origin unknown to us; we are not conscious of them until they have taken their place in the world of objects and we have to look on them with the eyes of a stranger. It is not a matter as has too often been said, of substituting their unconscious subjectivity for consciousness, but of showing the subject to be like an inconsistent illusion in the midst of an objective universe.[4]

This time, Sartre's criticism falls into the most indefensible arbitrariness. In virtue of what should we admit such an *a priori* definition of the subjective? He proceeds as summarily as the professors of psychology who tried to negate psychoanalysis by simply denying the idea of the unconscious. One can criticize the idea, and on the basis of this criticism conclude that the idea itself must be revised, but does this in any way permit the avoidance of Freud's remarkable explanations and the many and various facts that his research has brought to light? Not only that, but Sartre's criticism here dealing with the limits of subjectivity is completely gratuitous. He could validly maintain that there are two quite distinct types of subjectivity: a perfectly clear consciousness, sure of possessing itself and, on the other hand, the other forms of subjectivity which take in the unconscious, the subconscious and the supra-conscious. But there is absolutely no rational or experimental motive for excluding them from subjectivity in order to cast them into nothingness or to connect them with exterior objectivity, for they are too actively alive in man to let themselves be annihilated or cast into the exterior world. Moreover, these rigid categories that Sartre puts down like a grid over the manifestations of surrealism so as to judge them by the principles of his doctrine are only a Procrustean bed unable to contain the reality-in-fact of surrealism and, more generally, of the life of the mind.

At the moment when the series of word-images or of pictorial forms engendered by automatism rises up, even if one wrongly claims that this source has nothing subjective about it, the fruit it bears becomes *ipso facto* subjective, since by definition it appears in the domain of consciousness and incorporates itself into it. It should be remembered that the automatism of the surrealists is not identical to that of the mediums. While the latter's is purely mechanical, the arm being directly moved by a foreign force, that of the former cannot happen without the intervention of an awareness which acts as a turntable, the lever without which the hand of the painter or the poet would remain lifeless. Surrealist activity then does have initially to do with subjectivity since it manifests forms which appear directly to the consciousness without the intervention of the exterior senses. Besides, all human thought is in some degree indebted to this interior output. Totally clear thought, transparent to itself from A to Z, is a pure fiction, an entity that exists nowhere in this world.

We have perhaps to find the real motive then for the violent reaction of Sartre against surrealism in the fact that such affirmations seriously infringe on the categorical opposition Sartre tries to set up between the *pour-soi* and the *en-soi.* Since there exists an area of the mind in which these two categories are in intimate communication, it is their opposition, the basis of the whole Sartrian architecture, which turns out to be the illusion.

It is logical then that he sees automatic writing like an enemy torpedo tearing open the phantom ship of the *pour-soi* and letting in the waters of the *en-soi.* If this surrealist project were able to succeed, it would mean the prompt scuttling of the consciousness; but Sartre thinks rather that this attack of surrealism against the transcendence of the *pour-soi* is only an illusion. The fact, however, is there, and we prefer to believe the event rather than the doctrine: the subconscious is the living synthesis of the *en-soi* and the *pour-soi.* It does not let itself be torn in half by these two categories. Why then won't the ship let itself be sunk? Simply because there is no ship. The ship is a fabrication, but the *pour-soi* and the whole of the subjectivity are not. The subjectivity is not a water-tight vessel, it is a fish in the waters of objectivity. A *poisson soluble,* in that these waters traverse it continually and constitute its being, and yet at the same time an indissoluble fish, because it is the constant presence, the living force, the figure commanding these currents of life that sustain it as *être en-soi* and *pour-soi.*

When Sartre withdraws to his rear lines, then, maintaining that automatic writing turns out only inconsistent products, we respond that he has only to analyze them closely to see that they form a close-woven fabric and that they have a meaning which can certainly be elucidated. The most frenzied poetry has a sense that cannot be denied by a prior refusal of any possibility of consistence and meaning.

Thus we can truly say that automatic writing bears out into the exterior objective world the projection of a world that is also objective but in suspension within the subjectivity. No matter what Sartre says, the aim of surrealism is in no way "to annihilate the real in annihilating oneself along with it"; it is false that "nothingness glimmers on the surface, a nothingness which is only the endless sparkling of contradictories." [5] Like prose, poetry—especially surrealist poetry—is an unveiling, even though it unveils something other than prose unveils. While the theme of the latter is the depiction of the rational and the daily in their opaque thickness, the theme of the former is revelation, that is, the unveiling of the irrational and the sacred, of the marvelous which shines through at the very heart of the ordinary.

Surrealism is above all science of the imagination, not at all theoretical but concrete; not passive, but dynamic. It is the setting in motion of the forces of the imaginary and an exploration of the imaginary worlds. Does it necessarily follow that it is of little value, a vain passion for mirages and that "the purely imaginary and the praxis are hardly compatible"? [6] In no way. In the physical world itself, mirages are optical phenomena and the object of scientific study, for they become illusory only in that the mind of the traveller connects them mistakenly with a real oasis; but insofar as the eye sees them, without interpreting them falsely, they have a real existence as mirages. In the same way, the imaginary is not purely inexistent. It is an illusion insofar as the dreamer relates it falsely to an objective exterior presence or attributes to it unreal powers. But as a mental phenomenon, the imaginary exists objectively within the mind, and as such is the object of scientific study or of what one could perhaps call the science of ideas.

There is, moreover, between the mirage and the imaginary this main difference, that while the mirage is only an accidental and inoperant phenomenon of nature, sterility itself, the imaginary is a power ceaselessly at work in the life of the mind, its great force for fecundity and action. The imaginary is to the mental just about what water is to terrestrial life. It is the great bringer-forth of myths, without which neither revolutions nor philosophies would be born— and their myths are not their falsest part, for the falseness of the myth lies not in what it expresses but in our pseudo-rational modes of interpreting it.

It is very tricky to try to set up a category of the unadulterated imaginary, for this would no doubt be an outpost never to be reached. The most fantastic imaginary always contains some root in reality through the exterior forms it draws upon for the figuration of the images it presents to the mind. It is also real because of the real tension of the mind it expresses, since it cannot be born except under the action of such an impulse. In any case there exists no pure abstraction to which we can give the name of the pure imaginary. This formula has no other reality than to express the willed attitude of the negator of the imaginary. What does exist is really an intra-. mental world of which almost everything has still to be discovered. This would be enough to justify surrealism's claim that it is pursuing not invention but discovery.

I will add further that it is very imprudent to try to separate in any radical way this intra-mental world from the extra-mental one. The action of sexual complexes in the imagination is a good example of the power of the objective over the subjective. The same holds true for the action of social complexes, a study that has been gravely neglected.

One can answer that these facts in any case indicate that these phenomena are limited: it is always the objective which weighs on the subjective and not the inverse, but this is only a so-called statement of fact. In effect, the subjective and the imaginary, after having been submitted to this exterior action, react in their turn on the objectivity, marking man's comportment with new impulses. The imaginary is not a vague, up-in-the-air force, however great its liberty; it remains part of the machinery of existence, a dialectic moment between two exterior stances. To act on the imaginary is to act on the myths, and who today can seriously deny that to act on the myths is to act on individual and even social existence?

There is still another way for the subjective to bite directly into objectivity. It is through the whole set of possibilities proposed to it by the phenomena already irrefutably brought to light by telepathy. The other phenomena falling under the general title of objective chance can be rather hotly contested, but telepathy is a fact that everyone, or almost everyone can experience and grasp, if he wants to.

To conclude, let us say then that there is on the one hand an exterior world that is the prerogative of physical science, and that surrealism in no way contests its right to it. The negation, pure and simple, of the value of science is due only to that childhood malady of surrealism which led, at a certain period, to a tendency toward a kind of magic idealism; but to attack surrealism on the basis of something which it has long since outgrown is to no purpose.

On the other hand, there is an interior world which is the prerogative of surrealism and, moreover, of all the modern methods of exploration that it would like to unite in the name of this common undertaking. It is high time that a certain childhood malady of modern science refrain from contesting surrealism's right to this world.

Finally, these principles hold only to the extent that the work methods can be differentiated. The two worlds, interior and exterior, communicate by hundreds of pores, hundreds of capillary vessels. The more men progress, each in his own field, the more they will discover numerous areas of overlapping between the two zones that were originally separated; there will finally be born a single common science, impossible to define at this present moment, but which must come, for it will be the result of the nature of things, of the basic unity of the world, of man and of the cosmos.

Analogies between Science and Surrealism

Before analyzing more closely the scientific tasks of surrealism and the way in which these are carried out, it might be useful to point out several striking indications which are evident signs of certain convergences between physical science and the surrealist movement.

It has not been sufficiently stressed that surrealism came to birth in the era of the great revolution in the physical sciences and mathematics brought about by Einstein, Niels Bohr, Riemann, Heisenberg, de Broglie and many others. The surrealists themselves rarely alluded to it. Breton makes only one passing reference to Einstein (*Pas*, p. 10), but he returns to it in a very significant fashion, even though without naming Einstein, when he writes:

> Belief in an absolute space and time seem ready to disappear. . . . We know today, thanks to the film, how to make a locomotive *arrive* in a painting. With the widespread use of the slow-motion and the

high-speed camera and our becoming accustomed to seeing oaks spurting up and antelopes gliding, one feels an intense excitement in wondering what must be these local times one hears spoken of. (*Pas*, p. 103)

It is possible that, for a scientist, this metaphorical translation of relativity seems simplistic and fallacious, and so we do not use it at all as a scientific truth, but as a revelatory indication of the preoccupations of surrealism. If the surrealists denied the absolute value of the limits of space and time, it is not only because they were lead to do so out of magico-poetic considerations, but also because of the more or less valid perspectives opened up to the imagination by modern physics.

If, on the one hand, there were very few scientists in the group which formed about Breton, one will note, on the other, that among the predecessors of surrealism there were men who joined scientific activity and avant-garde poetry. There is, for instance, Lewis Carroll, the author of *Alice in Wonderland*, who also wrote mathematical treatises. In like manner, Charles Cros, who takes a place beside Lewis Carroll as a poet in the *Anthologie de l'humour noir*, was one of the inventors of the phonograph and the author of abstracts on color photography, modern scientific alchemy, and the principles of cerebral mechanics.

The solidity of the scientific principles of Edgar Allan Poe is much more doubtful, but the fact is that he was haunted by this sort of thing. In *Eureka* he claims to give a new cosmogony which is at once poetic and scientific. As for Jarry's pataphysics, it is clearly a caricature of science, but even with this paradoxical bias in attitude, it witnessed to the attraction of science on the poet. Suggestive of this is his trying to give a description of the time-machine thought up by H. G. Wells. The meeting of these two writers is a remarkable example of the conjunction of attraction existing between the poetic marvelous and the scientific marvelous in modern minds.

Another typical case is found in the fact that Cros, like Wells, was passionately interested in the idea of communication between humans and the hypothetical inhabitants of other planets.[7] To give another example, the first pages written by Wells in *The War of the Worlds* are not without similarities to those of Breton in the *Great Transparent Ones.*

Nor is it by chance that Villiers de l'Isle-Adam, cited also in *L'Anthologie de l'humour noir,* raises Edison to the dignity of an authentic magician, uniting the scientific marvelous with the poetico-religious marvelous; nor is it any less significant that Roussel professed the greatest admiration for Jules Verne and was curiously inspired by him.

The plastic analogies existing between science and surrealist poetry or painting should also be stressed. The machine, for instance, plays an important role in the mythologies of Roussel, Duchamp, Ernst, and also Kafka. It is not by chance that the poets discover mental automatism at the time when the scientists are inventing masses of automatic machines. Nor is it chance that enables both these groups to represent the unforeseen and the unknown.

Once more, these are only analogies. There is no question here of maintaining that the two modes of activity are identical or interchangeable; on their two distinct levels, however, they correspond to each other in a remarkably parallel way.

The romantic doctor and philosopher, Malfatti de Montereggio, describing the beginnings of electricity or, more precisely, the work of Galvani, wrote this amazing sentence:

> For man's hand, become suspect, he substituted a metallic conductor.[8]

Does not this maxim which forcefully sums up the whole tendency of modern science ring with a surrealist sound? Doesn't it recall Breton's decision which led him to confide his hand no longer to the calculations and fantasies of art and doctrine, but to the automatic impulses of the unconscious? Man's hand has become suspect for the surrealists also and they tend to metallize it directly through automatism. They want to make a new sorcerer's wand of it that will indicate the gold-lodes of the subconscious, or the needle of a new compass that is attuned to the pole-star of the wonderland.

A frequent objection to surrealism and to Freudianism as well is that their method for recording the content of the unconscious is liable, by systematizing it, to deform it. This is an evident danger; however, it is possible to prepare for it by a willed impartiality of observation as well as by auxiliary techniques which have still to be perfected. In any case, this difficulty itself is but one more analogy with the obstacles contemporary physics must handle: the phenomena observed are so sensitive that they react to the instrument of observation.

The consistent use of the vacuum in the methods of modern physics also has its correspondence in telepathy and modern poetry. Concentration of mind is based, to a certain extent, on mental vacuum, for it is impossible to unveil the phenomena of the infinitely small except by putting aside the massive presence of the realities which ordinarily hide it. Thus, the infraconscious or the supra-conscious can appear only when the habitual content of the consciousness is laid aside.

In a further comparison, the modern poetry of the surrealists and some others tends to bring about a disintegration of images and language in the same way that modern physics tends to bring about a disintegration of matter.

Physics has come to recognize enormous groupings of atoms in all the molecules which make up the materiality of the universe. It has been able to decompose these groupings as well as, paradoxically, the atoms themselves. At will, and in ever wider ranges, physics breaks through the barriers that nature imposed on human power. It advances with giant steps toward the fulfillment of the old dream of the alchemists: the transmutation of matter.

Again, from this point of view, the work of poetry is curiously analogous. It is striking to note what a large part of our study of surrealism has been devoted to the idea and the methods of mental disintegration. It is along these lines, moreover, that poetry has been able to create the very special type of poetic discontinuity of which Rimbaud's *Illuminations* and Hölderlin's *Poems of Madness* are the main prototypes. It is Joyce, though, and the American novelists like Faulkner who have continued it, as have, in another way, Breton, Péret, Tzara, Leiris, Desnos, Arp, etc. Roussel himself, in spite of the classical form of his narrative, uses the disintegration of words as his basis.

Through these very works, however, we see that in modern poetry as in contemporary science, this tendency toward disintegration is only for the sake of reintegration, in the sense that both are working to bring about new regroupings of force on a superior level, each in its own field.

What is surrealist science, then? What is its nature, what are its aims and its implications?

Surrealism's Scientific Tasks

If the primitive mentality is deformed by animistic prejudices which we sometimes rightly find astonishing, the Western mind for its part pays homage to the most ridiculous of positivist mentalities. Getting rid of them by becoming aware of their presence is all the harder in that they are common to the most varied types of occidental man: to the man in the street with his taste for solid common sense, to the cultivated man with his classical formation, to scientists and to militant marxists. For all of these, poetry is a gratuitous dream, and dreams are nothing but the vain picturing of the unreal. As for hallucinations, myths, the enigmatic words of automatism, and the strange happenings of objective chance, who could possibly take such eccentricities seriously? Everything that is eccentric, that is, everything outside that platform of security where Western man has chosen to set up housekeeping, all that is, in his eyes, suspect. He sees in them only rare and isolated events, events whose existence is extremely dubious and whose meaning is incomprehensible or divested of the most elementary certitude.

This is not a new attitude. Our ancestors scoffed at the supposition of the poles' existence, and the seamen of old saw only ghosts and chasms of perdition where Columbus glimpsed a path that would link the two extremities of the world by an unknown short cut.

We should feel no surprise, then, if our contemporaries, faced with the first explorations of automatism, disintegration and objective chance, see there nothing but shadowy or perilous phantoms. This matters but little. We have tried to show how these new explorers proceeded, what signals they recorded, what messages they transmitted to us from their observatories, what early results they consigned to their writings. What we would like to do now is show in a general outline the panoramic view of the new world into which they ventured.

The Field of Exploration

In every case, the direction taken by their investigation converges on the same point. Automatic writing and objective chance, black humor and illumination, disintegration and the orientation toward the supreme point: each is meant to burst open the enveloping gangue, to tunnel through the mountain closing off our valley, so as to open up to us the way to the wonderland which, in the eyes of the surrealists is none other than the totality of the world. Breton put strong emphasis on this when he wrote:

> A work can be accepted as surrealist only to the extent in which the artist has made himself reach out to the whole psychophysical domain (of which the domain of the consciousness is only a small part). . . . Automatism leads straight to this region. (*Peinture*, p. 94)

This is probably the best definition of a surrealist work that can be proposed, because it is not based on any particular aspect of surrealism but on the concordance of all its appearances, tending as it does to rise in a dialectic manner above all the antimonies, even those of waking and of dreaming and of disintegration and automatism, to open up to man the avenues of the supreme point. In other words, it brings out the fact that the deepest reason for the surrealist accomplishment has always been the initiation of the Great Work. The error of the aesthetes and of many artists has been, not to set their sights on beauty, but rather to devote themselves to the worship of fragments of beauty in a separatist spirit, as though an object of beauty could be basically isolated from the hidden and unique source of all beauty in this world. For the surrealist, it is not merely a question of being more complete, but rather of restoring the sense of the deepest reality and of its *sacred* value. While ordinary language projects into the mind only partial images of human reality reduced to the area of social existence and its immediate surroundings, authentic poetic language attempts to project an integral image of human reality grasped in all its profoundness, down even to that point at which it seems to become lost in unknown abysses.

Even though these requirements are laid down just in the fields of art and of literature, it becomes immediately evident that their unavoidable consequence is a displacement of their frontiers and an infinite extension of their zone of action which becomes as vast as the universe, known and unknown. Note should be taken here that it is important, among other things, to distinguish between surrealism in the restricted sense and surrealism in the general sense. While the former designates all the strictly surrealist methods, notably automatism, disintegration, and objective chance, even though there exist beyond these many other techniques specific to other sciences, generalized surrealism is the integral teaching that attempts to make the dialectical sum of all the others in order to win for humanity the knowledge and the possession of the supreme point. That is why, in spite of the limits (in any case, still quite distant) of restricted surrealism, the object of the investigation of generalized surrealism is as vast as the whole world. It is moreover presumable that, as the still separated sciences make progress, these will come more and more closely together, even the physical and mental sciences, forming, like the world itself, a single whole.

In any case, we will limit ourselves at this time to defining the field of exploration of restricted surrealism. This is what Breton is designating with precision when he assigns to art that immense mission which is its alone:

> Art, constrained for centuries to stray hardly at all from the beaten paths of the ego and the super-ego, cannot but show itself avid to

range in every direction over the wide and almost virgin territory of the id. (*Position*, p. 58)

His dream is to throw open all its floodgates. (*Position*, p. 59 and *Point*, p. 227)

The term *id*, borrowed from Freud, is perhaps not very well chosen; let us say simply that he is referring to the widest sector of the unconscious.

If we could make a cross section of the poetic thought of the times, we would find that its roots penetrate deeply into the libido which is to the human mind what the geological substratum is to the plant. It is in the *soi* (the id) that are deposited all the mnemonic elements, the residue of innumerable previous individual existences. Automatism is nothing but the means the mind uses to penetrate and dissolve this soil in order to dig into it; it parallels the mechanical action by which vegetal roots are able to thrust stones aside and to weaken firm foundations. (*Humour*, p. 226)

The expression "previous individual existences" introduces a certain ambiguity into Breton's sentence. Is he alluding to hereditary traces, to the residue of the collective unconscious or only to the paralleling of our existences by those no-man's-lands of forgetfulness which separate us successively from our childhood and then from our youth? Let us retain only the last of these hypotheses, the only one to fit in with the Freudian ideas to which constant reference is made in this area, and let us see how, elsewhere, Breton defines the relationship of automatism and the mnemonic elements:

For the question, 'How does a thing become conscious?,' there is an advantage, says Freud, in substituting another: 'How does a thing become preconscious?' The answer: 'Through association with corresponding verbal representations.' A little further on he becomes more precise: 'How can we bring suppressed elements into the (pre-) consciousness? By determining, by means of analysis, those intermediary preconscious members which constitute verbal memories.'
These verbal representations which Freud presents to us as 'mnemonic elements coming mainly from accoustical perceptions' are precisely

what make up the raw material of poetry. 'Outworn poetic ideas,' confided Rimbaud, 'played a great role in my alchemy of the word.' More particularly, the whole thrust of surrealism in the last fifteen years has consisted in obtaining from the poet the flash revelation of those verbal elements whose psychic charge can be propagated by the makeup of the perception-consciousness system (as it has been to obtain from the painter from fastest possible projection of the mnemonic remainder in the optical order). I shall never grow tired of repeating that automatism is the sole dispenser of the elements on which the secondary task of emotional amalgamation and the passage from unconsciousness to preconsciousness can validly work. (*Position*, p. 54)

We can see in the attraction of the mnemonic elements a phenomenon analogous to the Proustian attempt to regain the *temps perdus*. The causes of this attraction are evident; they are the immediate result of the definition Breton gives of that total psychophysical domain he hopes to conquer by plunging into the *soi:*

Freud has shown that at this abysmal depth there reigns the absence of contradiction, freedom to break away from the hemming in of the emotions that comes from repression, intemporality and the replacement of external reality by a psychic reality that has to submit to no other principle than that of pleasure (*Peinture*, p. 94).

A psychoanalyst would find in this an evident nostalgia for childhood or even a return-to-the-womb complex. This could be true in part, but only in part, for many other things enter in. Let us note in passing the difference between Proust and Breton; the former owes to chance alone the reappearance of the past in his moments of ecstasy. Breton attempts to provoke these manifestations and to stabilize them by calling less on emotivity and more on the technique of automatism. In both instances, however, there is the bringing about of vast reassembling of the consciousness above and beyond the divided times it has experienced.

On the other hand, it must be emphasized that these mnemonic elements are not sought after for their own sake, the shreds of a past now forever changed; their main interest resides in the fact that they form a kind of crossroads between the past and the present, between memory and the nether unexplored reaches of the mind. This is why they are not just the deadwood of a past consciously relived, but are symbols charged with a thousand mysterious meanings and with an overflowing emotivity. Symbols: this means that they are like clouds suspended at the horizon of two tangential worlds, charged with their beams and their contradictory reflections. Their enigmatic force comes from this double nature, from the extreme tension between the two worlds whose projection they are.

This permits us to notice readily the immense difference between surrealism and psychoanalysis: while Freud is interested in symbols only to pass through them down to the lower psychophysical zone which serves as their basis, so as to dissolve them if he can and to root out the neuroses which may be associated with them, Breton, without losing interest in the examination of these foundations, turns more toward the upper regions which serve as their firmament and keystone. Symbols are not epiphenomena, superstructures whose sufficient origin is their base: they come into being suspended between the two worlds of the unconscious and the superconscious, of the mind's sub-levels and of the interior heavens of the past and the future. It is because of this latter duality that they have both a mnemonic and a prophetic function. Both are important to surrealism, because both have a role to play in the reascension toward the eternal zone that is beyond the antimonies of time.

The goal of surrealism can be then neither the copying of external forms nor dreaming alone; it must be to lead the poet to conquer in

> the immense reserve from which symbols come forth fully armed to spread through the work of a few men, into the life of all. (*Position*, p. 57)

Breton is, moreover, happy to see that even outside surrealism such preoccupations are becoming more lively and widespread:

> I do not see any fundamental antagonism, for example, between Pierre-Jean Jouve, who estimates that in his actual experience 'poetry is faced with multiple condensations through which it is able to achieve the symbol—no longer under the control of the intellect, but rising up, awesome and real—'; Tristan Tzara, according to whom the ideas of identity and imitation, whose meaningless use in the interpreting of a work of art constitutes the principal argument of those who would like to assign to it the role of a means of propaganda, are henceforth replaced by those having to do specifically with a process of symbolization; and André Malraux, who states that 'the work of the artist in the West consists in creating a personal myth through a series of symbols.' (*Position*, p. 55)

While other works in general, though, waver toward compromises with strange and untimely interruptions, surrealism remains unshakeably centered on the myth. It is, above all, life and knowledge of the myth. Through the synthesis it attempts to bring about between modernity and the hermetic tradition, between materialism and esoterism, it bears alone the great *weltanschauung* of surreality in which are integrated the real and the unreal, matter and fantasy.

It is true that one could claim to see a major contradiction in the attitude of surrealism in regard to the myth. On one hand, Breton proclaims the necessity of a "mythic comportment" (*Amour*, p. 153) and defines surrealism as "the way to create a collective myth" (*Position*, p. 13), and we have seen him try with all his energy to develop the powers of automatism and to deliver man up to his phantasms. There is no doubt that he is trying to arouse a tidal wave of the unconscious.

But, on the other hand, it is the same Breton who writes:

> On return to what is called normal existence, what a sweeping away of projectors and resolute job of cleaning up will have to take place in that vast and dark region of the *soi* where myths take on boundless proportions in the same time that wars are fomented. (*Situation*, p. 29)

A page further on, he again makes clear that he sees in surrealism:

> a preparation along practical lines for breaking into the mythical life, one which at first assumes, on a vast scale, the aspect of a clearing away. (*Situation*, p. 30)

This is no doubt a public service undertaking, a proposal for a new descent by Orpheus into the underworld, animated this time, however, by the desire to crush forever the tyranny of the subterranean powers.

But isn't there a contradiction between the two tasks—that of opening up the well of the abyss in order to set free in the world the real power of the myths, and that of going down into this same well in order to wrest the power from the subterranean rulers? It is true that there is an undoubted antimony, but it does not constitute an absurd contradiction; it is a dialectical, that is, surmountable, contradiction.

Breton ceaselessly works to bring about a reduction of the marvelous by drawing on the techniques of Freud and Marx, and yet he works no less precisely to keep these methods of reduction within their due limits and to uphold the irreductible value of a certain core of the marvelous.

Moreover, the analysis of myths, their reduction and submission to human intelligence is not possible except precisely *after* their being brought to light, their surging up out of the subconscious. The two attitudes of surrealism, far from being incompatible, are the two indispensable moments of its exploration. The real danger is in letting ourselves react emotionally to the myths without knowing that it is this which is urging and animating us. Refusing to distinguish them in the shadows amounts only to a confirmation of their power. Anonymity makes them impossible to get rid of.

There is a much more real contradiction to be found in the other doctrines which claim to pull down certain myths in order to build new ones on the ruins of the old. The same holds true for psychoanalysis and for Marxism. It is much better deliberately to recognize oneself as a generator of myths, as surrealism has done, for self-criticism always remains open.

This does not mean at all that these myths anymore than any others are sheer illusions. To see the myths as nothing but trumpery is a simplistic position which has long since had its day. If marxism makes a myth of economy, it is because it does place an enormous and really exorbitant weight on our whole life, and even in a certain measure on our apparently purest and most disinterested ideas. The same is true of sexuality. Such forces become myths, in the pejorative sense of the term, only when they go beyond the real limits of their ability to act and therefore to be explained, and when they lay claim, in the minds of those whom they obsess, to the ability to account for all reality and all illusion.

Likewise the surrealist experience, in the measure that it proposes myths, does not fill the world with sheer illusions. It draws these myths into the light of day from the dark regions where they were hiding in order to act on man. They become myths, in the pejorative sense we already mentioned, only if instead of trying to X-ray them and make them as clear as possible, the poets want to make new idols of them. The surrealist is then in no way antiscientific when he extracts the matters and forces which are hidden in the lower levels of the consciousness and in the fabric of the unconscious. His attitude becomes scientific or antiscientific only in the following moment, after this extraction of the precious metals of poetry, according to whether he is content to play with these diamonds like an artist concerned for elegance or to venerate them as do certain primitives, or if, on the contrary, he wants to manifest in their regard only that admiration which is worthy of science and which consists in studying their nature and in using them for the victorious transformation of the world.

In these meta-sensitive domains, and in the present state of science, there can be no descent into hell in the proper sense of the word descent. The only possible form of exploration consists in projecting the image of the underground currents onto the screen of the consciousness at the level at which it is fixed. No one can reproach the surrealists for opening the well of this abyss, for it has always been open for all men; like the psychoanalysts, the surrealists do no more than reveal to men that the well is open, something men were unaware of. The only question that still goes unanswered is to find out if, by their attitude, the surrealists are working to purge humanity of the tyranny of the mythological powers or, on the contrary, to increase that power.

Reading the statement made by Breton to the students of Yale, which assigns surrealism the task of cleaning up the region of the *soi*, one might think that surrealism is above all else a therapeutic. Breton insists on this with force:

> But, you will ask me, how is this region to be approached? I tell you that only surrealism has bothered to look for a concrete solution to this problem, that it has truly set foot in the arena and taken its bearings, and that for all useful purposes and in view of an undertaking which goes far beyond its numerical forces, it has been alone in placing a few lookouts at distant intervals. . . . A persistent faith in automatism as an instrument of investigation, a persistent hope in the dialectic (that of Heraclitus, of Meister Eckhart, of Hegel) for the resolution of the antimonies that burden man, the recognition of the aims of nature and the ends of man in the eyes of this latter, a desire for permanent incorporation in the psychic apparatus of black humor which alone, at a certain temperature, can play the role of escape valve, a preparation along practical lines for breaking into the mythical life, one which at first assumes, on a vast scale, the aspect of a clearing away, such are or remain, at this hour, the basic orders of surrealism. (*Situation*, p. 29)

This statement is perfectly clear, and one can do no more than rally to it. However, an ambiguity persists in surrealism. It does not come at all from the recourse to auto-criticism, as is often erroneously supposed. The science of myths has a double task: projection and interpretation. Without doubt, the other methods which claim to compete with surrealism in this task believe they apply themselves with equal energy to these two aspects of their undertaking. It is surrealism, however, that wins the day, first of all because surrealism is an open doctrine which can, without losing its integrity, use to its own advantage the techniques of its competitors, something they cannot do. Besides, psychoanalysis, and even more so, sociology and Marxism gather up only the remains of myths, their traces in books, social and political facts, the remembrance of dreams, the psychoanalytic confessions of the ill. The surrealists, on the contrary, themselves plunge into the high sea of myths: by giving themselves up to automatism and objective chance they themselves live the mythic life, they immerse themselves in it, they continually discover new myths which the other explorers that have remained ashore can only make out from afar. It follows from this that the surrealists' understanding of the mythic life is not limited by a bookish, medical, or political outlook; they have become citizens of the mythic worlds and know them from the inside, and so they have incomparable possibilities for exploration. Not only that, but this situation gives them another privilege from the interpretive point of view. While their competitors consider the myths only in order to reduce them, doing so in a partially arbitrary manner by bringing them down to their least common denominator, the surrealists experience in themselves to what extent each of these systems of interpretation is partial, and they invite the consciousness to seek continually deeper, from myth to myth, the supreme secret of the world.

The Three Levels of Interpretation

From the beginning of this work, we have tried to define the cosmology of surrealism, to show into what general picture the surrealist myths fit. Then by studying the role of disintegration and of automatism in literature and painting we have shown how surrealism provoked the manifestation of the myths in suspension in the subjectivity. Finally, moving to objective chance, we have tried to give a glimpse into the way in which myths and the forces of mystery could effectively intervene in outward life. Now that we have set out to confront surrealism and science, it is incumbent on us to look into the possibilities for the scientific interpretation of this body of research. What do these possibilities mean? What is their experimental value?

Surrealism claims to descend "into the heart of the interior wonder-world" (*Manifestes*, p. 147), but not for the sake of blind enjoyment; a real exploration is at stake. Breton is searching for "palpable proofs of an existence other than that which we think we lead." (*Manifestes*, p. 149) It is not enough just to explore; it is up to the explorers to be exact, to know how far they have gone and into what lands they have adventured. The task of interpretation cannot rightfully be separated from that of exploration. The chief interest of Breton's work is that he never forsakes the one in favor of the other.

> It is up to us to seek to perceive more and more clearly what is going on, all unknown to man, in the depths of his mind. (*Manifestes*, p. 143)

What he is after is not the breaking down of the mind, but rather bringing ever more light to bear on it, and so he notes with intense interest while pondering the correspondences between automatism and chance:

> The practice of psychic automatism in every domain has been found capable of widening considerably the field of the immediately arbitrary. This is the important point: that arbitrariness, upon examination, had a violent tendency to deny that it is arbitrary. (*Position*, p. 145)

At the same time it becomes more and more certain that these signals are not indecipherable:

> The signs in question could not be retained for their immediate strangeness nor for their formal beauty; this for the very good reason that from this time forward, their decipherability is proven. (*Position*, p. 58)

The exigetical methods of psychoanalysis are important here, but so also is the constant development, in our times, of the poetic consciousness:

> The poetic works of the end of the last century which seemed the most definitely secret or the most frenzied are becoming every day more completely illuminated. (*Position*, p. 60)

This is why Breton insists on the guidelines which the surrealists must lay down for themselves:

> Surrealism, passing beyond any preoccupation with the picturesque, will, I hope, soon go on to the interpretation of automatic texts, in the form of poems or not, on which it will bestow its name, and whose apparent bizarreness will not be able, in my opinion, to survive this test. (*Point*, p. 127)

It is regrettable that, up until now, the surrealists have far too much neglected this task as well as that of the systematic exploration of automatism and of objective chance. They have instead tried too hard to exploit aesthetically the riches surrealism has brought them; I personally believe that this attitude is one of the main causes of the crisis in the growth of surrealism during recent years. What is important, then, is to work systematically to organize the terrain gained from the unknown and to undertake new exploration.

Since automatic writing and objective chance take in very complex and heterogeneous phenomena in the perhaps boundless region of the *soi*, what must first be done is to establish with what levels of reality the constellations of the myths can be identified.

In spite of this extreme complexity and their sibylline aspect, the texts of automatism and modern poetry are decipherable, as Breton has stated. This is a main point and it is important to clarify it more and more.

On this point, Sartre, in *What is Literature?* [9] showed as much force and precision in defining the function of prose as he did misconception in regard to poetry. For him, prose is eminently transparent, an unveiling of reality in the consciousness by means of layers of brightness projected by language. Poetry, on the contrary, seems to him to be a grouping of words that are perhaps delightful but opaque, even if they seem to be of crystal. They have neither theoretical nor practical utility; their end is in themselves. They evoke the human condition from an extra-human, almost divine, viewpoint; it is the world seen wrong way round, and is therefore a useless illusion.

It is paradoxical to join so much penetration to so much blindness. It is perfectly true that poetry, great poetry at least, is placed in the perspective of the zenith, but why judge it in advance as opaque and consequently indecipherable and vain? This is perhaps due more than anything else to a lack of intuitive feeling for poetry and to a continuing adhesion to the old classical prejudices according to which modern poetry is incomprehensible; Sartre's philosophy, by proclaiming the radical opposition of the *en-soi* and the *pour-soi* and by declaring the final absence of meaningfulness in the world, must of necessity anchor him in that misconception.

Poetry shines so gleamingly, so blindingly, that at first it is totally disconcerting, but even so, it is transparent. The difficulty is to find the angle of transparence. The clearest glass seems deprived of all transpareney if one persists in looking through it at the angle under which it reflects the sun, and this is what Sartre does with poetry.

He does not accept the fact that poetry might have an angle of transparency. He does not accept the fact that it might have a positive meaning, because this would lead to a conclusion unacceptable to his philosophy of existentialism. His refusal of the positive value of poetry as revelation, that is, as superior unveiling of the world, is logical, because the value of poetry implies the value of its symbols, and consequently the existence of a cosmic symbolism or, in other words, of an *ars poetica* of the world, which includes man and the universe in an harmonious unity. It rises above the quarrels of the *en-soi* and the *pour-soi* to affirm that the divorce between them is not irremediable.

The unveiling that poetry brings about is naturally not precisely the same as that of prose. It does not progress along the ordinary lines of the perspective on life. It takes the opposite, the contrary stance, so as to emphasize the presence of certain unusual and flashing lights which radiograph ordinary appearances. Poetry is the plunge of the awareness into the abysmal regions where life shows itself to be other than it seems. It places itself at the zenith of life, or sometimes at the nadir, each time bringing into sight the celestial spaces that offer themselves to man's conquest, in spite of the black clouds which sometimes close in on the life beneath them. Poetry is for man what astronomy is for science: the discovery of the worlds of light without which earth would be only a black star lost in the night.

The only problem is to define the nature and the value of these worlds of light. These constellations of myths exist in suspension in the vast region which Breton, after Freud's example, calls the *soi*. This name, however, is far too equivocal and indeterminate, and it is important to determine to what exactly it corresponds. This meaning cannot be defined in advance; it can only be the result of experimentation, and this experimentation has only just begun. As soon as one becomes unwilling to hazard wild guesses, it becomes clear that the content of this region, and therefore of the myths themselves, must be distributed in the prolongation of the three essential levels of reality, in the personal unconscious, the collective unconscious and the cosmic unconscious.

The personal unconscious. Under the title of *The Psychopathology of Everyday Life*, Freud made an essential advance contribution to the criticism of objective chance. He investigated a certain number of prophetic dreams, unusual coincidences, revelatory lapses, bewildering impressions of *déjà vu* and current superstitions in order to show that all these cases could be elucidated by the use of psychoanalysis properly so-called. He congratulated himself on dissipating what he considered their apparent mystery and bringing them down to the level of simple illusions or revelatory manifestations of the single individual unconscious. Thus these reminiscences, bizarre coincidences, and premonitions did not originate in an authentic morveilleux, but were simply illusions due to the pathology under consideration.

I am therefore different from a superstitious person in the following way:

I do not believe that an event in whose occurence my mental life plays no part can teach me any hidden thing about the future shape of reality; but I believe that an unintentional manifestation of my own mental activity *does* on the other hand disclose something hidden, though again it is something that belongs only to my mental life. I believe in external (real) chance, it is true, but not in internal (psychical) accidental events. With the superstitious person it is the other way round. He knows nothing of the motivation of his chance actions and parapraxes, and believes in psychical accidental events; and, on the other hand, he has a tendency to ascribe to external chance happenings a meaning which will become manifest in real events, and to regard such chance happenings as a means of expressing something that is hidden from him in the external world.[10]

It is this system which is sometimes claimed to be in line with the attitude of the surrealists in regard to objective chance. But let us see how, in the same work, Freud concludes:

In point of fact I believe that a large part of the mythological view of the world, which extends a long way into the most modern religions, *is nothing but psychology projected into the external world.*[11]

The role of psychoanalysis would then be to bring all this metaphysics back to its point of projection, that is, to "reduce" it to a "psychology of the unconscious." Later, however, Freud had to withdraw to a less intransigent position. In a lecture on occultism in which he was attempting to demonstrate that a certain number of cases of telepathy could be traced to personal illusions, he did not believe that he could in any case deduce from this an absolute negation of telepathy, anymore than a positive declaration in its favor. One of the favorable arguments which seems most to have impressed him and kept him from considering telepathy as a hypothesis to be ruled out in advance was the unresolved question of the way in which

The common purpose comes about in the great insect communities; possibly it is done by means of a direct psychical transference of this kind.[12]

Freud's use of this motive is paradoxical, for he would only have had to study the results obtained in our day by explorers in telepathy, much more convincing than these suppositions about animals of whose psychisms we are profoundly ignorant.

Whatever be the case, telepathy is a fact that cannot be rejected for reasons of dogma, not even in the name of positivism or materialism. It is a field of science, and it is enough to explore it methodically, taking care to scrutinize closely cases of telepathy, like all the marvelous, or so-called, phenomena, either to confirm their authenticity or to unmask their illusion.

Freud has given a remarkable analysis of a wonderful tale by Jensen, *Gradiva*, the story of a young German archeologist, always lost in the clouds, who thinks he sees one day at high noon in the ruins of Pompeii, the flesh-and-blood phantom of an ancient and yet young and beautiful Pompeian girl.[13] He discovers soon afterwards that this supernatural apparition is in reality none other than his cousin and contemporary, Zoe Rediviva Bertgang. However, the young man is not so badly made a fool of by destiny since in this unusual way he comes back to earth and, on this earth, to love.

Probably a certain number of the phenomena of objective chance have to undergo a similar reduction of their supranormal reach, without their poetic beauty being for all that, in any way impaired; but are they all reductible in this manner? That is the question that must be asked about each one; no general simplistic law allows this examination to be dispensed with.

It is possible also that, in a general way, poetry is a force for disorientation, without there always being present the certainty that this force leads to a higher orientation or to a fall into the most useless of confusions. This last danger is always to be feared, and so requires that the accomplishments of poetry be put to the test of psychoanalysis and all the possible procedures of reduction.

One has only to read *Don Quixote* to notice that very often the attitude of the knight-errant is identical to the poet's. He thinks he spies a marvel in the countryside when there is only a mirage before his eyes. In all the wide world that Sancho Panza judges to be as prosaic as his own common sense, Don Quixote on the contrary discerns only knights, magicians and fantastic signs; we have as witness the well-known episodes of the windmills, the fulling-hammers, the cave of Montesinos and the poor Dulcinea of Toboso.

One remembers how in *La Prisionnière* Proust alludes humorously to what he calls the Dostoevskian side of Madame de Sévigné. Sometimes, instead of presenting things in logical fashion, beginning at the beginning with the cause, the vivacious letter-writer shows first of all the unusual and fallacious effect, bringing it out in a disconcerting way, cut off from its cause and the natural setting that made things seem familiar. This way of seeing things may be rare in a Frenchwoman, but it is constant with Cervantes. Through the eyes of Don Quixote, it is first of all the marvelous effect, the poetic mirage that springs up before us, until the eyes of Sancho reveal to us the lowly pretext for the phantasmagoria. The whole art of Cervantes lies in this blending into a single dialectic unity of the contradictory movements of the knight and the simple fellow who accompanies him.

The modern marvelous is the direct inheritor of the marvelous of the historical novels that inebriate Don Quixote. One such sentence taken from the passage about the night in which the fulling-hammers echoed seems to come from one of those gothic novels that enchant Breton—and all of us:

> The night, as has been said, was dark, and they had happened to stray beneath some tall trees, the movement of whose leaves in the soft wind made a gentle but alarming sound; so that, taken all together, the solitude, the locality, the darkness, the roaring of the water, and the rustling of the leaves produced a horror and dread.[14]

One could, in the same way in our times, write a work that would take up again these eternal themes of fantasy and terror, continuously opposing to them the prosaic sayings of the descendants of Sancho Panza.

I will use as another example the importance that many occultists attach to the *Centuries* of Nostradamus. Others, it is true, rank his predictions with riddles undeserving of attention, but one can wonder if, following the line of Sandomir's thought, another interpretation might not be possible.

For Nostradamus, he tells us, there is neither progress, as we would speak of it today, nor even history; there is only a burning chaos of disordered events among which a minority of essential types guarantees a cyclic recurrence: famines, epidemics, conflagrations, and massacres.

Moreover, certain places, designated by a sort of curse or more probably by geographic fatality, become the theatre for these. For example, on the surface of the globe, a certain number of places become indispensable as passages or stopovers necessary to human movements. This is true independently of the passage of time. In this way, the "astrologer" has no trouble keeping in his predictions a number of fixed points that he is sure in advance will have a role to play; to these he assigns an archaic name, the better to indicate this timeless nature. One can then explain, without having to credit the "prophet" with a miraculous foresight of happenings, those amazing sequences that over several epochs were thought to have been taken from actual events. Take, for example, this eternal communiqué about the wars of Italy:

Naples, Palerme et toute la Sicile
Par main barbare sera inhabitée,
Corsiq, Salerne et de Sardaigne l'isle:
Faim, peste, guerre, fin de maux intentée.[15]

As Sandomir points out, *main* here signifies troops (*manus* in Latin); *barbare*, foreigner; *inhabitée*, another Latinism (rather than the French *habitée*), for inhabited.

All these images, moreover, are given without any order, and the interpreters of Nostradamus have not in general been shy about taking their material at random from the *Centuries*, one might say helter-skelter, in such a way that they have not had much trouble finding here and there the material they need for images from which they can compose "prophetic" visions.

One has only to think of the imagination's extraordinary faculty of effervescence, and of the facility with which it finds its way, or thinks it finds its way about in the most hopeless confusion of images (as Leonardo da Vinci very well knew, since he advised his pupils to gaze attentively at the spots on old walls until they found in them the outline of an idyll or a battle) to understand more easily how a poet as gifted as Nostradamus was able to pack into his quatrains so many scintillating images that the reader could find in them almost at will the evocation of the events of his epoch. How can the imagination miss being stirred and set in motion, given the sole condition of a minimum of poetic complicity?—especially since the images of the *Centuries* are brilliant and rapid, elliptical and flashing, carried along by the current of a truly incantatory inspiration.

It must be added that places are not the only obligatory relays along the course of history. Men's name, like place names, titles, emblems, coats of arms, and allegorical myths will almost always summon up a few mythological commonplaces, so that the use of one of these keywords of allegorical history is almost bound to carry along with it some trait of the future history of our planet.

If one wonders why there is so much chaos, so much muddle in the *Centuries*, it is easy to answer that this is the best way to reflect the chaos and muddle of history.

> These words set one into the other with a rigor that borders on hardness, these rich sequences of sonorous catastrophes, these cruel and many colored medleys of sumptuous proper names, these comets' tails and monsters' heads weaving in and out through the vast display of time, all call out invincibly, but also secretly repel.
>
> Like Mallarmé, Nostradamus is a 'lover of words'. He tests verbal forces with the same severity. Mallarmé, we know, dared to dream of an absolute book which would be indistinguishable from the world itself and which would have made real the creative claim that Genesis attributes to the divine Word; he left only its preface. Nostradamus, although he did not complete it, advanced further into this impossible undertaking; in his thousand-odd quatrains, the order and chaos of

the universe are so present that, when it comes down to it, the future itself is really forced to reproduce the poem.[16]

It is important to insist on the example of Nostradamus, for if any authentically prophetic credit could be awarded him, the great poet of the *Centuries* would also be one of the great explorers of objective chance. To reduce his work to an admirable technique of apparently premonitory disorder is, inversely, to open the way noticeably to the reduction of similar mirages.

One can indeed wonder if, in certain poetic texts of high quality, the reflection and the richness of the images are not such that everything in them is foreseeable in advance. But then what is happening today is in on way distinguishable from what happened yesterday, nor from what will happen tomorrow. Everything happens in such a way that one might very well say nothing of it is foretold. In the same way, one might say that a dictionary is a prophetic work, because tomorrow will be found in it all the words needed to tell future history. Nor would a mirror be any less prophetic, in this regard, because it will be able to reflect all the images that one day or another will be presented to it.

We can ask ourselves questions of this nature about Breton's poetry, especially about the night of the sunflower. Keeping in mind that there are places of election for geography and the history of peoples, it is permissible to think that there are also places chosen by Breton in his personal geography of Paris and in the history of his wanderings about the capital. It would not then be so strange that the night of the *Tournesol* took place in a spot that he loved, or that his walk took him and the woman along a well-known path in the vicinity of the Tour Saint-Jacques. On that axis of references a constellation of images familiar to Breton arose when he wrote his poem *Tournesol;* is it then so strange that years later he was able to find a similar constellation when once again he began the same trajectory?

The mystery of the night of the sunflower is in no way dissipated by this. A gleam of enigma still persists at the heart of this night: are the habitual laws of Breton's way of acting enough to account for it? It would be risky to say so. There are, moreover, other examples which do not fit into this type of interpretation, like Nadja's red window and the house of discord.

The marvelous does indeed exist, that is undeniable for anyone who has ever been its lucid witness or for those who attentively examine the facts reported by serious witnesses. The interest we have in it makes it a necessity for us to inspect it, to test it as harshly as possible with every method capable of reducing it to nothingness, as gold is tried with the greatest care before it is pronounced free of all impurity and blending. That is why we must first make ourselves methodically reduce, if possible, all the phenomena of objective chance to aberrations of the personal unconscious. Only what remains can be accepted as the authentic manifestation of objective chance.

The collective unconscious. If the phenomena attributed to objective chance prove resistant to individual psychoanalytic critique, they then ought evidently be brought to the level of the collective unconscious, as a second resort. The idea of a collective unconscious can be held suspect. Almost anything legendary or mythological, in the worst sense of these terms, has been stuck under this heading. It has been made one of those absurd entities like the soul of France or the soul of humanity, terms to be used if need be in the rhetoric of official speeches or in the attempt to inject a little warmth into an artificial academicism, but these entities, which are valid metaphors expressing the French spirit or humanity's common destiny, confer no personality on these abstract realities.

One wonders if, in the mind of the public—another useful abstraction—these "collective souls" that are spoken of with no relationship to any religious belief and which are as uncomfortable with theology as with atheism, do not in some way correspond to an elementary conception of the "great transparents." They are in fact situated a little higher, by definition, along the animal scale, since from their invisible balcony they dominate the floating mass of beings that we are and who compose that mass. This would be rather like the mental mountains of crystal that lie at the extreme limit of our inward horizons. It is these, in any case, I mean all those national souls, which would be most liable to spark the great atmospheric disturbances of the mind, the wars and revolutions which upset humanity.

In reality, this collective mythology is no more misleading than the individual mythology. It only expresses in a rather excessive way what takes place in the collective unconscious, just as the latter translates individual complexes.

If the soul of France as a personal entity situated above human persons is a fiction, the community of the French is on the other hand a very concrete reality which can be considered as bound much more intimately together than by any exterior signs uniting them. This is where telepathy can very well be brought back into play. It is from this point of view that the spirit of the times or the spirit of the nation, like the spirit of a church spire, recovers the full force of its reality.

It would be foolhardy to reduce the phenomena of telepathy either to the deliberate experiments conducted for the purpose of bringing these phenomena to light, or to the examples of it which spontaneously happened to the persons concerned. There is quite probably an incessant exchange of currents of images and feelings which travel through the vast network of human minds and wash against them on every side; but their area of penetration in man is located below the level of consciousness, and he is unaware that such images and feelings arise, not from his personal unconscious, but from the chorus of other unconsciousnesses. Perhaps the poets are the only ones to suspect that through their intuition they were sometimes in contact with other spirits; these are perhaps only other human spirits. Would not inspiration then be a kind of fertilization by the intromission of a foreign spirit into that of the poet? It is perhaps not without meaning that Aragon once devoted an article to the succubae.[17] If the above were so, then one would have to take away their demoniac aspect and consider them rather as anonymous and unconscious genies who fecundate poetry. They are the Muses, human Muses, terribly distracted since they act without being aware of it. Doubtlessly, and especially, they are beloved women, as so many poets require. And yet, is it not rather a male role that they assume, for the fruit of their love is the poet, the native femininity of the poet which accepts the burden of that love and gives it birth. They disappear in the shadows, or die magnificently in a ray of the poet's glory, like the males of the hive, while the poet reigns in the midst of this glory, golden with honey, rich in celestial offspring, winged, a bearer of honey, the honey of his poems, like the queen bee reigning in the midst of her Pantheon of delights.

It is probably just such telepathic currents which in great part justify that sense of communal ecstasy during celebrations so definitely noticed by Nietzsche and Durkheim.

We are on a level of fantasy here, but it is a human fantasy which no longer calls on extra-human and literally fabulous beings, and so the most positive history can be clarified by it, as Breton indicates:

> The fantastic, which is radically excluded by the application of any password such as socialist realism, this fantastic, on which surrealism has never ceased to call, constitutes in our opinion the key par excellence allowing the hidden content to be explored, the way of touching on the secret depths of history which disappear beneath the web of events. It is only at the approach of the fantastic, at that point where human reason loses control, that the deepest emotion which not being apt to project itself into the setting of the real world, has in its swiftness no other outlet than to respond to the eternal beckoning of the symbols and myths. This seems to me the most opportune time to redirect attention to that extraordinary crop of English novels of the end of the eighteenth century known as gothic novels *(Limites)*.

These novels crossed the Channel and were the forerunners of a flurry of gothic novels (especially those of Sade) in France also, as well as of the arrival of the Terror itself. It has been said often enough that the playing at shepherds of Rousseau and the queen's "Hameau" had by their "naiveté" served to introduce the reign of the scaffold. It would probably be less dialectic, but just as admissible, to see in these terrifying works of fiction one of the preliminary signs of the spirit of the times, hours in which fictions came out of the tapestries woven by the printing press to incarnate themselves tragically in a Europe undergoing radical and sudden change from Paris to Madrid and Moscow, torn from its orbit down as far as the Pyramids, by the genies born of the revolution. Perhaps England was able to escape from the full force of this because it is an island, to give credit to one of those ideas of elect places, like those of Nostradamus, and on the other hand in virtue of a sort of catharsis due to the fact that it was itself the originator of the gothic novels and could gorge itself on these instead of on blood really shed.

Such perspectives will naturally not convince minds which are sure of the absolute validity of their good sense and which keep credibility within limits. As far as method is concerned, they are perfectly correct. One must never accept without question what must remain only a hypothesis as disconcerting at base as the supposition, in other times, that the earth could turn around the sun. Certain religious minds took offense, but the materialists of the day could only laugh as though at an evident violation of the sacrosanct laws of the weight and solidity of the globe on its base, or rather what at that time one took to be those laws. To bypass this obstacle, it was necessary for the defenders of the new hypothesis to be able to offer certain substantiating proofs. This same thing is uncumbent on all those who would formulate hypotheses on the role of telepathy and the fantastic in history; moreover, these hypotheses must be unified, otherwise how can the field that they are liable to open up be recognized?

It would be a good idea to reexamine in this same light the question of the "occult sciences." It might be supposed that, aside from the too numerous number of cases of vulgar hoaxes, the instrument-objects prized by the seers are not just absurd fetishes. In the tarot deck, the coffee-dregs, the crystal ball, they find instruments that will project under their bodily eyes the views that they discover with difficulty in the zone of their subconscious where they enter into communication with that of their clients and even with others.

In an analogous way, it is also possible that some hallucinatory disturbances, unusual encounters and verified presentiments are manifestations due to unknown phenomena of telepathy. This would explain in a rather positive way the viewpoint Breton proposes:

> The sympathy of feeling which exists between two or several beings seems to put them onto solutions that separately they would pursue in vain. The nature of this sympathy would be nothing less than to make pass into the domain of favorable chance (antipathy into that of unfavorable chance) encounters which are inexplicable when they happen to one alone, and which fall back into the accidental. It brings into play to our advantage a real second finality. (*Amour*, p. 50)

In this way, in the telepathic networks which unite all mankind, there would form smaller "magic" circles joined to one another, capable of sometimes drawing others into their orbit, which would be the secret of a number of spells and collective attractions. Speaking of his strange walk with Giacometti, Breton says,

> Two individuals who walk along together constitute a single machine with dynamic influence. (*Amour*, p. 47)

Who can explain to us the role of these circuits of intermental thought in what Breton calls the finding of windfall-objects, in poems in several voices or even, through automatic writing, the work of one hand? When is man ever sure of being completely alone? Do those sentences which "knock at the window" come from another human being, linked by hidden affinities, who will never know that his message has been transmitted? How many calls cross this way at night? When will the great diviner come who will teach them to recognize and answer each other? The least indication could be of the greatest aid here:

> I am deeply convinced that every perception recorded in the most involuntary manner, as, for example, words addressed to no one in particular, carries in itself the solution, symbolic or otherwise, to a difficulty one has reached within oneself. One has only to know what direction to take in the maze. The frenzy of interpretation begins

only when the man who is poorly prepared takes fright in this forest of signs. (*Amour*, p. 12)

Since art has already taught us so much about ourselves, what then of the new forms of spiritual art exercises, of collective master-pieces, which will be born of this new and intimate form of subjective communication?

It is here that are formed, no doubt, those myths having a rare power of attraction and a great poetic beauty: the archetypal symbols. There is no need to ascribe to them any other origin than the common achievement of man, through the intervention of their myths and individual symbols in the night of the unconscious. It is the accumulation of individual myths and their development in the invisible history of the unconscious which is perhaps all that is needed to trace in outline above our dreams the towering architecture of the great myths which exalt or frighten humanity.

Thus in the nocturnal hemisphere is accomplished that "putting in common of thought" (*Manifestes*, p. 171) of which Breton speaks, yet without the self's becoming one of its myths; quite the contrary, for it is all these human *moi* which are the projectors of these X-rays and the unwitting architects of this palace of myths which could well merit the title of the Great Work par excellence.

Here is one more reason for not believing that there exists a strictly individual "inspiration". Not only does man always draw the raw material of his inspiration and a part of its forms from the fundamental ideas he first received from his education and also from what he learns in his daily dealings with people, but also the region that poetry explores is not a private property sheltered behind the wall of private life in a kind of interior dead-end, or in an extra-human world. The region each poet explores is but the view he has as he goes his own path, of the nocturnal hemisphere that all men inhabit, that all dreams and all poems help to recompose, and whose landscapes are valid for everyone. Every unconsciousness, every dream, every poem communicates in a same universe which is only the unexplored side of that universe in which men of flesh and blood come and go.

The question then is to know whether objective chance, in the measure in which it is not reductible to illusions of the individual unconscious, leads back to manifestations of this great nocturnal gathering of men in the collective unconscious, or whether, in the case of certain phenomena, it is necessary to go even further and to recognize the intervention of a third instance: the subterranean action of the cosmos in man's unconscious.

The Cosmic Unconscious. The conception current in Europe holds as evident that man and nature form two worlds, juxtaposed but irremediably isolated by impassable barriers. In spite of the existence of the human body and the instincts that link us in thousands of ways to nature, the world is considered as sheer matter and a monster of insensitivity, and man as a complex of intelligence and feeling which is imprisoned in the human body.

It is this vision that inspires the Platonicians with the notion that the body is the tomb from which the soul dreams of rising. It is also the source of the Cartesian opposition between spirit and extension, that of the theories of parallelism as well as that of Sartre's antithesis between the *pour-soi* and the *en-soi*. This vision is the starting point from which branch out in opposite directions the Western or Hindu idealists who consider the world as an illusion and a degradation of the spirit, and the materialists who instead treat the spirit like an epiphenomenon, a by-product of matter, the mother of all reality.

If, on the contrary, it is admitted that nature is something other than brute matter, and man something other than a spirit sequestered in this inanimate matter, one is led to suppose that there can exist a cosmic unconscious with which man might communicate in the farthest reaches of objective chance.

For example, who moved the impression of an earthquake into Goethe's mind? Was it telluric emanations, or else the subconscious of the inhabitants of Messina? Similar questions could be asked about the "house of discord."

There are indications that favor a telluric influence in singular facts which naturalists are said to have pointed out. Thus before the catastrophe of Fourvière, it seems that horses put up an insurmountable resistance to being led, as they ordinarily were each day, into their stable located on the spot where the disaster took place. How are certain migrations of birds and fish to be explained without some intimate communication between these animals and some kind of still very mysterious impulse which nature must give them? Does not every instinct, with the certainty that characterizes it, presuppose that the being animated possesses "information" about nature, preceding any habitual exercise of the sensations? How could an accord so infallible and of which man, paradoxically, in spite of his intelligence, is the only one to be in large part deprived, be possible if the instinctive powers were not previously accorded with those of nature, on the strength of a veritable cosmic harmony of which the fantasies of Bernardin de Saint-Pierre are only the wild caricature. No caricature can prevent the existence of the original from which it is inspired.

Besides, if man had no cosmic role, and if the cosmos had no human meaning, how could this cosmos have engendered man? The rationalist separation of man and the cosmos is a pure abstraction which could be born only in the brain of intellectuals in the setting of urban life. Yet, at the peak of this metropolitan life, surrealism is like a great rush of outside air suggesting a more conscious return to the primitive feeling for the unity of the destiny of matter and man. As Breton wrote:

> Even though order, aim, etc. in nature are objectively distinguishable from what they are in man's mind, it still happens that natural necessity can come into harmony with human necessity in an extraordinary and troubling way, so that the two determinations are seen as indiscernible. (*Amour*, p. 32)

He concludes by this sentence which treats especially of objective chance:

> Chance would be the form under which exterior necessity shows itself as it makes it way through the human unconscious (to make a bold attempt at interpreting and reconciling Engels and Freud on this point). (*Amour*, p. 35)

Of course it may seem beforehand and totally unrealistic for nature itself to intervene to conduct the course of automatism in our literary exercises of our daily way of acting. Such a view lends itself to a secularization of the idea of Providence that is as indefensible from the religious viewpoint as it is from the atheistic. It will be objected that it is completely foolhardy to try to link the phenomena of objective chance in automatic writing and in life to the hypothetical interventions of a no less hypothetical cosmic unconscious.

Yet these views of surrealism can be criticized only in the event in which that criticism attributes nature with plans, a will, an intention. More precisely, it does not attribute these to nature on its own account, but supposes that the surrealists consent to this arbitrary, almost paranoiac, attribution to nature of a subjectivity equivalent to human nature's, just as Sigmund Freud does when he analyzes the superstitious mentality. But is the attitude of the surrealist superstitious? Does he really attribute a conscious or semiconscious design to nature? Nowhere does this appear.

It is rather in biology that one could find the first indications of the intuition which inspires surrealist hope. In the different manifestations of instinct in animals we can come directly upon the finest examples of the way in which exterior necessity makes its way through the animal sensibility. The quest for food, the great migrations, the phenomena of mimesis, and the instinct for procreation show in an amazing way how the individual being can be led in a really divinatory fashion by some images and certain fundamental impulses through the mazes of existence.

In other words, if the expressions the *soi* and the unconscious, with which psychoanalysis has supplied surrealism, have the misfortune to be insufficiently precise; if progress consists not in rejecting them under pretext of imprecision but rather in bringing to them all the precision possible; if, finally, the first of these progressions in precision is to consist in carefully distinguishing the three levels of individual unconscious, collective unconscious, and cosmic unconscious, it must be stressed that this last zone does not possess frontiers relatively as precise as the two others and that it contains sectors which are probably quite heterogeneous. However, the first of these sectors to be dealt with is that which makes up the very stuff of our biological existence, that of the life we lead in common with the other animals.

Animal instinct seems to us to express itself only through objective, divinatory and imperative conduct. In this respect, we generally meet with frustration because of the excessive light of our consciousness which bestows on us liberty of action only by at the same time placing us in a state of indetermination, that is by depriving us of the divinations of determinism. This is still no reason for thinking that the umbilical cord which links us to mother earth and even to the whole of the cosmos is cut. We are unaware of it only if we too continue to be linked to it by a thousand instincts through which she communicates her impulses to us. In the very measure in which their hold on us does not immediately provoke decisions which are more hers than ours, the current which was mounting up through these instincts ceases to act on the motivating force which pulls us along and instead finds itself, at the point of connection with the consciousness which cuts it off, changed into images which propose themselves wildly to the awareness. In these images in which we thought to encounter only the purely subjective, we instead come up against projections of nature just as direct as the information from our outward senses.

The world of the *soi* in which the myths float in suspension like clouds and constellations is visible only from the privileged observatory of the consciousness which remains this side of the individual epidermis. But why should it be any less real than the world that the sensitive extremities of that epidermis observe, those other privileged observatories which are our outward senses?

Why, moreover, should this world that man discovers in the nocturnal hemisphere of the *soi* be a world entirely different from that which we discover outwardly? Isn't it rather identical, but revealed according to another cross-section?

Finally, while our outward senses, in spite of their smallness and their inability to set themselves free of the narrow limits of the human form are even so capable of enlightening us on a multitude of forms and phenomena observable in the infinitely vaster sphere of their perceptual reach, why should our inability to feel through the world of the *soi* be limited to synesthesia, and be unable to have a perceptual reach of its own, infinitely more vast than the limits of our epidermis? We are too far from having explored all the depths of nature and the bonds which unite us to it to be able to maintain restrictive theories on such subjects.

Roger Caillois has written remarkable pages on the biological value of myths, whose interest goes far beyond that of the categorical imperatives he has since thought he could impose on literature; one cannot but feel intense regret at his abandoning this wonderful insight which he one of very few to explore.

> Be that as it may, if we want to understand the ultimate function of myths, it would seem necessary to strike out in this direction, and going even beyond psychoanalysis, address ourselves to biology, interpretating as need arises the sense of its basic concepts by their repercussions in the human psychism, such as psychology presents them. Comparing the most finished examples of the two divergent evolutions of the animal kingdom, evolutions ending respectively in man and in insects, it ought not be too difficult to find correspondences between one and the other and more especially between the behavior of the one and the mythology of the other, if it is true, as Bergson holds, that the mythic representation (the quasi-hallucinatory image) is destined to provoke, in the absence of instinct, the behavior that its presence would have set in motion.[18]

He takes up this important idea again a little further on:

> Here, conduct, there, mythology. . . . men and insects make up part of the same nature. To some extent, the same laws govern them. Comparative biology has to do with both. Their respective behaviors are mutually explanatory. Of course there are considerable differences, but these too, when taken into account, must help to clarify the answers. . . . Fantastic images arise in place of the act set in motion.[19]

There exists then at least a sector of the fantastic which far from being gratuitous, expresses in us the most objective and determinant action of nature. From this point of view, the question raised is much less knowing how apparently individual and subjective automatism can be attached to the cosmic unconscious than knowing in what measure it is detachable from it.

We can see, in any case, that the world of the myth is far from being the inconsistent fairy tale, the naive and epiphenomenal superstructure it is customary to believe. Its iridescent flowers are no less rooted in the soil than those of the fields. Shall we say that the humid warmth of the *soi* is comparable to that of a forcing-shed which gives them fabulously complicated forms and unexpected colors? But aren't greenhouse flowers also products of the earth?

It would however be rather arbitrary to try to bring the whole world of myths down to a mere projection of biological realities. Besides the expression of the other sectors of the unconscious that it contains, it certainly conceals in its tangled lines the transposition in hallucinating forms of many other cosmic forces.

Thus it is fitting to bring into the light the expression it gives to metapsychic phenomena other than telepathy (this being only a manifestation of the collective unconscious). If it is likely, as Breton says, that exterior necessity comes through in the human unconscious, the reverse is almost as likely. Along certain paths which, though still mysterious, are destined to be brought to light as the pioneers work on them, the unconscious or even the human consciousness makes its way through the unexplored depths of nature. While instinct appears to be strictly divination, it can be admitted that it is not the only possible form of authentic divination.

Marxists dislike making an attentive examination of metapsychic phenomena. They would rather start by holding them to be fake, without making the least effort to unravel the authentic from the illusory. They might, in cases of strict necessity, put off such an examination under the pretext that this kind of learning is to be reserved for post-revolutionary times, but why inflict delay on the psychic sciences more than on the physical sciences? But even this shoddy treatment is not enough for them. It is indeed difficult to grasp these metapsychical phenomena while treating them as reflections of the struggle between the classes; however, to admit their objectivity would be to open a serious wound in the side of materialism.

How is it to be tolerated that mental forces are capable of entering into action far from their material support, how can they be granted such liberty in their comings and goings, such a hold over matter and space? The weight of matter is in no way suppressed by this, but it could be seriously lightened, and that would be enough to upset the doctrine of the primacy of matter, a consequence hard to reconcile with the orthodox interpretation of Marxism.

In a word, the network of mythic images in suspension in the world of the *soi* is, it is obvious, closely connected to all the forces of biological and psychic life with which the universe is shot through; the task of the surrealists will be to explore these connections without allowing themselves to be stopped by the iron curtain of a dialectical materialism which represents only a methodical localization of the dialectic.

Matter is permeable to our senses, as much to those coiled in the shadows of the *soi* as to those which emerge visibly at the frontiers of the human epidermis. It is permeable also to our intelligence.

To anyone who has advanced along the paths of modern physics, it appears that the notion of brute matter, a notion upheld in the Middle Ages and up to the early part of the nineteenth century, is now a phantom that is being dissipated. It was the primitive myth which served as the foundation of materialism; however, the more physico-mathematical science progresses, the more it becomes clear that the material mass that passed for a stuff immovable and impenetrable to the spirit is being resolved into an essentially dynamic reality, without representation for the senses, but permeable to mathematical understanding. The opaque and unintelligible appearance of matter exists only at the level of the routine opposition between the abstract and the concrete. The activity of the intelligence which created the instruments of physics and the methods of mathematical analysis is forcefully tearing apart a veil that was taken to be impenetrable; it is delivering its attacks on the deepest levels of materiality so that the very idea that we had formed of this materiality is becoming completely outworn.

What results from this is the extraordinary and really fantastic fact is that the levels of matter which we approach, not naturally, but in violation of our status as animals, are seen to be intelligible. What other meaning does this have, if not that man and the cosmos speak the same language, which is that of mathematics. And yet what is there in more apparent opposition than physico-mathematical methods and those of poetry? How is it possible to compare them?

To formulate such objections is to lose sight of the fact that physico-mathematics and surrealist poetry have in common this essential point: both are based on symbolism. The realm of symbolism takes in, of course, extremely diverse areas, but their heterogeneity, extreme as it may be, is nevertheless brought together in this unique realm of symbolism.

Surrealist poetry is completely symbolic, and not allegoric, that is, it does not fabricate disguised representations of already known realities, but instead receives fully formed from the unconscious unrecognizable projections of realities of which there is no advance information.

That mathematics is symbolic is a fact so generally recognized that there is no point in insisting upon it. Modern physics also owes more and more to these same principles. The best proof of this is in the fact that it can have direct recourse to mathematical symbolism to express the ideas to which it attains. Even these realities become so difficult to represent that in the cases where it is still possible to imagine a figuration of the areas of the universe discovered by mathematics and its instruments, physicists recognize that these figurations have only a symbolic value. They are pulling further and further away from the illusions of a naive realism.

If the vision that my eyes give me of this table is true only on the scale of size, being then only a partial symbol of its materiality, the other ways in which a physicist would picture it in its different dimensions are also only other fractional symbols. One could even add that they are often so contradictory that it becomes impossible to reconcile them directly; Louis de Broglie writes:

> In order to account for phenomena on the atomic scale, we are obliged to use 'complementary' descriptions. By this is meant descriptions which complement each other but which are, strictly speaking, incom-

patible. According to Niels Bohr, each of these descriptions is an 'idealization' which allows us to picture certain aspects of the phenomena under study, but not all the aspects of these phenomena.

The best known instance of these complementary descriptions is furnished by the two descriptions of matter and light by means of waves, on the one hand, and corpuscles on the other. The use of one or the other image is seen to be necessary for the interpretation of some phenomenon or other; but all attempts to the contrary, the images remain irreducible in terms of each other and can be connected only by considerations of a statistical order.[20]

This same physicist remarks also:

It is evident almost before starting that the idea of a corpuscle conceived of as the abstract limit of a grain of sand, or the idea of force conceived of as the abstract limit of a biceps or the tension of a spring was not likely to represent something exact at the interior of an atom.[21]

The cause of this inability to grasp directly the new reality detected by mathematics and the instruments of physics is clearly pointed out by Bachelard:

We must not forget that we picture things with our retina and not with the help of a mysterious and all-powerful faculty. This is a fact that Jean Perrin has ingeniously demonstrated. We cannot go any lower through the use of the imagination than we can through the use of sensation. There is no use in labeling the image of an object with a number to show its smallness; the imagination does not follow the mathematical bent.[22]

In these infra-sensitive areas opened up by physics, as well as in those of poetry or mysticism, any attempt at direct visualization is doomed to failure. Our only help lies in the enigmatic ways of seeing offered by mathematical and poetic symbols.

Mathematical symbols, it will be objected, express pure objectivity, while poetic symbols never leave the realm of subjectivity. This is a fallacious opposition: while mathematical symbols have to do with scientific objectivity, they are nonetheless the product of the subjectivity; on the other hand, while the poetic symbols arise from the depths of the subjectivity, it cannot be *a priori* denied that they might deal with other levels of objectivity. The only real problem is to find out what these levels are and to make an exact inventory of what they contain.

Mathematical symbols correspond to certain hieroglyphs inscribed in cosmic reality, but there is no valid motive for claiming that only they are able to exercise this function. Other types of symbols based not on numbers and on algebra, but on forms and images can be discovered and perfected in order to reveal the presence and action of other cosmic hieroglyphs.

The modern mind explodes the old theories that enclose matter within itself, the *soi* within itself, literature within itself, as though matter were brute matter, inhuman and unintelligible, as though the *soi* were nothing but a shadowy region shut away within the individual unconscious, as though literature were only a lot of fictions having no relationship with life. On the contrary, the modern mind interconnects these realms, for none of them. without being arbitrary, can abstract itself from the cosmic whole. In the same way, the three levels of the individual unconscious, the collective unconscious and the cosmic unconscious, which we distinguished for the purpose of showing the necessary states along the way to acquiring an awareness of the multiplicity of the world of myths, are in no less perpetual interaction and intercommunication.

Even though it comes out of a civilization which is founded on a radical separation of all the domains of life into a rigorous caste system that ignores the universal intercommunication of all things in the unity of the cosmos, surrealism has, at a superior stage of evolution, rediscovered the intuitions of the ancient and primitive peoples which affirm this extremely rich unity of the world and its close correspondence with the human person. This is what Breton means when he speaks of a return to a complete animism. Of the painter Matta, he writes:

> With him, everything is seen on the level of first and not of second sight tends to be conceived of along the lines of *total animism*. From

the time of romanticism, when it can be observed in its early stages, up through Lautréamont and Rimbaud, this animism has never stopped growing and at the same time improving. Nowadays, of course, there is no longer question of wondering if the rock thinks or the flower suffers, still less of looking on the world as a meeting place of prisoner souls, some of them borne along towards a fall, others ascending; present-day animism has pulled itself too free of the chilly quagmires of sin for that. What remains, what is coming to culmination is the certainty that nothing is in vain, that everything we consider has a decipherable language which can be heard in unison with some human emotion. (*Peinture*, p. 192)

Surrealism is not a return to a past age and outdated ideas. It is the discovery, at the high point of the modern stage of evolution, of a conception of the world which corresponds on a new level to the magico-animist conceptions. Opposed not only to the old conceptions because of the outworn beliefs that were mingled with these, but also to the drying-up and the ruinous fragmentation of life by the positivist-scientific civilization, surrealism is a conception of the world which today affirms anew the universal correspondence of all things and the conviction that man is, through his sensitivity and intelligence, less in discord than in harmony with the cosmos.

Man can sense everything, decipher everything, on condition that he turn aside from preconceived notions and ready-made views, that he plunge his lucid consciousness into the abyss of the unconscious which is not a separate world, but is at the same time the abyss of cosmic reality.

Far from being an extra-cosmic being, man is a bit of the cosmos; far from being an insignificant epiphenomenon of that cosmos, man discovers in himself such abilities of investigation and understanding of the total cosmos that he shows himself to be, on the contrary, its greatest source of light, its very awareness. And far from nature's being a blind and unintelligible mass, it reveals itself as so profoundly receptive to human sensitivity and intelligence that one can no longer reject the idea that man and the cosmos were naturally preordained for each other. It is in man that the way to the supreme point is found.

Nature is an enigma, but a decipherable enigma which ceaselessly calls to man for discovery and understanding. "It is possible that life is asking to be deciphered like a cryptogram." (*Nadja*, p. 150) Breton takes up this same idea later when he says of the painter Gorky:

> For the first time, nature is treated here like a cryptogram on which the sensible earlier imprints of the artist affix their grid in order to decode the very rhythm of life. (*Peinture*, p. 198)

There must be, then, a pre-established harmony between man and the cosmos. And why not? A harmony already exists between the mind and the body and, on the other hand, between the body and the universe. Man's first body is the flesh, but after that, there is the earth and, on a larger scale, cosmic matter which are man's greatest body. The macrocosm is the primordial mold, the matrix of microcosms. The body might very well be the privileged locus for the exercise of personal sensitivity and intelligence, but from this infinitesimal observatory, their powers radiate in all directions throughout the immensity of the universe. Signs and symbols exist in the social world of man only because they exist also in the world of the *soi* and in the universal reality of nature. The cosmos is not an unmarked parchment that man at whim sprinkles with signs, it is a great living body, already starred with signs that man did not think up but discovered.

The poet on the lookout for mythic images does not differ essentially from the scientist on the lookout for mathematical signs, nor from the savage on the lookout for traces of animals in the jungle; each of them is following his respective path in quest of the secret of the world's life. None of these symbols exists completely apart from the others, even though in the present state of man's exploration of the universe it is impossible to bridge the gap between them. Each poses the more general problem which is that of the universal symbolism from which all the others derive. Mathematics and myths, in man, are only parts of a cosmic symbolism. With this in mind, one understands how far-reaching is this declaration by Breton:

> Even with all reservations made about its principle, esoterism at least offers the immense interest of sustaining in the dynamic state the system of comparison, that unlimited field at man's disposal which provides him with the relationships likely to draw together the most apparently distant objects and which partially reveals to him the universal symbolism. (*Arcane*, p. 152)

It is because of this perspective whose amplitude takes in the whole of human and cosmic life that, in spite of the objections of Sartre and Mounin, surrealism holds the supreme point of view encompassing all the others. It alone proposes to undertake that sort of confederation of all the forces of humanity, those of science and of revolution, of psychoanalysis and of historic materialism, of sociology and of metaphysics, of the inward life and of love in order to lead man to the supreme point. From the human and the cosmic point of view, there can be no higher ambition, no more complete synthesis, because any other question represents only a particular aspect of these.

Just as the social revolution has objectives which are proper to it and which are independent of the methods of surrealism in its restricted sense, automatism, disintegration, and objective chance, while having nevertheless as its mission to straighten the ways for surrealism in the general sense, that is for the total liberation of man through the realization of the wonderland, so the science of the physicists has its proper object which is completely outside restricted surrealism; but when finally this science has placed the entire universe at the disposition of human desires and human understanding, it will become clear that its mission will have been none other than to straighten the ways for this same total liberation.

It is only when cosmic and social determinisms have become completely submissive to man that he will have the immense base he needs for the building of the wonderland. Just as real socialism cannot be set up in one country alone, total surrealism cannot be set up in a single area of reality.

When all the provisional tasks have been completed, then all symbolisms will be gathered into an undivided whole, immensely rich and diverse, but universal; all the forces for the metamorphosis of existence will be gathered into a single prodigious power which also will be at man's complete disposition. Then the time of surrealism will truly have been surpassed and it will make place for the very fullness of surreality.

POSTSCRIPT

This book was in no way meant to exhaust its subject; on the contrary, it is intended to show that on every side, surrealism sees new fields of exploration and asks new questions. Here and now, surrealism poses numerous other problems: those of poetic illumination and expression, those of the relationship of poetry and the revolution, of symbolism and automatism.

We have, for the time being, put to one side these vast, too vast, fields of research in order to confine ourselves to the examination of the basic concepts of surrealism, first of all because these are the basis for its experimentation, and then because their importance is almost always misunderstood.

As for the relationship of poetry with religion and atheism, I have presented my own position elsewhere, clearly enough to make it unnecessary to come back to the question here.

We shall have reached our essential goal if we have been able to show, if not to the aesthetes, at least to the men who care intensely about the future of humanity in this world, the true nature of surrealism and how far-reaching is its experience.

Surrealism has wrought the boldest doctrine of our era, the most perfect of all those that Prometheism could conceive of, for it assigns to humanity the task of reaching a goal that encompasses all the others.

Even now, in the comportment it inspires, it is synthesizing the most daringly modern spirit with the sense of an hermetic tradition whose origin is lost in the night of time. It imparts a lucid orientation to our progression in those central realms of life in which blend into one both waking and dreaming, the real and the imaginary.

Above all, by proposing that man smash the barriers behind which occidental customs close him off, and that he take for his own a supreme goal which is nothing less than the total possession of the objective and subjective universe, surrealism pushes aside the short-sighted antimonies that would make man subservient either to the primacy of pure intellect, or to the primacy of matter. It removes from these extra-human categories the right to dispute the supreme polarization of the dialectic of existence. It reveals in man the living source in which are united the antagonistic but indissociable worlds of the objective and the subjective. It sees in him the melting pot in which will be worked out the birth or the rebirth of the supreme point, the central point which, gathering in all the energies of the cosmos, progressively makes them its own in order to command the development of the universal dialectic.

In a word, even though this expression is not pronounced in the writings of the surrealists, one can say that in all its teaching and its practice, against abstract philosophies and against dialectical materialism, what it is ultimately proposing is a dialectical humanism. What we have hoped to do here is to give the keys to it.

NOTES

Chapter I

1. Swiss village; scene, in September, 1915, of an international socialist meeting seeking an immediate peace. (translator's note)

Chapter II

1. The *Zohar* is ascribed to a thirteenth-century Spanish Jewish mystic, Moses of Leon. It embodies the Kabbalistic traditions of that time and is, in part, a commentary on Genesis. The universe is divided by its dual cosmogony into empires of light and of shadow. (translator's note)
2. *Le Zohar* II, 126b, trans. by de Pauly (Paris: Leroux), Vol. IV, p. 5.
3. *Le Zohar* I, 20a, Vol. I, p. 121.
4. John Dee, *La Monade hiéroglyphique* (Paris: Chacornac, 1925), p. 23.
5. Nicolas de Cuse, *Oeuvres choisies* (Paris: Editions Montaigne, 1942), p. 480.
6. de Cuse, *Oeuvres*, p. 520.
7. Valentin Andréae, *Les Noces chymiques de Christian Rosenkreuz*, edited by Auriger and Chacornac (Paris: Chacornac, 1928), p. 64.
8. Rene Guénon, *Le Symbolisme de la Croix* (Paris: Véga, 1931), p. 66.
9. Guénon, *ibid.*, p. 72.
10. Henri Martin, *Études d'archéologie celtique.* (Paris: Didier, 1871), p. 290.
11. Eliphas Lévi, *Histoire de la Magie* (Paris: G. Baillière, 1860), p. 528.
12. Arnaud Dandieu, *Marcel Proust, sa révélation psychologique* (Paris: F. Didot, 1930), p. 58.
13. Cahiers G.L.M. 7 (1938).
14. That is, their basic make-up would be different from ours. (translator's note)
15. August Strindberg, *Inferno* (Paris: Le Griffon d'Or, 1948), p. 161.
16. Julien Gracq, *André Breton* (Paris: J. Corti, 1949), p. 39.
17. *Ibid.*
18. Eliphas Lévi, *Dogme et rituel de la Haute-magie* (Paris: G. Baillière, 1856), p. 87.
19. Marcellin-Pierre Berthelot, *Les Origines de l'alchimie* (Paris: Steinheil, 1885).
20. André Festugière, *La Révélation d'Hermès Trismégiste*, Vol. I: *L'Astrologie et les sciences occultes* (Paris: Gabalda, 1944).
21. Lévi, *Dogme et rituel*, p. 371.

277

278

22. Jacques Combe, *Jérôme Bosch* (Paris: Tisné, 1946).

23. Emile Grillot de Givry, *Musée des sorciers, mages et alchimistes* (Paris: Librairie de France, 1929).

24. A.-J. Pernety, *Dictionnaire mytho-hermétique* (Paris: n.p. 1787), V° Fontaine de jouvence.

25. de Givry, *Musée*, p. 392.

26. Jacques Gengoux, *La Symbolique de Rimbaud* (Paris: Editions du Vieux-Colombier, 1947).

27. See Breton, *Amour fou*, especially Chap. IV.

28. Berthelot, *Origines de l'alchimie*, p. 90.

29. Pernety, *Dictionnaire mytho-hermétique*. Vʳ Matière, pp. 272ff.

30. Lévi, *Histoire*, p. 200.

Chapter III

1. Jean-Edouard Spenlé, *La Pensée allemande* (Paris: A. Colin, 1934), p. 100.

2. Edgar Allan Poe, "The Poetic Principle" in *The Book of Poe*, ed. by Addison Hibbard (New York: Doubleday Doran and Co., 1934), pp. 65-86.

3. André Breton and Paul Eluard, "Notes sur la poésie," *Révolution surréaliste* 12, p. 53.

4. *Ibid.*

5. Julien Benda inveighed against literature that was intuitive rather than intellectual. (translator's note)

6. John Keats, in a letter to George and Thomas Keats, December 28, 1817. ". . . . *Negative Capability*, that is, when a man is capable of being in uncertainties, mysteries, doubts, without any irritable reaching after fact and reason." *Complete Poems and Selected Letters* (New York: The Odyssey Press, 1935), p. 528.

7. cf. Charles du Bos, preface to *Ecrits en Prose d'Hofmannsthal* (Paris: Editions de la Pléiade [1927]).

8. Wladimir Weidlé, *Les Abeilles d'Artistée* (Brussels: Desclée De Brouwer, 1936), p. 217.

9. Arthur Rimbaud, Letter to Paul Demeny, May 15, 1871, in *Complete Works, Selected Letters* (Chicago: University of Chicago Press, 1966), p. 306.

10. Rimbaud, "Alchimie du verbe," in *Une Saison en Enfer II, op. cit.*, p. 194.

11. Marcel Proust, *A la recherche du temps perdu*, Vol. III: *Le temps retrouvé* (Paris: Gallimard, 1954), p. 867.

12. Rimbaud, "Alchimie du verbe," *op. cit.*, p. 194.

13. These psychologists were especially interested in sensory perception. (translator's note)

14. Leonardo da Vinci, "Precepts of the Painter" in *The Notebooks*, Vol. 2 (New York: Reynal and Hitchcock, n.d.), p. 250.

15. Max Ernst, *Oeuvres de 1919 à 1936* (Paris: Cahiers d'art, 1937), pp. 16-18.

16. *Ibid.*, p. 20.

17. *Ibid.*, p. 22.

18. *Ibid.*, p. 20.

19. Edgar Allan Poe, *The Complete Tales and Poems* (New York: Random House, 1938), pp. 643-644.

20. *Ibid.*, p. 644.

21. *Ibid.*, p. 644.

22. Karl Jaspers, *Psychopathologie générale* (Paris: F. Alcan, 1934), p. 534.

23. *Ibid.*, p. 533.

24. cf. Jean and J.-R. Trabaud, *Guide thérapeutique du médecin practicien* Vol. VI: *Les Maladies de la jeune fille et de la femme* (Paris: Vigot frères, n.d.).

25. Georg Wilhelm Friedrich Hegel, *Esthétique*, Vol. II (Paris: Editions Montaigne, 1944), p. 342.

26. Marco Ristitch, "L'humour, attitude morale," *Surréalisme au service de la révolution* 6, p. 38.

27. *Ibid.*, p. 38.

28. Fyodor Dostoevsky, *The Possessed* (New York: Random House, 1936).

29. Raymond Roussel, *Comment j'ai écrit certains de mes livres* (Paris: Pauvert, 1963), p. 18.

30. *Ibid.*, p. 13.

31. Fulcanelli, *Les Demeures philosophales* (Paris: Schemit, 1930), p. 36.

Chapter IV

1. Plato, *Phaedrus* in *Dialogues*, trans. by B. Jowett. Vol. 1 (New York: Random House, 1937), pp. 248-249.

2. Plato, *Ion* in *Dialogues*, Vol. 1, p. 289.

3. Antoine Giraud, *L'Automatisme dans l'art* (Paris: Rivière, n.d.), passim.

4. James Leuba, *Psychologie du mysticisme religieux* (Paris: F. Alcan, 1926), p. 355.

5. *Ibid.*

6. *Ibid.*

7. Ludovic Halévy, "Carnets," *Revue des Deux Mondes* (12-15-37), p. 827.

8. Henri Ghéon, "Aridité et inspiration," *Etudes carmélitaines*, October 1937, p. 29.

9. Johann Eckermann, *Conversations with Goethe*, trans. by John Oxenford (London: J. M. Dent, 1930), pp. 233-234.

10. Maurice Betz, *Rilke Vivant* (Paris: Emile Paul, 1937), p. 122.

11. Maria von Thurn und Taxis, *Souvenirs sur Rainer Maria Rilke* (Paris: Emile Paul, 1936), p. 211.

12. *Ibid.*, p. 174.

13. Francis Gérard, "L'Etat d'un surréaliste," *La Révolution surréaliste* 1, p. 29.

14. Jules Monnerot, *La poésie moderne et le sacrée* (Paris: Gallimard, 1945), p. 50.

15. "De derrière les fagots" means literally "from behind the woodpile." It is used in speaking of something—often a bottle of wine—that has been brought out of hiding "from behind the woodpile" for a special occasion. (translator's note)

16. Franz Kafka, *Journal Intime* (Paris: Grasset, 1945), p. 85.

17. Virgil, *The Aeneid*, VI, v. 268ff.

Chapter V

1. In antiquity, a land so remote that the sun did not shine there. (translator's note)

2. Max Ernst, *Oeuvres de 1919 à 1936* (Paris: Cahiers d'art, 1937), p. 46.

3. *Ibid.*, p. 28.

4. Sidney Hook, *Towards the Understanding of Karl Marx* (New York: John Day, 1933), p. 95.

5. Paul Nougé, "Les Images défendues," *Surréalisme au service de la révolution* 5, pp. 24-25.

6. Cited by Eluard in *Donner à voir* (Paris: Gallimard, 1939).

7. Friedrich Nietzsche, *La Volonté de Puissance*, Vol. 1 (Paris: Gallimard, 1936-37), p. 217.

8. Issue devoted to "L'Objet," *Cahiers d'Art* 1-2 (1936).

9. Louis Leprince-Ringuet, *Les Rayons cosmiques* (Paris: Albin Michel, 1945), pl. 29-32.

10. René Sudre, *Introduction à la métaphysique humaine* (Paris: Payot, 1926), pp. 192-193.

11. Man Ray, in an interview given to *La Flèche* circa 1937-1938.

12. Raoul Ubac and Jean Lescure, "L'Envers de la Face," *Exercice de la pureté* (printed privately).

13. cf. *Minotaure* 12-13, pp. 60-61.

14. Paul Morand, *Clarisse* in *Tendres stocks* (Paris: Nouvelle Revue française, 1921), pp. 63-64.

15. Salvador Dali, "Objets surréalistes," *Le Surréalisme au service de la révolution* 3, p. 16.

Chapter VI

1. A further dimension of meaning is added if one remembers that the French word "tournesol" refers to a sensitive chemical substance that takes on a different color when exposed to an acid or a base, as well as to the sunflower. A translation of the poem follows:

The Night of the Sunflower

The traveler who crossed *les Halles* at summerfall
Was walking on tiptoe
In the sky despair rolled its great and lovely arms
And in the handbag there was my dream that flask of salts
That only God's godmother has breathed
Torpor spread like vapor
In the café *Au chien qui fume*
Where the pros and the cons had just come in
The young woman could be seen by them only with difficulty and from the
    corner of the eye
Was I dealing with the ambassadress of saltpeter or with the white curve
    on a black background that we call thought
The innocents' ball was in full swing
The lanterns caught fire slowly in the chestnut trees
The lady without a shadow knelt on the *Pont-au-change*
In *rue Gît-le-coeur* the sound of the bells was no longer the same
The promises of nights were finally kept
The homing pigeons the emergency kisses
Joined the breasts of the beautiful stranger
Darts under the crepe of perfect meanings
A farm was prospering in the heart of Paris
And its windows looked out on the Milky Way
Only nobody lived there yet because of the chance comers
Unexpected guests that are known to be more devoted than the ghosts
Some like this woman seem to swim
And a little of their substance enters into love
She interiorizes them
I am not the plaything of any sensorial power
And yet the cricket singing in the cinder hair
One evening near the statue of Etienne Marcel
Gave me a knowing wink
André Breton, he said, pass (Tr. note)

2. Carrouges includes among the keywords *ici l'on dine/l'ondine* which do not occur in the poem itself; however, the earlier incident to which they belong

prefigures the joyful mystery of the night of the sunflower and is evoked in the discussion of these themes. See *Amour*, chapters I and VII. (translator's note)

3. Mary Webb, *Gone to Earth* (New York: Dutton, 1917). David Garnett, *Lady into Fox* (New York: Alfred A. Knopf, 1923).

   [Vercors was inspired by Garnett's novel to write one with a fox-into-lady theme: *Sylva.*—translator's note.]

4. Pierre Mabille, "L'Oeil du peintre," *Minotaure* 12-13, pp. 53-56.

5. Johann Eckermann, *Conversations with Goethe*, p. 22.

6. Goethe, *Autobiography: Truth and Poetry*, p. 433.

7. Eckermann, *Conversations*, pp. 233-234.

8. Yves Delage, *La Nature des images hypnagogiques et le rôle des lueurs entoptiques dans le rêve* (Paris: 14, rue de Condé, 1903).

9. Albert Béguin, *L'Ame romantique et le rêve* (Paris: J. Corti, 1939).

10. M.J.L. Hervey de Saint-Denys, *Les Rêves et les moyens de les diriger* (Paris: Amyot, 1869), published anonymously.

11. *Ibid.*, p. 232.

12. *Ibid.*, p. 263.

13. Béguin, *L'Ame romantique*, Vol. 2, p. 58.

14. Hervey de Saint-Denis, *Les Rêves*, p. 73.

15. Eliphas Lévi, *Histoire de la Magie*, p. 239.

16. Hofmannsthal, *Ecrits en prose*, p. 79.

17. In the Genesis mystery as well, the woman is the only treasure—a living treasure—that man brought away from Paradise.

18. Georges Hugnet, *Petite anthologie poétique du surréalisme* (Paris: J. Bucher, 1934), p. 153.

Chapter VIII

1. Georges Mounin, *Avez-vous lu Char?* (Paris: Gallimard, 1946), pp. 64-65.

2. *Ibid.*, p. 86.

3. Jean-Paul Sartre, *Situations II* (Paris: Gallimard, 1948), p. 216.

4. Sartre, *Situations II*, p. 215.

5. Sartre, *ibid.*, p. 217.

6. Sartre, *ibid.*, p. 324.

7. Charles Cros, *Poèmes et proses* (Paris: Gallimard, 1944), p. 240.

8. Johann Malfatti de Montereggio, *Etudes sur la mathèse* (Paris: Le Griffon d'or, 1946), p. 69.

9. Jean-Paul Sartre, *What is Literature?* trans. by Bernard Frechtman. (New York: Harper and Row, Colophon ed., 1965).

10. Sigmund Freud, *Complete Psychological Works*, Vol. 6: *The Psychopathology of Everyday Life* (London: The Hogarth Press, 1960), p. 257.

11. *Ibid.*, p. 258.

12. Freud, *Complete Psychological Works*, Vol. 22: *New Introductory Lectures on Psycho-Analysis* (London: The Hogarth Press, 1964), p. 55.

13. Freud makes a thorough study of this story in *Complete Psychological Works*, Vol. 9: *Jensen's 'Gradiva' and Other Works* (London: The Hogarth Press, 1959), pp. 3-95.

14. Miguel de Cervantes, *The Adventures of Don Quixote* (Baltimore: Penguin, 1950), p. 149.

15. Edgar Léoni, *Nostradamus: Life and Literature* (New York: Nosbooks, 1961), p. 310.

16. Sandomir, "Nostradamus," *L'Arche* 22, p. 104.

17. Louis Aragon, "Entrée des succubes," *Révolution surréaliste* 6, pp. 10-13.

18. Roger Caillois, *Le mythe et l'homme* (Paris: Gallimard, 1938), p. 23.

19. *Ibid.*, p. 81.

20. Louis de Broglie, *Matière et lumière* (Paris: Albin Michel, 1937), p. 308.

21. Louis de Broglie, *Continu et discontinu* (Paris: Albin Michel, 1941), p. 69.

22. Gaston Bachelard, *Le nouvel esprit scientifique* (Paris: Presses Universitaires de France), p. 132.

BIBLIOGRAPHY

The works of André Breton to which Carrouges refers are listed below in chronological order of their publication date. For the surrealist periodicals, I have indicated the more readily available facsimile reprints published by the Arno Press, New York. The general bibliography has been expanded to include works of related interest, several of which contain more extensive bibliographical material. (Translator's Note)

I. Selected Works by André Breton
    Title
    Short Form
    Les Champs magnétiques (with Philippe Soupault). Paris: Au Sans Pareil, 1920.
    Les Pas perdus. Paris: Gallimard, 1924 .... *Pas*
    Nadja. Paris: Gallimard, 1928. .... *Nadja*
    L'Immaculée Conception (with Paul Eluard). Paris: J. Corti, 1930.
    Le Revolver à cheveux blancs. Paris: Editions des Cahiers libres, 1932
    .... *Revolver*
    Les Vases communicants. Paris: Editions des Cahiers libres, 1932 .... *Vases*
    Point du jour. Paris: Gallimard, 1934 .... *Point*
    Qu'est-ce que le surréalisme? Brussels: Henriquez, 1934.
    Position politique du surréalisme. Paris: Sagittaire, 1935 .... *Position*
    *Misère de la poésie, l' "Affaire Aragon" devant l'opinion
    publique.* Paris: Editions Surréalistes, 1932 .... *Misère*
    L'Amour fou. Paris: Gallimard, 1937 .... *Amour*
    "Limites non frontières du surrealisme." *Nouvelle Revue francaise,* 2-1-37.
    .... *Limites*
    Anthologie de l'humour noir. Paris: Sagittaire, 1940 .... *Humour*
    Situation du surréalisme entre les deux guerres, Algiers: Fontaine, 1945
    .... *Situation*
    Le Surréalisme et la peinture. New York: Brentano's, 1945 .... *Peinture*
    Manifestes du surréalisme. Paris: Sagittaire, 1946 .... *Manifestes*
    Arcane 17. Paris: Sagittaire, 1947 .... *Arcane*
    Martinique, charmeuse de serpents. Paris: Sagittaire, 1948.
    Flagrant délit. Paris: Thésée, 1949.

II. Surrealist periodicals
 La Révolution surréaliste. Reprint, with a cumulative table of contents
 added, of the serial published in Paris 1924-1929. New York: Arno Press
 [1968?].
 Le Surréalisme au service de la révolution. Reprint, with a cumulative table
 of contents added, of the serial published in Paris 1930-1933, superseding
 La Révolution surréaliste. New York: Arno Press [1968?].
 Minotaure. Authorized reprint edition in four volumes including a specially
 prepared cumulative index. New York: Arno Press, 1968.

III. General Bibliography
 André Breton et le mouvement surréaliste. *Nouvelle Revue française* 172,
 special issue. Paris, 1967.
 Andréae, Valentin. *Les Noces chymiques de Christian Rosenkreuz*, edited by
 Auriger and Chacornac. Paris: Chacornac, 1928.
 Aragon, Louis. "Entrée des succubes." *Revolution surréaliste* 6, pp.
 10-13.
 Bachelard, Gaston. *Le Nouvel Esprit scientifique*. Paris: Arcan, 1934.
 Balakian, Anna. *André Breton: Magus of Surrealism*. New York: Oxford
 University Press, 1971.
 _____. *Surrealism: the Road to the Absolute*. New York: Noonday Press,
 1959; Dutton, 1970.
 Bataille, Georges. *Histoire de l'oeil*. New edition. Paris: Pauvert, 1967.
 Béguin, Albert. *L'Ame romantique et le rêve*. 2 vols. Paris: J. Corti, 1939.
 New edition in one volume, 1946.
 Berthelot, Marcellin-Pierre. *Les Origines de l'alchimie*. Paris: Steinheil, 1885.
 Betz, Maurice. *Rilke vivant*. Paris: Emile Paul, 1937.
 Brechon, Robert. *Le Surréalisme*. Paris: A. Colin, 1971.
 Broglie, Louis de. *Continu et discontinu*. Paris: Albin Michel, 1941.
 _____. *Matière et lumière*. Paris: Albin Michel, 1937.
 Butler, Samuel. *Erewhon Revisited Twenty Years Later*. New York: Dutton,
 1920.
 Caillois, Roger. *Le mythe et l'homme*. Paris: Gallimard, 1938.
 Carroll, Lewis [Dodgson, Charles Lutwidge]. *Alice's Adventures in Wonderland
 and Through the Looking-glass*. New York: Macmillan, 1966.
 Cervantes, Miguel de. *The Adventures of Don Quixote*. Baltimore: Penguin,
 1950.
 Combe, Jacques. *Jérôme Bosch*. Paris: Tisné, 1946.
 Cros, Charles. *Poèmes et proses*. Paris: Gallimard, 1944.
 Cuse, Cardinal de. *Oeuvres choisies*. Paris: Editions Montaigne, 1942.
 Dali, Salvador. "Objets surréalistes." *Surréalisme au service de la révolution*
 3, pp. 16-17.

Dandieu, Arnaud. *Marcel Proust, sa révélation psychologique.* Paris: F. Didot, 1930.

Dee, John. *La Monade hiéroglyphique.* Translated by Grillot de Givry. Paris: Chacornac, 1925.

Delage, Yves, *La Nature des images hypnagogiques et le rôle des lueurs entoptiques dans le rêve.* Paris: 14, rue de Condé, 1903.

Dostoevsky, Fyodor. *The Possessed.* New York: Random House, 1936.

Eckermann, Johann. *Conversations With Goethe,* translated by John Oxenford. London: J. M. Dent, 1930.

Eluard, Paul. *Donner à voir.* Paris: Gallimard, 1939.

Eluard, Paul, and Breton, André. "Notes sur la Poesie." *Révolution surréaliste* 12, pp. 53–55.

Ernst, Max. *La Femme 100 têtes.* Avis au lecteur par André Breton. Paris: Editions du Carrefour, 1924.

————. *Oeuvres de 1919 à 1936.* Paris: Cahiers d'art, 1937.

Festugière, André-J. *La Révélation d'Hermés Trismégiste,* Vol. I: *L'Astrologie et les sciences occultes.* Paris: Gabalda, 1944.

Freud, Sigmund. *The Standard Edition of the Complete Psychological Works.* Translated by James Strachey. 23 Volumes. London: The Hogarth Press, 1953–1964.

Fulcanelli. *Les demeures philosophales et le symbolisme hermétique dans ses rapports avec l'art sacré et l'esotérisme du grand-oeuvre.* Preface d'Eugène Canseliet. Paris: Schemit, 1930.

Garnett, David. *Lady into Fox.* New York: Alfred A. Knopf, 1923.

Gengoux, Jacques. *La Symbolique de Rimbaud.* Paris: Editions du Vieux-Colombier, 1947.

Gérard, Francis. "L'Etat d'un surréaliste." *Révolution surréaliste* 1, pp. 29–30.

Gershman, Herbert. *The Surrealist Revolution in France.* Ann Arbor: University of Michigan Press, 1969.

————. *A Bibliography of the Surrealist Revolution in France.* Ann Arbor: University of Michigan Press, 1969.

Ghéon, Henri. "Aridité et inspiration." *Etudes carmélitaines* (October 1937), pp. 25–30.

Giraud, Antoine. *L'Automatisme dans l'art.* Paris: Rivière, n.d.

Goethe. *Autobiography: Truth and Poetry, From My Own Life.* Translated by John Oxenford. Vol. I. London: Goerge Bell and Sons, 1897.

Gracq, Julien. *André Breton, quelques aspects de l'écrivain.* Paris: J. Corti, 1948.

————. *Au Château d'Argol.* Paris: J. Corti, 1938. English translation (*The Castle of Argol*) by Louise Varese. New York: New Directions, 1951.

Grillot de Givry, Emile. *Musée des sorciers, mages et alchimistes.* Paris:

Librairie de France, 1929. English translation *(Picture Museum of Sorcery, Magic, and Alchemy)* by J. Courtenay Locke, New York: University Books, Inc., 1963.

Guénon, René. *Le Symbolisme de la Croix.* Paris: Véga, 1931.

Halévy, Ludovic. "Carnets." *Revue des Deux Mondes,* 12-15-37, pp. 810-43.

Hegel, Georg Wilhelm Friedrich. *Esthétique.* 4 vols. Paris: Editions Montaigne, 1944.

Hervey de Saint-Denys, M.J.L. *Les rêves et les moyens de les diriger.* Paris: Amyot, 1867 (Published anonymously).

Hofmannsthal, Hugo von. *Ecrits en prose.* Introduction by Charles du Bos. Paris: Editions de la Pléiade [1927].

Hook, Sidney. *Towards the Understanding of Karl Marx.* New York: John Day, 1933.

Hugnet, Georges. "Petite rêverie du grand veneur." *Minotaure* 5 (1934), p. 30.

Janet, Pierre. *Neuroses et idées fixes.* 2 vols. Paris: Alcan, 1898. 2nd edition.

Jaspers, Karl. *Psychopathologie générale.* Translated by Kastler and Mendousse. Paris: Alcan, 1934.

Juvet, Gustave. *La Structure des nouvelles théories physiques.* Paris: Alcan, 1933.

Kafka, Franz. *Journal intime.* Translated by P. Klossovski. Paris: Grasset, 1945.

Keats, John. *Complete Poems and Selected Letters.* New York: The Odyssey Press, 1935.

Lautréamont, le Comte de [Isadore Lucien Ducasse]. *Oeuvres completes.* Paris: J. Corti, 1938.

Léoni, Edgar. *Nostradamus: Life and Literature.* New York: Nosbooks, 1961.

Leprince-Ringuet, Louis. *Les Rayons cosmiques: les mésotons.* Paris: Albin Michel, 1945.

Leuba, James H. *Psychologie du mysticisme réligieux.* Translated by Lucien Herr. Paris: F. Alcan, 1926. English Translation *(The Psychology of Religious Mysticism),* New York: Harcourt, Brace and Co., 1925.

Lévi, Eliphas [Abbé Constant]. *Dogme et rituel de la haute-magie.* Paris: G. Baillière, 1856. English translation *(Transcendental Magic)* by Arthur Edward Waite, New York: McKay, 1923.

––––––. *Histoire de la magie.* Paris: G. Baillière, 1860. English translation *(History of Magic)* by Arthur Edward Waite, New York: McKay, 1914.

Mabille, Pierre. "L'Oeil du peintre." *Minotaure* 12–13, pp. 53–56.

Malfatti de Montereggio, Johann. *Etudes sur la mathèse, ou anarchie et hiérarchie de la science, avec une application spéciale de la médecine.* Translated by Christian Ostrowski. Paris: Le Griffon d'or, 1946.

Martin, Henri. *Etudes d'archéologie celtique.* Paris: Didier, 1871.

Marx–Engles. *Etudes philosophiques.* Paris: Editions sociales internationales, 1935.

Masson-Oursel (Paul), de Willman-Grabowska (H.de), and Stern (Ph.). *L'Inde antique et la civilisation indienne.* Paris: La Renaissance du livre, 1933.

Monnerot, Jules. *La Poésie moderne et le sacrée.* Paris: Gallimard, 1945.

Morand, Paul. *Clarisse* in *Tendres stocks.* Préface de Marcel Proust. 2nd ed. Paris: Nouvelle Revue française, 1921. English translation *(Green Shoots)* introduced by A. G. Walkley. Freeport, N.Y.: Books for Libraries Press [1971].

Mounin, Georges. *Avez-vous lu Char?* Paris: Gallimard, 1946.

Multhauf, Robert P. *The Origins of Chemistry.* New York: Franklin Watts, 1967.

Nietzsche, Friedrich. *La Volonté de puissance.* 2 vols. Translated by G. Bianquis. Paris: Gallimard, 1936–1937.

Nougé, Paul. "Les Images défendues." *Le Surréalisme au service de la révolution* 5–6, pp. 24–28.

Panly, Jean de. *La Cabbale, pages classées du Zohar.* Paris: Editions du Chant nouveau, 1946.

Péret, Benjamin. *Le Déshonneur des poètes.* Mexico City: Poésie et Revolution, 1946.

––––––. *La parole est à Péret.* Mexico City: Editions surréalistes, 1942. 1942.

Pernety, A. J. *Dictionnaire mytho-hermetique dans lequel on trouve les allégories fabuleuses des poètes, les métaphores, les énigmes et les termes barbares des philosophes hermétiques expliqués.* Paris [n.p.], 1787.

Plato. *Dialogues.* 2 vols. Translated by B. Jowett. New York: Random House, 1937.

Poe, Edgar Allan. *The Book of Poe.* Edited by Addison Hibbard. New York: Doubleday, Doran & Co., 1934.

––––––. *The Complete Tales and Poems.* New York: Random House, 1938.

Proust, Marcel. *Á la recherche du temps perdu,* vol. IV: *Le Temps retrouvé.* Paris: Gallimard, 1954.

Ribémont-Dessaignes, Georges. "Histoire de Dada." *Oouvelle Revue française* (o.s.), 6-1-31, pp. 867–879 and 7-1-31, pp. 39–52.

Rimbaud, Arthur. *Complete Works, Selected Letters.* Translation, Introduction, and Notes by Wallace Fowlie. Chicago: University of Chicago Press, 1966.

Ristitch, Marco. "L'humour, attitude morale." *Surréalisme au service de la révolution* 6, pp. 36–39.

Roussel, Raymond. *Comment j'ai écrit certains de mes livres.* Paris: Pauvert, 1963.

Sandomir. "Nostradamus." *L'Arche* 22, pp. 98–104.

Sartre, Jean-Paul. *Situations II.* Paris: Gallimard, 1948, 1949.

_____.*What is Literature?* Translated by Bernard Frechtman. New York: Harper & Row, (Colophon edition), 1965.

Spenlé, Jean-Edouard. *La Pensée allemande, de Luther à Nietzsche.* Paris: A. Colin, 1934.

Strindberg, August. *Inferno.* Paris: Le Griffon d'Or, 1948.

Sudre, René. *Introduction ă la métaphysique humaine.* Paris: Payot, 1926.

"Le Surréalisme." *Europe*, special issue. September–October, 1967.

Le Surréalisme. Colloquium directed by Ferdinand Alquié at Cérisy in 1968. Paris: Mouton, 1968.

Thurn und Taxis, Marie von. *Souvenirs sur Rainer Maria Rilke.* Paris: Emile Paul, 1936.

Trabaud, Jean and J.-R. *Le Guide thérapeutique du médecin practicien.* 13 vols. Paris: Vigot frères, 1940–1944.

Ubac, Raoul, and Lescure, Jean. "L'Envers de la face." *Exercice de la pureté.* Printed privately.

Vaché, Jacques. *Lettres de Guerre.* Paris: Au Sans Pareil, 1919, 1949.

Vandier, Jacques. *Egypte: Anciennes religions orientales.* Paris: Presses Universitaires de France, 1944.

Viatte, Auguste. *Victor Hugo et les illuminés de son temps.* Montréal: Editions de l'Arbre, 1942.

Vinci, Leonardo da. *The Notebooks of Leonardo da Vinci.* 2 vols. Arranged, rendered into English, and introduced by Edward MacCurdy. New York: Reynal & Hitchcock, 1948.

Walpole, Horace. *The Castle of Otranto* in *Shorter Novels, Eighteenth Century.* London: J. M. Dent, 1903. French translation (*Le Château d'Otrante*) by Dominique Corticchiato, Paris: J. Corti, 1933.

Webb, Mary. *Gone to Earth.* New York: Dutton, 1917.

Weidlé, Wladimir. *Les Abeilles d'Aristée.* Brussels: Desclée, De Brouwer et Cie.; 1936.

Wells, Herbert George. *The War of the Worlds* in *Seven Science Fiction Novels.* New York: Dover, 1950.

INDEX